GETTING STARTED IN
Woodworking
SKILL-BUILDING PROJECTS that TEACH the BASICS

Aimé Ontario Fraser

The Taunton Press

To my readers—Be kind to yourself and remember
the sooner you make mistakes, the faster you'll learn.

Text © 2003 by Aimé Ontario Fraser
Photographs © 2003 by Sloan Howard
Illustrations © 2003 by The Taunton Press, Inc.

The Taunton Press, Inc., 63 South Main Street, PO Box 5506, Newtown, CT 06470-5506
e-mail: tp@taunton.com

Distributed by Publishers Group West

EDITORS: Carolyn Mandarano and Helen Albert
JACKET/COVER DESIGN: Ann Marie Manca
INTERIOR DESIGN: Mary McKeon
LAYOUT: Mary McKeon and Cathy Cassidy
ILLUSTRATOR: Melanie Powell
PHOTOGRAPHER: Sloan Howard

LIBRARY OF CONGRESS CATALOGING-IN-PUBLICATION DATA:
Fraser, Aimé Ontario
  Getting started in woodworking : skill-building projects that teach
the basics / Aimé Ontario Fraser.
     p. cm.
Includes index.
  ISBN 1-56158-610-2
 1. Woodwork. I. Title.
  TT180 .F73 2003
  684'.08--dc21

                                   2002151755

Printed in the United States of America
10 9 8 7 6 5 4 3 2 1

The following manufacturers/names appearing in *Getting Started in Woodworking* are trademarks:
Accuride®, K-Body™ clamps, Quick-Grip® clamps, Workmate®.

ABOUT YOUR SAFETY:
Working wood is inherently dangerous. Using hand or power tools improperly or ignoring safety practices can lead to permanent injury
or even death. Don't try to perform operations you learn about here (or elsewhere) unless you're certain they are safe for you. If something
about an operation doesn't feel right, don't do it. Look for another way. We want you to enjoy the craft, so please keep safety foremost
in your mind whenever you're in the shop.

Acknowledgments

Getting Started in Woodworking grew out of the "Absolute Beginner" series of classes I taught at The Woodworkers' Club in Norwalk, Connecticut, the Marc Adams School in Whiteland, Indiana, and WoodenBoat School in Brooklin, Maine. I love my students. They're always an inspiration to me, and their questions and comments make me a better teacher and writer. This book couldn't have happened without them.

While beginning woodworkers are at the heart of this book, the outstanding people at The Taunton Press are at its head. Helen Albert is ever my champion and editor, and as my sometime co-teacher, she's well aware of problems beginning woodworkers face. John Lively, president of the company, saw the potential in my approach, as did publisher Jim Childs and editor in chief Maria Taylor. These three were strong supporters from the start. The capable Carolyn Mandarano helped me work out the details, and when the going got rough I counted on her for more than words. Her warmth always cheered me up. Rick Mastelli's excellent suggestions helped give the book its accessible structure. Copy editor Diane Sinitsky kept everything straight and helped me write more clearly. Fast, calm, and utterly capable, Sloan Howard is a great photographer to work with in the shop. Wendi Mijal, Rosalind Wanke, Mary McKeon, and Cathy Cassidy in the art department brought the words and photos to life on the page. I'm truly honored to work with all of them.

A number of people in the business of woodworking have helped me do a better job teaching and writing: John and Ginny Matchak, owners of The Woodworkers' Club, who pushed me to teach more; Pete Hopkins of Porter-Cable, who is always happy to loan me tools for classes and photo shoots; Mark Duginske of Woodworking FastTrak, who cheerleads and keeps me up to date on trends in the business; Dick Anderson of System Three Resins, a loyal supporter in many ways; Gary Meixner at American Clamping, who tries to make sure I always have enough clamps; Steve DeMonico, who sets good things in motion; David Powell and Stan Watson of DMT, brilliant guys who are always ready to find answers to arcane questions; and Jeff and the guys at Torno Lumber and Hardware in Westport, Connecticut, my local lumberyard.

Finally, I must acknowledge the daily doses of love, support, and maintenance provided by my family—Lois, Becca, and Justin. They've taken care of me with everything from cups of tea to impromptu late-night lip-synching performances, all while putting up with noises from the shop at odd hours, my absences while writing late into the night, and a sometimes embarrassing preoccupation with furniture design and construction—all with cheerfulness and unwavering support.

Contents

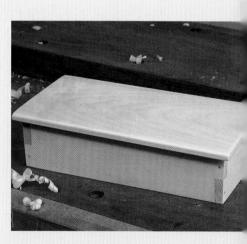

Introduction

Wood is an antidote to the stresses of modern life. From the rough-hewn beams of an old barn to the elegant simplicity of a handmade box, we're drawn to wood. Luxury car makers know this and accent the interiors of their highest-priced models with bird's-eye maple and walnut burl.

Wood is a material with a wholly human scale. Trees are part of our lives, and we watch them through the seasons. We understand how they live and grow. Their wood is not too hard to work but is strong enough to accomplish almost monumental human tasks such as building bridges and shoring up hillsides, yet delicate and soulful enough for making a cradle. Unlike the heroic scale of steelmaking or the hurtling electrons in a microchip, the processes of woodworking are familiar in scale and easy to accomplish using tools that have changed very little over the centuries.

Woodworking is satisfying on many levels. It's a physical activity, with lots of lifting, carrying, planing, and using your arm, leg, and back muscles. It's work that connects you with real life, not with a screen. It's working in a medium where nothing is a given. Each piece of wood is different, and you must see how it acts and work with it.

This requires a great deal of creativity and resourcefulness.

Doing woodworking connects you with the real world in a new way. As you learn to use tools and materials, you'll have a new understanding of the way things work. You're able to shine the light of knowledge on some of the mysteries of everyday life, such as why floors squeak (the joints move), the reason drawers stick in the summer (high humidity causes wood to swell), and why the coat rack fell off the wall (the screws were not long enough to anchor the weight in the soft drywall).

How to Use This Book

This book is designed to teach you the basics of woodworking while you build five useful, good-looking projects for your home. The projects become more complex, with each one building on the skills you learned in earlier projects. You progress from a simple handmade box to building a bookcase that requires the router to complete and finally to a complex cabinet that teaches you how to use a table saw.

Detailed Tools and Materials lists in each chapter show you exactly what tools and materials you need to buy and give the essential information you'll need to make your selection. The first two chapters, "Tools for Woodworking" and "Materials," provide more information on setting up a shop, making wise purchases, and getting the most out of your materials.

The how-to section of each chapter begins with measured drawings, which you should study before you begin and periodically during the building process. They show the projects from different viewpoints, with details called out so you can understand how the piece goes together.

You'll learn how to build the project with detailed step-by-step instructions. These are amplified with tips called Work Smart and Work Safe that not only tell you what to do but also what not to do and what to look out for.

The step-by-step instructions are supplemented with Skill Builders, which isolate critical skills and provide even more detailed instructions for ensuring success. The first Skill Builders teach you how to accomplish basic operations such as using a drill and sharpening your tools; others teach you how to use a router and how to cut simple joints on a table saw. If you want to practice skills before working on your project, take some extra time with Skill Builders and do the operations two or three times with scrap wood.

A woodworker's Glossary at the back defines woodworking terms you might not know; each word in the glossary appears in bold text the first time it is used. A Resources guide lists contact information on the tools and materials used in this book, along with a selection of useful books you might like to add to your library. Finally, check out the book's companion website at www.aofraser.com, where you'll find relevant articles, measured drawings of variations, a photo gallery of readers' work, and more.

By the time you've worked your way through the projects in this book, you'll have a strong foundation of woodworking skills that cover everything from how to use a plane to making a crosscut sled for safe and accurate table-saw work.

The Larger Lessons of Woodworking

In addition to teaching practical skills, the projects illustrate more general philosophical lessons, which I find stand me in good stead in a variety of life situations.

- Mistakes are inevitable. Don't focus on the mistakes; focus on the lessons you can learn from them (Simple Handmade Box).
- Perfection doesn't matter; success does. Don't get hung up on measurements (Outdoor Easy Chair).
- Take up a challenge you can meet. Stretch yourself but not too far (Rustic Old-World Coffee Table).
- Think ahead and do all you can to control the outcome (Classic Bookcase).
- Time spent planning saves time (Top-Drawer Lateral File).

This book offers you the best way to get started in woodworking: Get started. As one of my mentors used to say, experience starts when you begin.

Tools for Woodworking

It doesn't take a big investment to get started in woodworking. You can build the first three projects in this book with a few well-chosen tools. By the time you've built a couple of boxes, a chair, and a coffee table, you'll have the know-how and experience you need to make wise choices as you add new tools to your collection.

To qualify as well chosen, a tool has to meet three criteria. First, it must be the right tool for the job. The wrong tool is hardly better than no tool at all. Second, it must be a quality tool—well designed and well made so you can adjust and tune it to do the work. Third, the tool must be comfortable for you. It has to feel good in your hands as you use it.

A good rule of thumb for buying tools is to stick with the upper-middle price range. That way you get quality components, thoughtful design, and good value. Low-end tools are often built to a price point and don't have the features, accuracy, or reliability you need to do good work. On the other end of the scale, professional-quality tools are meant to be used and abused eight hours a day for years at a time and are heavier, more powerful, and more expensive than necessary for a small shop. ■

Where to Get Quality Tools

Start your search for tools at the lumberyard favored by local contractors. Stores that supply the pros usually offer no-nonsense tools with a track record of quality. Although carpentry tools meant for homebuilding are sometimes different from those used for woodworking, there is enough overlap that you should be able to find most of the items you need to build the projects in this book.

Your nearby hardware store is another good source, but watch out for low-priced "homeowner" tools meant only for occasional use. Such tools may seem like a bargain, but if you're serious about woodworking, you'll soon outgrow them.

At home centers you'll find a dizzying selection of tools in a wide range of prices—everything from light-duty "homeowner" tools to huge construction-site tools much heavier or more powerful than you'll need for woodworking. But you'll have the chance to compare the fit and feel of each tool and find plenty in the upper-middle price range. Remember, you get what you pay for. A deal that seems too good to be true probably is.

If you're lucky, you live near a woodworkers' store, a place dedicated to supplying the needs of those who build to finer tolerances than is customary in carpentry. Woodworking on this level requires quality tools, and these stores offer a full range of hand and power tools. You can expect knowledgeable and attentive service; quite likely the salesperson will encourage you to test-drive the tools. Have a good look around while you're there, since woodworkers' stores typically stock items such as premium lumber and fasteners, traditional finishes, and fine decorative hardware that you won't find at a lumberyard, hardware store, or home center.

If you don't have a woodworkers' store nearby, you can also shop via catalog or online. Check out woodworking magazines and online search engines, and get on several mailing lists—each company has its specialty (see Resources on p. 198). Some offer only the highest-quality tools, others specialize in hardware, some specialize in hand or power tools, and others are known for their innovative design. Most woodworkers keep the catalogs as a reference; they're a great source of education and inspiration.

Good tools properly maintained can last for generations, but older tools are increasingly difficult to find. I've not had much luck at yard sales or tool swaps, but a friend who works at it occasionally finds something worthwhile. Online auctions are a good source for antique tools, but with a knowledgeable international audience willing to bid, real bargains are rare.

▼ Woodworkers' specialty stores stock tools and materials you can't find at a lumberyard or home center. You can expect knowledgeable and attentive service, and the sales staff is likely to encourage you to try before buying.

Keep in mind that old tools almost always require expert cleaning and tuning, so they may not be the best choice for beginning woodworkers.

Workbenches

The workbench is your most important woodworking tool. Everything comes together there. You'll use it for laying out, planing, chiseling, routing, assembling, and more. To do woodworking with any degree of success, you need a proper workbench.

I'm not saying the first order of business is to build yourself a fancy workbench. In fact, that's a bad idea. Building a good bench is a fairly advanced project; you can't build a proper workbench without a workbench to build it on.

You can do good work on a less than perfect bench, but you'll be frustrated if your bench doesn't have the following characteristics:

- Height about halfway between your hip and your waist (36" is right for someone about 5' 9" tall)
- A smooth, flat wooden surface that's light in color
- Enough size and weight to keep it from jumping around when planing
- Overhanging edges you can clamp to
- A woodworking vise to secure workpieces

The height is important to your comfort and health. Working for long hours at a bench that's too high or too low makes things more difficult than necessary and can lead to shoulder, arm, and back problems.

> **WORK SMART**
>
> Don't sand the surface of a workbench; minute particles of grit left by the sandpaper will lodge in the surface and mar your projects. Plane or scrape it smooth.

A Shop of Your Own

Most woodworking gets done in less than perfect shops. You don't really need much to do great work—just enough room to spread out your tools and materials; plenty of light; adequate heat when it's cold; and room to stow your tools, lumber, and partially completed projects.

Most amateur shops are in a basement or garage, which is a good idea when power tools are involved. Power tools of all kinds produce a very fine dust that will cover everything in the house. A good dust collector at the source will get rid of most of it. If you still have a problem with dust, a shop air filter makes a huge difference in air quality in the shop and in the home. With the exception of saws, hand tools produce shavings rather than dust. A number of my friends and acquaintances have hand-tools-only shops in their apartments and living rooms.

A basement is a fine place for a shop provided it's dry and has a way to get lumber and plywood in and finished projects out. You can deal with a basement that is occasionally wet more easily than you can deal with a space that is always damp. You can clean up an occasional puddle and dry out in a few days. But a continually damp shop breeds mold and rust, and your lumber will have a higher moisture content than is ideal.

Garage shops have wider fluctuations of temperature and humidity than a basement shop, but they do have the advantage of big, wide doors. These are great for getting tools, materials, and projects in and out and for light and air when the weather's good. You might have more space in a garage shop, at least when the cars are pulled out, but don't forget to take into account the effect on your tools and projects when a rain-soaked or snow- and road salt-encrusted car pulls in.

With a little planning and ingenuity, you can get along in a surprisingly modest shop. And many woodworkers enjoy devising clever storage solutions that get the most use out of a small space.

■ Essential Qualities of a Woodworker's Bench

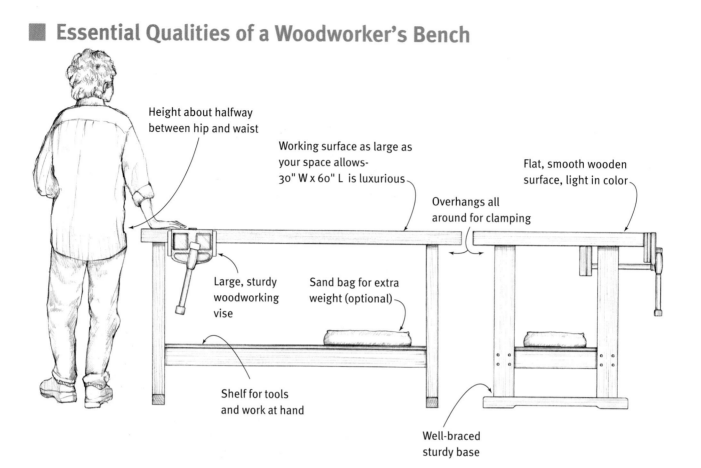

Height about halfway
between hip and waist

Working surface as large as
your space allows-
30" W x 60" L is luxurious

Flat, smooth wooden
surface, light in color

Overhangs all
around for clamping

Large, sturdy
woodworking
vise

Sand bag for extra
weight (optional)

Shelf for tools
and work at hand

Well-braced
sturdy base

A benchtop that's not smooth and flat will make it impossible to produce work that's flat, square, and true. The light color is important; a dark bench seems to suck all the light out of a room and makes it hard to see your work and set up your tools. If you already have a workbench with a dark or uneven top, you can fix it by planing it or covering it with ¾" birch plywood. If the bench is too light and jumps around in use, fasten it to the floor or a nearby wall. Or build a shelf beneath the bench and ballast it with bags of sand.

Workpieces almost always get clamped to the bench in some fashion, and small overhangs make the process a lot easier. Some benches have a thin facing around the sides to cover the end-grain plywood—these are hard to clamp to. If you have facing, make sure it's at least 1" thick for easy clamping.

If you can't get hold of your bench with a clamp, you can't do much woodworking.

Vises

You can actually do a lot of woodworking without a vise, but without one you'll spend a great deal of time inventing ingenious ways to hold things with clamps. A large, permanent wooden-jawed vise makes everything simple. Just put your work in the vise, crank it closed, and you're ready to go.

Make sure you buy a woodworking rather than metalworking vise. A woodworking vise nestles against the edge of the bench, with its top flush with the benchtop, and its large wooden jaws grip without marring. Woodworking vises are generally screwed or bolted to the underside of the bench. You'll never regret buying the best vise you can afford.

◀ A good wooden-jawed vise is necessary for successful woodworking. It holds the work securely without the hassles of clamping. Long pieces sometimes need an additional clamp.

Workbench options

There are an infinite number of creative solutions to the bench problem. You can build a sturdy table from simple parts or a kit, you can retrofit a garage-sale bench or worktable, you can buy a used bench, or you can buy a ready-made bench from a woodworkers' store.

Another clever and effective solution to the workbench problem is the Workmate®, an item that's something like a cross between a sawhorse and a vise (see the photo at right). Note the position of my left foot—you've got to steady the Workmate when planing. Even so, I've done some serious work over the years on mine, in boatyards and at friends' houses, trade shows, and even on the beach.

◀ The Workmate is a clever cross between a bench and a sawhorse. Even though Workmates are portable and easy to store, they are up to serious work.

Sawhorses

You'll need at least one pair of sawhorses around the shop, and if you have more, you'll use them. Stack lumber on them, use them for sawing plywood with a circular saw, put a sheet of plywood on top for a makeshift worktable—you'll think of other uses as well.

Your first pair should be high enough to let you work at a comfortable height, about hip high. For additional horses, consider a higher pair to serve as a worktable and a lower pair to use as an **assembly bench** (as a project progresses, it often gets too high for working comfortably on a benchtop).

You can make your own sawhorses, but when you're just starting at woodworking they can be harder to build than you think. Any hardware store or

WORK SMART

Whatever sawhorse you choose, make sure it has a wooden top. Sooner or later you'll saw through it by accident, and wood is kinder to sawblades.

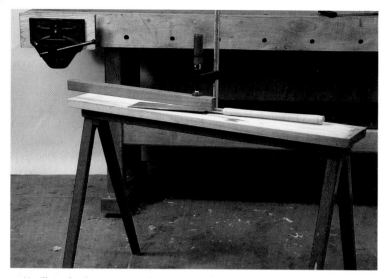

▲ You'll need at least one set of sawhorses in your shop. In addition to sawing, you'll use them for everything from stacking parts to serving as a workbench annex. Make sure they have wooden tops.

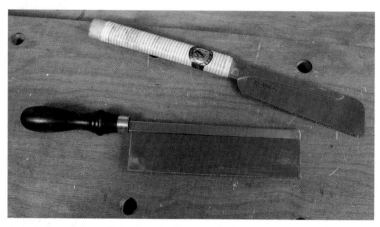

▲ A Western-style gent's backsaw is shown on the bottom; at top, a small Japanese-style backsaw. The Japanese saw has more teeth per inch for a smoother cut and greater control.

home center can offer several solutions to the problem, from inexpensive brackets for making your sawhorses from 2x4s to elegant folding sawhorses that are easy to store in a small shop.

Handsaws and Portable Power Saws

Square cuts are essential to successful woodworking. Without them, joints won't fit, tables wobble, chairs rock, and nothing comes out the way it's supposed to. If you can't cut perfectly square, you'll never be happy with your work.

There are any number of tools you can use to get square cuts—from the handsaw to the table saw. No matter which you use, you've got to keep two things in mind. First, you can't count on getting something square if you cut it freehand (even if you've drawn a perfectly square line). You need some kind of guide. Second, no matter how you cut it, the piece must be held against the fence (typically with clamps) so that it does not shift one millimeter during cutting. If the piece moves, it won't be square.

Backsaws

For precise cuts when doing joinery, you'll need a backsaw. So named because of the stiffener along their backs, these small saws have a relatively large number of teeth per inch to leave a smooth surface while providing maximum control. Backsaws come in several sizes and styles, but for the simple projects in this book buy a smaller dovetail or gent's saw, as shown in the photo at left.

Even making that distinction, you'll have one more choice to make—between a Japanese-style saw or a European style. The fundamental difference is that the Japanese saw cuts on the pull stroke, whereas the European saws cut on the push. Pulling the saw is less likely to bend it, so Japanese saws can be made of thinner material. That means a small kerf and less effort to saw. In addition, Japanese saws have more teeth, and they're ground in a way that makes them cut faster and more cleanly.

You'll get more control with a
Japanese saw, but many people prefer
the European saws because they are
easier to sharpen and sometimes a
wide kerf is desirable.

Miter boxes

The miter box guides a stiff-backed
handsaw so it makes perfectly vertical
cuts at a few preset angles—usually
90 degrees, 45 degrees, and 22½
degrees—and intermediate angles on the
more expensive saws. Clamp the wood
in place, and run the saw in the guides.
Miter boxes come in all shapes and
sizes, from mini plastic boxes for model
making to precision cast-aluminum saws
capable of crosscutting an 8"- wide board,
as shown in the photo at right.

Circular saws

Look around any construction site, and
you'll see that the hand-held circular
saw is the principal cutting tool. Where
pieces need to fit only within about ⅛",
you'll see carpenters using circular
saws freehand to crosscut, rip, miter,
and even cut long, smooth curves.
Woodworkers use them far less often—
typically only for rough-cutting plywood into dimensions easily run
through the table saw.

However, if you're on a budget, a
good circular saw coupled with accurate shopmade guides (see the sidebar
on p. 129 for how to build them can
double as a wide-board crosscut saw, as
a means to accurately cut plywood to
final dimensions, or even to rip wide
boards into narrower pieces.

I have several circular saws, both
corded and cordless, with blades ranging in diameter from 4" to 10". The one

▲ A large precision miter box can cut wood up to 8" wide. Clamp the wood in place
for accurate crosscuts or angled miters.

I reach for most often is a cordless
19.2-volt saw with a 6" blade, shown
on the left in the photo on p. 120. It's
light and easy to control and powerful
enough for most jobs. Best of all,
there's no cord to trip over, to catch on
the edge of the plywood, or to worry
about cutting through. Two batteries
are essential (see the sidebar on p. 12).

WORK SMART

When cutting plywood
with your circular saw, be
sure to use a many-
toothed blade intended
for cutting plywood. You'll
get a smoother cut with
less grain tearout along
the edge.

▲ Although more costly than a comparable corded saw, a battery-powered cordless saw like the 19.2-volt model shown on the left is more convenient. It can handle most small-shop jobs. Keep an extra battery on hand so you won't have to wait while the first one charges.

Corded Vs. Cordless Tools

Corded tools cost less than cordless tools, but I'm willing to pay for the pleasure of not having to deal with extension cords. It saves setup and cleanup time, and you won't ever trip over or get tangled up in the cord. The only time you really need a corded tool is when you're doing jobs that require high power and sustained effort, which is rare in small-shop woodworking.

For instance, a battery-powered circular saw has enough power and longevity to cut plywood for a cabinet or two. With two batteries and a fast charger, you'll rarely (if ever) deplete one battery before the other is charged. On the other hand, if you were a pro for whom minutes meant dollars, you'd want to cut a pile of parts without pause. In that case, you'd need a corded saw to keep up the pace.

Chopsaws

The chopsaw (sometimes called a mitre saw) is the motorized version of the miter box. It consists of a circular sawblade mounted so that it pivots downward to crosscut the wood. A miter saw is wedded to its table and fence, and they maintain their relationship no matter where the saw is moved, needing only occasional fine-tuning. A locking swivel mechanism allows you to cut any angle up to about 50 degrees on either side of square, as shown in the top photo on p 71. On a compound miter saw, the blade also tilts up to 45 degrees to cut the compound bevels required to fit crown molding into corners.

A miter saw with a 10" blade can crosscut a 6" board. The cost is similar to that of a precision miter box, although it has a smaller crosscut capacity. A 12" blade can crosscut an 8" board, but it costs considerably more than a 10" saw. The most versatile and expensive miter saws mount the blade and motor on a rail so they can slide in and out, increasing the crosscut capacity of a 10" saw to about 12".

Most chopsaws and precision miter boxes come with built-in clamps for holding your work, but you'll have to provide an auxiliary table for safe and accurate cutting of long boards (see the illustration on p. 94 for details).

Table Saws

A table saw is basically a circular saw mounted in a table (see the drawing on p. 15). With the turning blade fixed in one spot, you push the wood to make cuts. A table saw makes accurate crosscuts and also allows you to **rip** wide boards to narrower widths. You can also use it to make special cuts, including miters, rabbets, dadoes, and grooves. With the right jigs, you can make joints such as tenons, slip mortises, box joints, and more.

To get your table saw cutting square, straight, and true, the miter slots and fence must be fixed perfectly parallel to the blade, All new saws are aligned at the factory and probably survived transit unscathed, but this is such a critical point for accuracy and safety that you should check the saw before you use it. The owner's manual will describe how to check and align the saw. For a more detailed explanation, read one of the books on the table saw or setting up machinery listed in Resources on p. 198.

The table saw is the workhorse of a woodworking shop, but it must be used with care. With a blade turning in excess of 150 mph, every workpiece must be guided through the saw under the operator's complete control. If the piece wiggles as it goes past the blade or if the wood binds between the blade and the fence, the back edge of the blade can catch the workpiece, lift it off the table, and fling it back at the operator so quickly that evasive action is impossible.

Having the fence parallel to the blade is crucial to prevent binding and

B

Miter Box or Chopsaw?

A precision miter box costs about the same as a simple chopsaw. Which should you buy? There's no doubt that the chopsaw is faster than the miter box, but it still only takes a minute or so to crosscut a board by hand. The chopsaw is noisier than the miter box and decidedly more dangerous. The miter box has slightly greater capacity and needs no cord.

In the end, deciding which is right for you comes down to temperament rather than specs. Some people prefer speed, power, and technology. Others like the idea of working in a more contemplative manner, happily trading efficiency for quiet. Both ways are valid.

the resulting kickback, but every table saw should also have a splitter, as shown in the photo on p. 174. It holds the **kerf** open at the back of the cut, virtually eliminating binding against the back of the blade.

Choosing a table saw

Whatever your needs, you can find a table saw to suit. There are plenty to choose from—everything from portables costing less than $400 to powerful

$6,000+ saws with sliding tables large enough to hold a full sheet of plywood. As a beginning woodworker, you'll probably be looking at the smaller, simpler models with price tags of less than $1,000.

Benchtop table saws. Benchtop table saws are light enough to stow under a bench when not in use but powerful enough to fill the needs of many part-time woodworkers. Benchtop table saws can do every operation a larger, more expensive saw can do but not with the same aplomb. With their light-duty direct-drive motors, small tables, and slightly top-heavy design, benchtop table saws can make hard work of some big jobs. For instance, you'll have to cut thick hardwood in two or three passes, raising the blade a little each time, and cut long, heavy boards into smaller pieces to suit the small table. Even with an average price of around

$400, the accuracy of these small saws can be superb, and they are a great way to start woodworking in a serious way.

Contractors' table saws. Contractors' table saws are stationary job-site tools, heavy enough to require two people to move around and beefy enough to do hard labor. With large cast-iron tables and more powerful belt-driven motors, these saws are a step up from the benchtop saws in power and accuracy.

Many amateur woodworkers find that a contractors' saw offers more than enough power for their work. The saw's only serious limitation is in working with large, heavy workpieces. With open bases and cast-iron tops, these saws can be top-heavy and can **rack.** Expect to pay around $800 for a moderately accessorized contractors' saw.

Cabinet saws. Cabinet saws are the standard in small professional shops. Although they spin the same 10" blade,

TABLE-SAW RULES

You'll learn specific table-saw procedure when building the lateral file later in this book. In the meantime, here are a few rules to keep you safe and happily sawing for years to come:

- Never saw freehand. Always use a fence or jig.
- Always run a straight machined edge against the fence.
- Adjust the table so the sawblade is perfectly parallel to the miter slots and then adjust the fence to be perfectly parallel to the blade.
- Position your body so you're close to the saw throughout the cut and perfectly stable on your feet. Stand to the left of the blade.
- Never crosscut without a sliding guide.
- Never use the rip fence when crosscutting (even as a stop for determining length).
- Use a splitter whenever the cut allows it.
- Buy a good guard and use it.
- Use push sticks for pieces narrower than about 4".
- Use featherboards whenever possible.
- Always unplug your saw to adjust the blade, splitter, or fence.

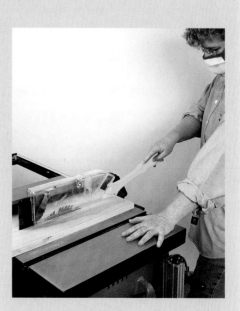

A Contractor's Table Saw

The table saw is all about straight and square and true. Set it up that way; guide and control your cuts with those concepts in mind, and you'll get great results every time.

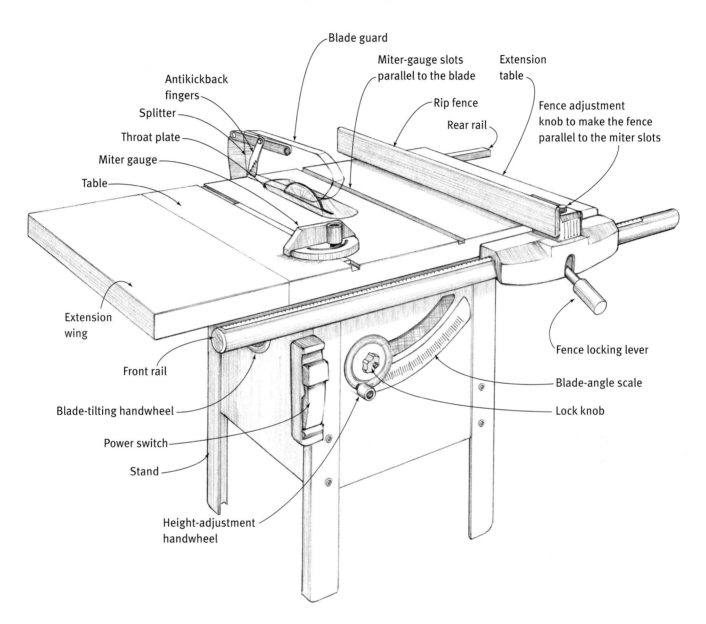

Blade guard

Miter-gauge slots parallel to the blade

Extension table

Antikickback fingers

Splitter

Rip fence

Throat plate

Rear rail

Miter gauge

Fence adjustment knob to make the fence parallel to the miter slots

Table

Extension wing

Front rail

Blade-tilting handwheel

Fence locking lever

Power switch

Blade-angle scale

Stand

Lock knob

Height-adjustment handwheel

a cabinet saw has greater power and precision than either contractors' or benchtop saws. Cabinet saws have higher-horsepower 220-volt motors, heavy cast-iron parts to reduce vibration, and larger tables. They're heavy duty in every respect. A typical cabinet saw weighs around 400 lb. and will cost from $1,500 to $2,200 depending on how you set it up.

Table-saw accessories

As delivered, your table saw will meet the basic standards of safety and functionality, but you'll need a few more items to get the most from it.

Table-saw blades. Your saw probably came with a ripping blade, with something like 24 teeth. It's the right blade to use for along-the-grain ripping cuts on solid wood, but the cut is too rough and aggressive for plywood, crosscutting, or for any kind of joinery.

A combination blade is designed to do most operations well, so you can crosscut, rip, make grooves, or cut joints with excellent results. The only time most people switch their combination blades for specialized blades is when they're working in particularly difficult materials. For instance, you can rip the solid wood for the lateral file with a combination blade, but if you were making three or four lateral files at once or using a dense hardwood like teak, your job would be easier with an aggressive rip blade (see the photo below).

The combo blade is the biggest section of the table-saw blade market, and you'll have many choices, no matter where you shop. You'll find blades with fancy laser-cut swirls at the edge to reduce noise, various combinations of teeth, slippery coatings, and lots of talk about the rake and grind of the teeth. You can delve as deeply as you want into the incremental advantages of those refinements, but what you really need is a well-made combination blade with 40 or 50 carbide-tipped teeth. Although the initial cost of a carbide-tipped blade is greater, it's so much harder than a non-carbide blade that it can cut twice as much wood before it needs to be sharpened.

Outfeed supports. The operator can control a moderately-sized workpiece on the infeed side of the table saw, but what happens to the wood after it's gone through the blade and off the edge of the table-saw table? This is a question you want to answer before you start sawing, because while you're sawing you should be focused on what's happening at the blade and nowhere else. The solution is some kind of support for the outfeed side of your saw.

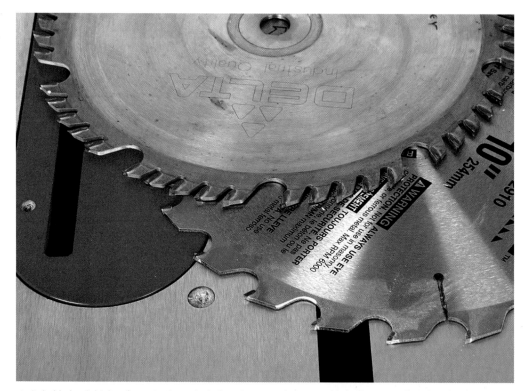

▲ A rip blade, right, has fewer teeth per inch than the general-purpose blade shown on the left. The general-purpose blade leaves a smoother surface but cuts a little more slowly.

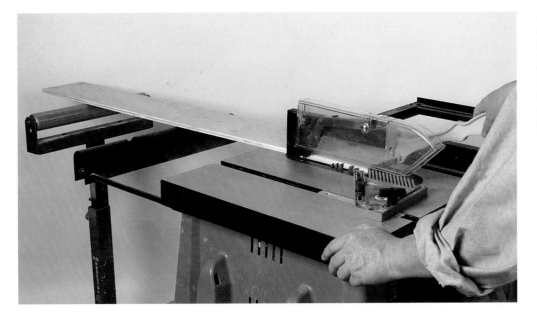

◀ The integral outfeed support (closest to the table) is always at the right height and won't tip over. For longer boards, you'll need an additional roller stand set some distance from the saw.

Integral outfeed supports are the best way to go. On some saws, they're in the form of an extension table bolted to the saw; on others they consist of a bar or roller that slides or bolts into place. Integral supports are always handy, always the right height, and they don't tip over.

Roller stands are adjustable in height, can be placed anywhere, and are useful secondary tables for dealing with very long workpieces (in which case you'll need one for the infeed as well). Look for roller stands that are not top-heavy and that have a wide footprint for stability.

Miter gauges. One of the cardinal rules of table-saw safety is never make a crosscut unless the workpiece is held with a guide that runs in the miter slot. Most table saws come with a miter gauge, a guide that is adjustable to cut not only square but just about any angle from 1 degree to 90 degrees, as shown in the photo at right.

To use the miter gauge, put the miter gauge in the miter slot and hold the workpiece tight against the protrac-

▲ The miter gauge shown below came with the saw. The shape of the head makes it hard to clamp anything to it. The miter gauge shown at top has a sliding fence you can clamp to and a more accurate protractor head.

tor head. Hold the work tight against the miter gauge, and push it past the blade. If the workpiece did not shift, you can draw the miter gauge back while keeping firm hold of the workpiece. You can use the slot on either side of the blade.

The miter gauge supplied with your saw often makes it hard to hold the workpiece tightly or to clamp it. Since it's only a few inches wide, it leaves a

▶ Long push sticks like the one shown at top keep your hands well clear of the blade. The push block below is useful when cutting rabbets and grooves.

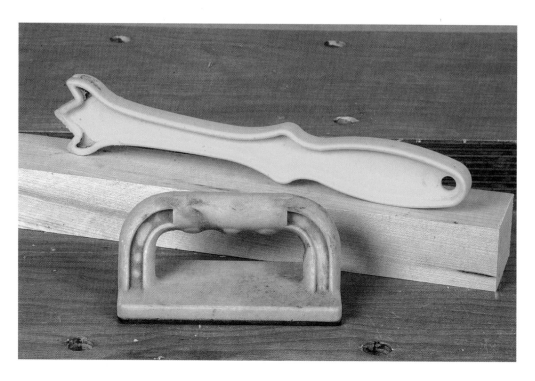

large workpiece unsupported. Add an auxiliary fence to the miter gauge that will allow you to clamp the work in place, and add stop blocks or other attachments to make your work safer and more accurate. You can add an auxiliary wooden fence, but you'll find that its length from the head to the blade must vary depending on the angle of cut. It's worth the expense to get an accessory sliding fence for your miter gauge or to buy an aftermarket miter gauge with a built-in fence.

Push sticks. You should use a push stick on ripping cuts where the workpiece is less than about 4" wide. That way, your hands will never get too close to the blade for comfort. There are dozens of push-stick designs, but I mostly use only two: a straight stick with a V in one end and a flat block with an angled handle.

For standard ripping, I use the push stick. It's long enough to keep your hands above the blade in any situation while maintaining control. A rubber-bottomed push block is the best push-

ing tool for those cuts where the blade does not come out the top of the wood, like rabbets, dadoes, and grooves.

Handplanes

I am continually amazed at the number of otherwise accomplished woodworkers who don't know how to use a plane. I can't imagine how they can build without this vital tool. No other tool gives such superb accuracy with complete control. You can clean up and round over an edge using a handplane in less time than it takes to get the router out of its box and its cord untangled. Unlike sanders or scrapers, a plane's long, flat sole guarantees flatness, and nothing beats it for leveling glue joints and face frames.

Planes are difficult to manufacture, and each one requires a significant amount of handwork before it's ready to be sold. The sole must be ground flat, the mating surfaces between the component parts need to be smoothed, and the handles attached. It takes time and money for a manufacturer to put out a plane with good fit and finish, and the price of a well-made plane will reflect that fact.

The less you pay for a plane, the more work you'll have to do to get it ready to use. You'll have to flatten the sole (use the same method as you use for flattening the back of a blade, as explained in "Skill Builder: Sharpening" on p. 66), file the inside of the cap iron and lever cap so they're flat and smooth, and lightly round the edges with a file.

Block Planes

Your first handplane purchase should be an adjustable-throat block plane. Sized to fit in the palm of your hand, this is the tool to use for final fitting or for lightly rounding edges. Most of the time, you'll keep the opening adjusted so the blade is about ¹⁄₁₆" from the throat. Set the blade deeper and open up the throat and you'll get a thicker, coarser shaving that hogs off material in a hurry. Conversely, raise the blade and close the throat for a thin, light cut.

Most manufacturers sell two models: a low-angle block plane good for all-around work, and a high-angle block plane suited for highly figured hardwoods. Get the low-angle plane first (see the top photo on p. 20).

Bench planes

This is the two-handed plane that's become the icon of hand woodworking. Bench planes come in a variety of sizes, from the 5½"-long number 1 to the 24"-long number 8. The longer the plane, the easier it is to get a truly flat surface. Before the days of jointers and planers, woodworkers needed several bench planes, but these days you'll do fine with a number 4 or 5 as your pri-

■ Bench Plane and Block Plane Anatomy

Master the plane, and you'll be a successful woodworker.

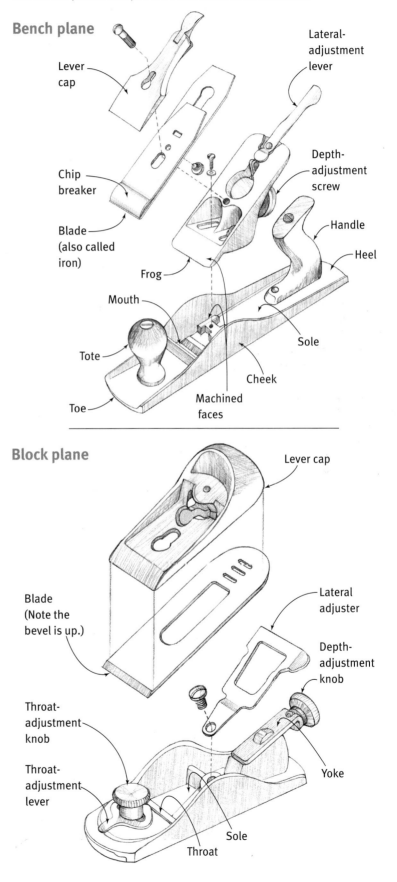

Bench plane

- Lever cap
- Lateral-adjustment lever
- Chip breaker
- Depth-adjustment screw
- Blade (also called iron)
- Handle
- Heel
- Frog
- Mouth
- Sole
- Tote
- Cheek
- Toe
- Machined faces

Block plane

- Lever cap
- Blade (Note the bevel is up.)
- Lateral adjuster
- Depth-adjustment knob
- Throat-adjustment knob
- Throat-adjustment lever
- Yoke
- Sole
- Throat

▶ Your first plane should be an adjustable-mouth, low-angle block plane like this one.

▼ For bigger jobs, you'll want a bench plane. The narrower one on the right is a bronze 04 bench plane.

mary plane. These planes have a 2"-wide iron. Some companies sell a number 4½ and a number 5½, which is the same size but with a 2⅜"-wide iron, which some people prefer because of its greater weight and slightly greater cutting width.

Bench Chisels

Chisels are for fine work. You'll use them to fit joints or remove a small amount of material with absolute con-

trol. Every woodworker needs a set of good, sharp chisels (see the sidebar on p. 74 for how to sharpen chisels). Learn to use a chisel well, and you're on your way to fine workmanship.

There are chisels for different purposes. For now, you need only a few bench chisels for general work. Your most likely source is a woodworking store rather than a home center or lumberyard. Carpenters prefer short butt chisels (they fit in a tool belt and are made to be struck with a hammer), whereas woodworkers need longer chisels for better leverage and handling when paring.

Wood handles look nice, but they're very expensive to make so that they're correctly aligned with the blade and don't split. Unless you're willing to pay more than about $30 per chisel, stick with a plastic version, as shown in the top photo at right.

The projects in this book only require two chisels—a wide one for cutting plugs (¾" or 1") on the chair and a narrower one (½") for cleaning out the ends of the stopped dadoes in the bookcase top. When purchasing chisels, you may want to buy a set—the price per chisel is often considerably less, and the deal often includes a box or canvas roll.

Corner Chisels

Until your chisel technique is perfected, it's hard to hand-chisel corners that are perfectly square. A special corner chisel can take the grief out of the process. Simple as they are, corner chisels are hard to sharpen, so take good care of the edge. Even though you'll almost always use it with a mallet, take thin paring cuts for control and to save the edge (see the bottom photo at right).

Mallets and Hammers

Mallets are for striking wood (or plastic) and have soft heads of materials like wood, leather, plastic, or lead. Hammers are for striking metal and have metal heads. And don't be tempted to make do when it comes to striking tools—use the right one for the job.

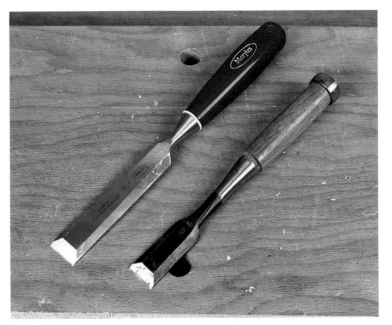

▲ Often more accurately made than all but the most expensive wooden-handled chisels, plastic-handled chisels like the one shown at left are a great value.

▲ A corner chisel makes it easy to cut perfect right angles. Though they look very different, these two corner chisels perform the same function. At left, a spring-loaded version; at right, a more traditional form.

Joiner's mallets

This classic wooden mallet is the time-honored tool for pounding chisels. It's an ergonomic masterpiece. The face is large, so you're likely to hit the chisel every time, and notice how the face angles back from the vertical. When it comes down, that angled face is square on the chisel, as shown in the photo at left below.

If you're strong, get a medium-sized mallet (about 20 oz.). If you're not strong, woodworking will do wonders for your upper body, but until then go with a lighter mallet. Leave the largest mallets to ship builders and timber framers.

Dead-blow mallets

A dead-blow mallet doesn't bounce much, no matter how you whale away. The head is filled with lead shot and oil. When the head comes down, the lead rushes forward, and the oil prevents it from bouncing back. The soft, nonmarring finish makes a dead-blow hammer the very best tool for coaxing wooden parts into place during assembly, as shown in the center photo below.

Warrington hammers

The Warrington hammer evolved to suit the needs of cabinetmakers, who

hammer only tiny brads or finishing nails. Whereas the classic carpenter's hammer has a claw for removing nails, the back of the Warrington hammer has a cross peen for starting brads without hitting your fingers. The Warrington is also fairly light for a hammer, weighing in at less than 10 oz. (see the photo at right below).

Measuring Tools

"Measure twice, cut once," woodworkers say with a knowing smile. True enough, but I know my limitations. I'm prone to reading the tape wrong, confusing sixteenths for eighths, transposing numbers, and measuring one thing and writing down another. Although I'm a competent mathematician, it's rare not to make mistakes when adding, subtracting, multiplying, and dividing fractions. Measuring twice, or even thrice, won't eliminate errors. If you don't want to make mistakes in

▲ Simple though it looks, the joiner's mallet is a triumph of form and function. The angled face ensures a square blow.

▲ A dead-blow mallet delivers force without marring. It's the ideal persuader for wooden joints.

▲ The cross peen on the back of a Warrington hammer is for starting brads without mashing your fingers.

measurement, don't measure—whenever possible, take direct readings with your tape or sliding square.

Tape measures

Woodworkers use smaller tape measures than carpenters. A 10' or 12' length is plenty long enough for laying out 8' sheets of plywood; sometimes a 16' tape is useful at the lumberyard when selecting boards.

Before buying a tape measure, pull it out to make sure the gradations are easy for you to read. Some tapes simply have lines at the finer gradations, which can be difficult to decipher. Other brands label the fractions at strategic points, and some advertise bold markings than can be seen without your reading glasses.

The hook end of the tape measure is a critical and often overlooked part. It should slide a distance equal to its thickness. That way, when you hook it over the end of a board, the first mark of the scale aligns with the inside edge of the hook, right on the end of the board. When you use it to measure the inside of an opening, the tape slides back against the hook so the scale measures from the outside of the hook.

Rulers

Tape measures are great for long lengths, but you'll need a ruler for anything less than a foot or two. Although you can get steel rules at an office-supply store, the best ones for woodworking are clearly marked on all four edges and read from right to left as well as from left to right. I like rulers that let me choose whether I want to read 32nds or 64ths of an inch and that are boldly marked so I can't read them wrong. Get a 12" rule first and 24" and 36" sizes as needed.

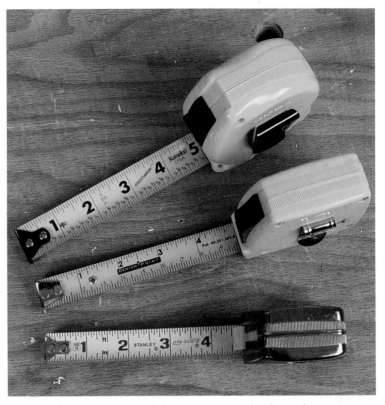

▲ Pick a tape measure with gradations you can see and understand.

Squares

Another excellent way to avoid measuring is by using a **combination square** or **double square.** These tools combine a square and a ruler in one handy tool (a combination square gives an accurate 45-degree angle as well). The ruler slides within the base, locking anywhere along its length, as shown in the center photo on p. 24.

You'll use a 6" square in nearly every project you build, sometimes alone and sometimes in addition to larger and smaller squares. I prefer a double square because it's more compact, and I rarely use the 45-degree side. Sometimes you'll have room to use the greater accuracy of a long blade, so you also need a 12" square. In this size, get the combination square, just so you'll have the 45-degree arm.

> **WORK SMART**
>
> The slots that allow the hook to slide can wear out on a well-used tape measure, causing it to read incorrectly. Check your tape measure from time to time to make sure it's accurate.

▲ You need a ruler with gradations up to ⅟₆₄th of an inch.

▲ You'll use a small sliding square like the one shown on the right more than any other tool in your shop. Shown at left is a 12" combination square.

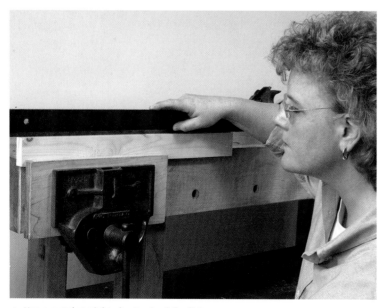

▲ Use a metal straightedge to check for flatness.

Sometimes even a 6" square is too large; it's then you'll need one that's only 4" long. It's handy (though expensive) to have a 4" double square, but an all-metal fixed-blade **engineer's square** is less costly and just as accurate. Don't bother to buy a fancy wood/brass try square with a fixed blade. They're too large to be useful and are notoriously inaccurate. I have a couple on the walls of my shop (gifts from well-meaning friends), but I don't use them.

Straightedges

To check for flatness, use a straightedge (shown in the bottom photo at left). The best straightedges are machined from steel, with a bevel edge on one side. They don't have a scale because they're not used for measuring. Aluminum is a good second choice and considerably less expensive. Start with one that's 24" long; when it's time to buy a 36", you'll understand why you need it and will feel better about paying the price.

Marking Tools

Most of the time, you'll make your measurement marks and labels with a sharp #2 pencil. Leave the fat, square pencils to the carpenters—they don't mark accurately enough for woodworking. The only time you'll need to use something else is when marking the hand-cut joints in the corners of the box. Then you'll use a layout or marking knife.

Layout lines made with a knife are more precise than those made with a pencil. The way the knife cuts through the fibers makes for a line you can see and feel as you pare or plane the surface back to it. You'll make your layout lines by drawing the knife along a metal straightedge, so one side of the knife is flat to snug up against the metal and cut right on the edge.

Some people use a pocketknife, but I don't think that works as well because the shape of the blade and the knife makes it hard to grip it tightly enough to make a clean line. I prefer to use a pair of marking knives, one ground with the bevel on the right, one on the left. Another kind of knife has a special pointed tip that puts both right and left blades on one tool (see the photo at right).

Cordless Drills/Drivers

You'll use your cordless drill/driver more than any other power tool in the shop, so take time to find one you like. Features are important, but your overriding concern should be to find a machine that feels good in your hand.

For most people, that immediately eliminates everything over 14 volts. The bigger battery packs produce higher **torque** and last longer between charges, but they're too heavy to be considered easy to use. Even a 14-volt drill is more than I want to lug around. Check out drills in the 9-volt to 12-volt range until you find one that suits. Any tool in that range will have enough torque and battery life for 99% of what you do as a woodworker. For that last 1%, you can compensate by drilling **pilot holes** (see the section on screws on p. 48 for more information) and by getting a second battery.

To function as both a drill and a driver, the tool must have two features— a high/low-speed switch and a **clutch.**

Using a Marking Knife

Put the flat edge against the ruler or straightedge with the bevel side out.

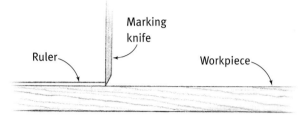

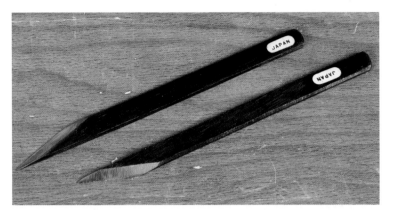

▲ Marking knives leave lines that are felt as well as seen. The most accurate way to cut them is by using a pair of knives, one with the bevel to the right, the other to the left.

The clutch disengages the drive when the torque reaches a certain level so the chuck can't turn, even when the trigger is depressed. You can hear the motor whirring and the drill makes a clicking sound, but the bit doesn't move.

Most drills have a collar near the chuck that lets you set the level of torque at which the clutch disengages. Use a low number for easy jobs such as when using small screws or soft wood and a high number where you'll need a lot of torque, say to drive a long screw. With a little experimentation, you can set the clutch to disengage so that the head of the screw is a little proud of the surface, flush with the surface, or even below the surface.

The numbers on the clutch dial aren't absolute; the setting will vary

WORK SMART

If your budget doesn't allow for a super-accurate metal straightedge, you can get by using a stiff metal ruler or a piece of accurately sawn plywood or MDF at least ¾" thick and 4" wide.

WORK SMART

Try operating your drill with your middle finger rather than with your forefinger. It gets your hand closer to the motor, which often makes the drill feel lighter and better balanced. It also frees up your forefinger for almost instantaneous reversals.

depending on the type and length of the screw and the hardness of the wood. Just beyond the highest number, you'll see a pictograph of a drill bit that indicates the fully engaged position used when drilling.

Sometimes a screw just needs another quarter turn to close up a joint. You have to go slowly to achieve that kind of control. To do it, you'll need a variable-speed drill—one that relates the bit-turning rpms to how hard you depress the trigger. You'll also want to set the high/low speed to low. Doing so changes the gearing inside the drill so that even when the trigger is fully depressed, the chuck won't turn at its highest speed.

Removing screws requires a reverse switch, so the chuck turns counterclockwise. You'll rarely use the reverse switch in drill mode—the proper way to remove a drill bit is to simply pull it out while it's still turning clockwise. On rare occasions bits do get stuck, and then you'll need reverse to extract it.

The position and design of the trigger and reverse switches are crucial to your enjoyment of the drill. A quality switch allows for smooth, virtually infinite variations in speed, and it should feel comfortable to operate. I like drills with the forward and reverse switches near the trigger, so I can change direction without changing my hand position.

Drilling Accessories

A drill is one of the most versatile tools in the shop, and well-chosen accessories make it even more so. For the projects in this book, you'll need drill bits, drivers, and a pocket-hole jig.

Bits

You won't need a whole set of drill bits to build the projects in this book, but it probably makes sense to buy a set anyway. The cost per bit is less, and they typically come in a case of some sort that keeps the bits from being dulled by improper storage. A small set of drill bits ranging in size from ⅛" up to ¼" will serve you well for the projects in this book.

For boring holes in wood, your best choice is a **brad-point drill bit,** shown in the left photo on facing page. The tip won't skate across the surface of the wood, and it tends to cut cleanly without tearing out. **Jobber's drill bits** have a simple angled point that is more likely to tear out the grain around the hole. For larger holes (such as the ¾" holes used to mount the tabletop fasteners in the coffee table project), use a **Forstner bit.** The teeth in the rim of the bit make it possible for you to start the hole with the edge of the bit off the apron and have the bit stay in place.

Most drill bits have round shanks, but it's worth the trouble to find smaller-diameter bits with the same hex shanks used on driver bits. You can also purchase hex-shank adapters for round-shank bits. The hex gives the chuck a better grip, but more importantly it can be used with quick-change attachments. These attachments can be a big saver of time and aggravation since they eliminate the need to loosen and tighten the chuck each time you change bits. Once the quick-change attachment is chucked into the drill, changing bits is simply a matter of pulling back the spring-loaded coupling and popping the bit in place.

▲ Brad-point bits, like the one shown in the center, are designed for cutting wood. Jobber's bits (left) are for other materials. On the right, a Forstner bit excels at cutting smooth large-diameter holes.

▲ If your bits have hex shanks, you can use a quick-change chuck. Just pull back the spring-loaded coupling to release the bit.

Driver bits and accessories

Just about every hardware store and home center has bins of driver bits of all shapes and sizes strategically placed so you'll pick up a few on your way out. Good idea. You can't have too many driver bits—they're easy to lose or misplace, and they wear out.

The 2"-long bits are the easiest to use. Shorter ones are hard to get into the chuck; longer than that and it's harder to drive the screw. The exception occurs when driving pocket-hole screws, where a 6" bit makes it easier to hold the drill at the correct angle.

If you're having trouble driving screws, you can get something like screw-driving training wheels. These are variously sized bit holders with a sheath that slides down over the screw to prevent tipping (see the left photo on p. 28). They're great to keep on hand for carpentry, when you're working on a ladder, and when you want to let your kids help.

A flexible shaft can solve difficult fastening problems. Sometimes it's the only way to drive a screw when there's too little room for any other tool in your shop. The shaft chucks into your drill/driver, and the other end has a socket for a driver bit. Hold onto the shaft at the collar near the bit and push hard. It's an odd feeling when the screw turns, and when it goes all the way in, be ready for a little kick. There's no danger in it, but it's unlike anything else and will surprise you.

Pocket-hole jigs and step drill bits

Essentially, pocket holes are stepped pilot holes set at a 15-degree angle and located near the end of a board (see the illustration on p. 29). They solve the problems of using screws to fasten corners. Screws set square to the face and driven from the outside of a corner joint have their threaded portion in end grain, which doesn't hold well. Plus, they're visible from the outside. Driving the screws at a slight angle gets the threads into face grain, where they can get a good bite on the wood. It also makes it possible to hide the screws by putting them on the inside. Assembled properly, with a bit of glue in the joint

▲ Training wheels for driving screws. With this setup, screws go in on the first try.

▲ Sometimes a flexible shaft is the only way to drive a screw in a difficult location.

and the screws taken up tight, a pocket-hole joint is very strong. It has other advantages as well. If the ends of the boards are square, the joint will end up square as long as the screws are tight. A pocket-hole joint doesn't require many clamps to assemble since the screws hold the joint in alignment while the glue dries.

The simplest commercial pocket-hole jigs have one or two hardened steel guides and clamp in place wherever you want to put a hole. When you're working on component parts, you'll usually have to secure the workpiece before clamping the jig to it. But sometimes it's handy to be able to clamp the guide on a finished or nearly finished project to strengthen a joint.

The most convenient jigs sit on the benchtop and have a lever-operated clamp to hold the workpiece in place. These jigs are easy to set up, fast, and secure. They're often sold as a kit along with a single-barrel or double-barrel guide and a special clamp for holding it in place (see the photo on facing page).

To make proper pocket holes, you need a **step drill bit**—a special type of bit that drills a hole with a larger diameter at the top, a shoulder, and then a smaller diameter at the bottom. This shoulder or step provides a solid surface for the head of the screw, whereas the smaller diameter creates a pilot hole for the screw.

Clamps

Clamps hold joints together while the glue dries, immobilize a piece of wood or a subassembly so you can work on it, and generally serve as an extra pair of hands.

Woodworkers love to wink at one another and say, "You can't have too many clamps!" It's tiresome after the first 100 repetitions, but we keep saying it because it is profoundly true. You'll be surprised how often you do something that requires nearly every clamp in the shop. And oddly, it continues to be the case throughout your woodworking life, no matter how many clamps you have.

Clamps come in all shapes and sizes, but most of your clamping only requires three types: **C-clamps, bar clamps,** and **panel clamps.** Any woodworking store or catalog will introduce you to other, more specialized types, but they're beyond what's necessary to build the projects in this book.

Bar clamps

There are several types of bar clamps, each one with its own advantages and disadvantages. A well-equipped shop will have some of each. These are the workhorse clamps—the ones you'll use in most situations.

C-clamps. Powerful, simple, and inexpensive, C-clamps are readily available in a wide range of sizes. They're not as convenient as some other types of throat clamps, but they do the job.

Adjustable bar clamps. Adjustable bar clamps, sometimes called F-clamps or bar clamps, have become the modern standard. The heads of these clamps are fixed in place, while the jaws (the part containing the screw) slide along a bar. These clamps are faster and have a greater useful range than C-clamps. Bar clamps come in lengths from 3" to more than 8', and in light-, medium-, and heavy-duty versions as well as

■ The Pocket Hole Screwed Joint

To make a pocket hole, you need a special jig and a step drill. Once the pocket hole is drilled, remove the jig, clamp the pieces together, and drive the screw.

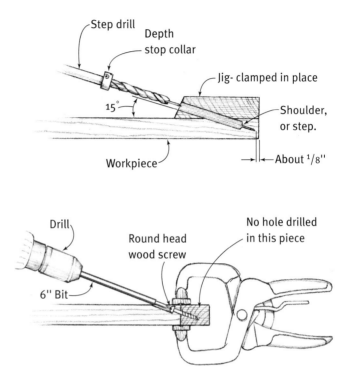

▲ The components of a pocket-hole kit—a double-barreled benchtop pocket-hole jig (back), a portable single-barreled jig (left), and a step drill.

standard and deep-throat configurations. Chances are you can find an adjustable clamp for just about any job. Several companies now make fast-action single-handed bar clamps, and every shop needs a few. Though generally not as powerful as clamps with handscrews, they're useful for holding a piece in place until you can get a bigger clamp on it.

Panel clamps

Panel clamps are large clamps with narrow jaws and are most often used for gluing up wide panels, such as a tabletop. Panel clamps have a very small throat, and they're typically set on the benchtop with the wood resting on the bars so all the component pieces of the glue-up are in the same plane to prevent twisting and bowing (see p. 126 for more information on making wide panels).

Because the height of the bar aligns the workpieces, it's important that all the panel clamps used on the bottom of a clamp-up are the same size and make. To keep uniform pressure on the joint, it's important to alternate clamps on the top and bottom.

There are many types of panel clamps. The projects in this book use fairly light-duty applications, so it

doesn't matter which you use. I'd suggest starting a collection with inexpensive light-duty aluminum clamps. Their light weight makes them easy to handle and position, and they are great for clamping in situations where the weight of a really beefy bar would tip over a project or cause some other problem.

Last but not least are pipe clamps, a clever invention that uses standard black iron pipe (available at virtually any hardware store for a very low price) as the bar. This option has the best cost/benefit ratio. The head threads onto one end of the pipe, and the jaw slips over the other end and slides along the pipe, jamming in place when tensioned (sometimes you have to whack it with a hammer to make it jam). Black iron pipe is sold in several standard lengths, so you can make clamps of almost any length by cutting the pipe or joining pipes together using standard plumbing parts. Make your pipe clamp glue-ups easier by using stabilizers to keep the heads from flopping around when not tensioned.

Sanding Tools

Nothing establishes your physical and emotional connection to your work like sanding. After sanding you come to know every inch of your work and can see the result of your care. The wood changes color, the edges soften slightly, and the oxidation and the marks of the milling tools disappear.

Random-orbit sanders

Most tool dealers offer a variety of specialized sanders, but the random-orbit sander is the best all-around sander you can buy. With a coarse paper, it can remove wood as aggressively as a

▼ From left to right: a Quick-Grip® fast-action clamp, a C-clamp, and an adjustable bar clamp.

belt sander but with more control. With fine paper, you can get the surface really smooth without losing flatness. It's easy to use, too. Unlike other types of sanders, a random-orbit just sits there until you move it—no pulling like an untrained dog on a leash.

The name random orbit refers to the way the disk rotates. It doesn't go around in perfect circles; if it did, the sanding action would be far too aggressive to leave anything remotely like a flat surface. Depending on the design of the sander, an offset drive shaft or lopsided weight degrades the rotation into a pattern that looks like it was drawn with a Spirograph. Combine that with the varied swaths of good sanding technique, and you end up with something like truly random abrasion.

A variable-speed control increases a sander's versatility. In most cases, you'll use the machine at max speed because max speed gives max material removal. That's the point, isn't it? But there are some times when you may want to lower the speed and therefore the aggressiveness. For instance, you want to lightly sand away the dust **nibs** on a sealer coat of varnish without cutting through the finish. Put 220-grit paper on the sander, reduce the speed, and go to it.

Get a sander with a pad that lets you use a hook-and-loop system for attaching sanding disks. Both the sander and the disks will cost a little more than one that uses stick-on disks. Hook-and-loop disks run cooler, and whereas sticky-backed disks are almost always destroyed in removal, you can reuse hook-and-loop disks. The other great advantage of the hook-and-loop system sander is that it has a better dust-collection system. Most models have some kind of onboard dust

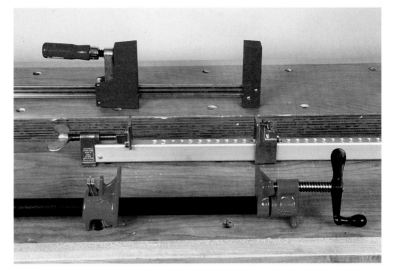

▲ Four kinds of panel clamps: a light-duty aluminum bar clamp, a cost-effective pipe clamp, a powerful solid-steel bar clamp, and a parallel-jawed K-Body™ clamp.

collection in bags or canisters, as well as provisions for connecting it to a shop vac for even better containment.

Whether you choose a 5" palm sander or a 6" two-handed sander is largely a matter of taste and strength (see the top left photo on p. 32). The 6" sander will make short work of big jobs, and some brands have an optional soft pad you can use to polish your car (or your furniture or boat). However, a 5" sander gets into small spaces and is lighter and easier to handle.

Hand-sanding blocks

I'm not a big fan of those clunky rubber sanding blocks sold in hardware stores and home centers. It's hard to load them with sandpaper, and they're too big for my hand. I prefer sanding blocks made of felt or cork or wooden blocks with felt or cork faces. You just wrap the paper around the block, and your natural grip holds the paper in place.

I also keep a long, two-handed sanding block for sanding larger surfaces by hand. It's actually sold as a push stick. When you cover the rubber bottom with sticky-backed sandpaper, it becomes an effective abrasive plane. It's perfect for smoothing difficult

▲ A 5" random-orbit palm sander (right) is light and easy to handle. A 6" random-orbit sander has almost 30% more surface area but requires two hands to operate.

▲ Hand-sanding blocks. The contoured wooden block shown on the left has felt on one side and cork on the other. At right left is a felt block.

grain, small pieces, or for a quick flattening or smoothing when you don't want to get out the power sanders.

Scrapers

The best way to deal with glue squeeze-out is to let it dry and remove it with a scraper. For that you need a big, two-handed scraper and a file to keep it sharp. A triangular scraper is the traditional choice; with three blades, you don't need to pause to sharpen very often.

Routers and Bits

When it comes to versatility, the router is the champion. With a router, the right bits, and guides, you can do almost any woodworking task: drill holes, cut grooves and housings, make identical parts, joint thickness boards, cut inlay, make moldings, cut curves, make complex joints, and more.

A router without a bit is as useless as a computer without software. And like software, you buy the bits you need to accomplish a specific job. There are hundreds of router bit profiles for sale, and as your woodworking advances, your bit collection will grow.

▲ This tool is actually sold as a push block, but with sticky-backed sandpaper, it makes an excellent long sanding board. Like a plane it leaves a smooth, flat surface.

The bits are held in the router by collets, as shown in the bottom photo on facing page. A cone-shaped collar surrounds the bit and squeezes tightly around it when the locking nut is cranked into position. All routers have collets to fit bits with ¼" shanks; most routers also have collets to handle ½" shanks.

Turning at over 20,000 rpm, a router bit can cut a profile into an edge effortlessly, leaving it so smooth it hardly needs to be sanded. But you can also mess up your workpiece in the blink of an eye. Mastering the router is all about learning to control it.

Bearings on bits, fences, and jigs help guide the router. In most situations, you'll run the router across the workpiece from left to right. This way, the forces of the counterclockwise rotation of the bit pull the router into the fence or guide. Routing in the other direction (called a climb cut) pushes the bit away. This type of cut has its uses, but for the most part you'll observe the left to right rule (see the illustration on p. 144).

To install a router bit, sink it all the way into the collet and then retract it about 1/16 in. Tighten the collet as much as you can. The depth of the cut is adjusted by raising or lowering the router motor within its base.

It's best to take light cuts with the router; it puts less strain on the motor and on the bits. Removing a substantial amount of material requires making multiple passes, gradually lowering the cutter until you reach the desired depth.

Choosing your first router

Being such a versatile tool, routers range in size from one-handed trimmers (roughly ½ hp and 3 lb.) to 18-lb. monsters packing 3+ hp. Your first router should be moderately powerful and easy to handle, so go with something around 1½ hp. Be sure to get a router that's capable of handling both ¼" and ½" shanks; if it can't it's not up to any kind of serious woodworking.

Before you buy any router, get your hands on it. It's a tool you must be

▲ A sharp, two-handed triangular scraper easily removes dried glue. Keep the edges sharp with a file.

◄ Router bits are held in place by collets. The one on the left is upside down showing its cone shape. The one at right is holding a template routing bit.

comfortable with. Are the grips comfortable for you? Is it easy for you to reach the switch? Check out the depth adjustment mechanism to see how easy it is to fine-tune and lock in place.

Although a plunge base router is not required for any project in this book, serious woodworkers will eventually need one. A plunge base lets you lower the bit into the work. It's ideal for making mortises, inlays, and any cut in the middle of a workpiece, but not preferred for most routing operations. Plunge routers don't have as great a cutting depth, and large ones can be unwieldy. Only use a plunge router when it's required.

WORK SAFE

Friction is all that holds a router bit in place. Make sure all the surfaces are clean and smooth. Don't oil them. And always tighten the collet nut as much as you can.

Router bits

Bits are made with ¼" or ½" shanks. A ¼" shank is appropriate for smaller-diameter bits, but larger, more complex bits need the extra strength and stiffness of a ½" shank. Some bits in the middle size range are sold with either size shanks, but you can't go wrong if you buy the larger shank. In theory the larger size one will cut cleaner and last longer, but the quality of manufacture is far more important than shank diameter. When buying bits, avoid no-name brands and remember that a good bit is not cheap to manufacture. It's another case of getting what you pay for.

Rabbeting bits

A rabbet is a groove or shoulder cut into the edge of a board, as shown in the illustration on p. 36. A rabbeting bit has a bearing mounted on its tip to guide the router. The bit is designed so that when the bearing is against the lower edge of the workpiece, the cutters remove wood from the top part of the edge, making a shoulder of a specified width. The width of the rabbet is set by the size of the bit and the bearing, and the depth is controlled by raising or lowering the motor within the base. These bits are available in sets with interchangeable cutters and bearings.

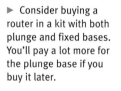

▶ Consider buying a router in a kit with both plunge and fixed bases. You'll pay a lot more for the plunge base if you buy it later.

Template bits

These bits have straight sides and a bearing mounted on the shank that's exactly the same diameter as the bit. It is made to follow a pattern (a template) exactly. Used with a straightedge to guide the bearing, this bit can straighten the edge of a board or smooth a rough sawcut. The bit can also follow all but the tightest curves. Called **template routing,** this method is most often used with a plywood or MDF template as a fast and nearly foolproof way of making multiple parts—either straight or curved (see the illustration on p. 36).

Classical pattern edge molding bits

The classical pattern is a specific profile that has a bead and a small cove. In an edge molding application, the bit has a tip-mounted bearing that runs along the edge of the workpiece, cutting the square corner into a complex profile that adds visual interest to an edge (see the illustration on p. 36).

Router accessories

There are hundreds of aftermarket accessories to increase your router's versatility, but there are only two I recommend from the start.

An offset base is important when routing edges or working on a narrow workpiece, as shown in the photo on p. 146. It gives you more surface area on the workpiece and therefore a little more leverage to keep the router vertical.

A router-bit depth gauge, shown in the bottom photo on p. 145, is the easiest way to adjust your depth of cut. The legs straddle the opening, making it easy to reference the depth from the base.

Shop Vacs

Until you get stationary machine tools, most of what you need to vacuum is fine dust made from sanding, routing, and sawing. This dust is both finer and more abrasive than household dust, and most home vacs can't handle it. The dust will abrade the working parts of the motor, and most of it is so fine that it's just blown back out into the air.

To protect your lungs and keep your house cleaner, get a dedicated shop vac with a 0.5-micron filter. Get the correct size floor and brush tools to use with it, since the ones you already have for your household vac probably won't fit the shop vac's hose.

The more you pay for your shop vac, the quieter it will be. So many woodworkers have inexpensive shop vacs that never get used because of the loud whining noise they make. You'll use a quiet vacuum more often.

Make sure to get the proper connector for attaching your shop vac to your random-orbit sander and table saw. It's also nice to have a vacuum designed with a built-in plug for the tool. This makes it so when you turn on the tool, the vacuum cleaner goes on. When you turn off the tool, the vacuum runs for a couple of seconds longer to clean the dust from the hose.

Safety Equipment

Safe woodworking begins with what you wear. Make sure to avoid loose clothing or jewelry that can catch on blades and cutters. Don't wear sandals in the shop; lightweight sneakers aren't much better. Go for substantial shoes or boots with a rubber sole to prevent slipping. To avoid splinters when stacking or moving lumber, wear

WORK SMART

Find a catalog of router bits and study both the shape of the bit and the illustrations of what the wood looks like after the cut. You'll learn a great deal about what routers can do, and you'll develop your ability to visualize the actual forms of objects from an engineering drawing.

■ Router Bits and Their Profiles

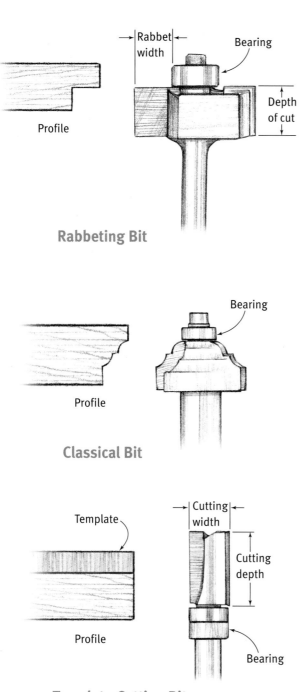

Rabbeting Bit

Classical Bit

Template-Cutting Bit

Tip- or shank-mounted bearings guide the router bit. While cutting you'll need these three bits to complete the projects in this book.

gloves. Soft leather or suede gloves are fine, but lightweight cotton gloves with a high-friction vinyl coating on the palms give you a strong, sure grip.

Remember that flying chips, loud noises, and airborne dust are as hazardous as a whirling table-saw blade. Buy and use the right safety equipment to protect your eyes, your hearing, and your lungs.

Safety glasses

Any kind of power tool, from a cordless drill to a router, sends chips flying. Keep them out of your eyes by wearing safety glasses with polycarbonate lenses and side shields. Many styles and sizes are available, so you should be able to find something that's comfortable and looks good.

If you wear eyeglasses, your eyes are protected from most kinds of dust, but without side shields, you're vulnerable to chips flying in from the side. You can get shields that slip over your glasses at the temples, or you can use goggles designed to be worn over your glasses. If you are serious about woodworking, it's worth the trouble to have an inexpensive pair of safety glasses with side shields made to your prescription.

Hearing protection

Whining power tools at close range will certainly damage your hearing over time, unless you reduce the decibel level by wearing hearing protectors. Choose a pair with a noise reduction rating of at least 22 decibels (db).

Earplugs, either reusable or disposable, offer the best value in hearing protection. Because they conform to the ear canal, they block out a lot of noise. Typical noise reduction ratings are in the 25-db to 27-db level. They are comfortable and nearly invisible, but some people find them difficult to insert.

Earmuff-type hearing protectors vary a great deal in their noise-reduction rating. The cheaper versions block out only 20 db, whereas the best go up to 30 db. You can also get earmuffs with stereo jacks or built-in radios, which could be pleasant to use when sanding or mowing the lawn but are too distracting to use when you need to concentrate.

Dust masks and respirators

Airborne wood dust is an irritant, a potential allergen, and a proven carcinogen. Wear a dust mask whenever dust is present—during sanding, sawing, routing, and sweeping up. You don't need a complicated respirator with cartridge filters; a light paper or cloth filter mask is enough but it must fit close to your face to work.

For protection against hazardous vapors or gases (like those found in oil-based paints), you should wear a heavy-duty respirator with charcoal filters.

WORK SAFE

If you suffer from carpal tunnel syndrome or any weakness in the hands or wrists, think about getting a pair of padded antivibration gloves for long bouts of power sanding. Vibration from the sander can be harmful to some conditions.

WORK SMART

Woodshop dust readily scratches plastic lenses of all kinds, so don't wipe off your dusty glasses with your shirttail or a paper towel. Blow the dust off, or use water or lens cleaner and a soft, clean lens cloth.

Materials

When you're eager to start a project, taking the time to get the right materials can seem like a drag. Eager to get going, you might be tempted to use whatever is at hand. Don't give this part of the building process the short shrift—the wrong materials can cause big problems. If you choose wrong, you'll have trouble fitting the joints or perhaps spending way more time than is necessary finishing (or refinishing). Worst of all, using the wrong materials can weaken your project and lessen its durability—it may come apart long before its time.

So, take the trouble to learn about your materials, and look forward to successful woodworking with a minimum of fuss and bother. ■

Solid-Wood Lumber

Picking the right wood for your projects can make the difference between success and failure. If you buy boards that are bowed, warped, or otherwise misshapen, you'll have a hard time getting well-fitting joints. And even if you do manage to make things go together, your work will lack the visual crispness that comes from straight lines.

Good results start with good lumber. Here's what you need to know to find it.

Rarely does a tree grow perfectly straight and upright. It could grow in all kinds of crazy situations—on a hillside, around fallen neighbors, or curved by the wind or from seeking the sun. Every cell of the tree bears the imprint of the stresses that shaped it. Yet when it comes time to make boards, every log is treated the same and run straight through a saw, sliced into uniform slabs, and stacked in a kiln to dry.

In the kiln, a complex program of heat, steam, and pressure evaporates the sap and moisture from the boards and reduces the moisture level to

■ Defects in Solid Wood

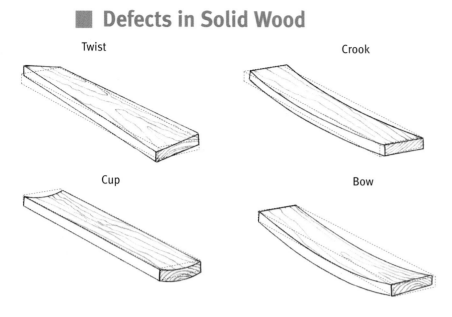

Twist

Crook

Cup

Bow

about 10%, which is the average moisture level that well-seasoned wood maintains over the years. As the moisture content falls, the cells shrink but not uniformly, and the boards **twist, cup, crook,** and **bow** to varying degrees, depending on the species, the thickness, and how and where the tree grew.

Once out of the kiln, the moisture content of the wood maintains equilibrium with the surrounding atmosphere. If you live in Winslow, AZ (one of the driest places in the United States), the wood will continue to lose moisture until it reaches about 7% moisture content. If you're in Lake Charles, LA (where the relative humidity averages 78%), the moisture content will rise to about 14%. Wherever the wood is, it will gain or lose moisture depending on the humidity of the air around it.

Each board gets bigger when the humidity is high and shrinks when the humidity goes down. That's why drawers are more difficult to open in the summer but glide smoothly in the dry winter months. Just how a piece of wood changes shape depends on where it was cut from the log (see the sidebar on p. 43).

Reading the grain

Upon leaving the kiln, the boards are milled flat and made into the rectangular planks you see at a lumberyard or home center. Twist, cup, and bow are removed in the process, but not always completely or for good. As the boards shrink and swell throughout their lives, they will continue to change shape according to their place in the original log.

When buying lumber, your first challenge is to find boards that are flat, straight, and square. Then you must figure out which boards will retain those characteristics once you get them to your shop. The clues are in the grain. Learn to read the grain, and you maximize your chances for woodworking success.

End grain. Check first for vertical end grain to find the most stable **quartersawn** boards. If the boards are narrow, select those with no pith. You might be able to find a wider board and rip away the pith using a tablesaw.

If there aren't enough quartersawn boards to complete your project, look for **riftsawn** stock, where the grain runs at around 45 degrees. These boards don't shrink much in width or thickness, but they do tend to become slightly diamond shaped.

Finally, select the best **flatsawn** boards, those with the flattest growth rings from the outsides of the trees. They cup less than boards cut nearer the center of the tree.

Face grain. Flatsawn boards have the familiar cathedral pattern along their length. Look for boards with a regular pattern, which indicates that the boards were cut from a fairly straight tree.

◼ Reading End Grain

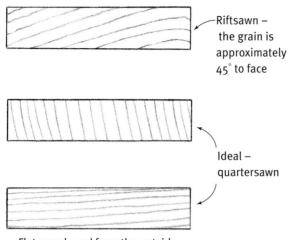

Riftsawn – the grain is approximately 45° to face

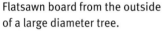

Ideal – quartersawn

Flatsawn board from the outside of a large diameter tree.

Avoid! Cut too near the pith, this board will cup severely.

◼ Reading Face Grain

Regular cathedral pattern

Multiple ellipsoids

The board came from a curved trunk. Boards with multiple ellipsoids are hard to plane and will likely bow.

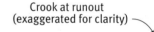

Quartersawn boards don't show cathedral grain on their faces.

Crook at runout (exaggerated for clarity)

Avoid flatsawn boards with multiple ellipsoids in the cathedral pattern. These occur when a straight board is sawn from a crooked tree. The internal stresses in the board will cause bow, twist, and other problems. It's a useful fiction to imagine that a board contains a "memory" of the whole tree and will always try to assume the shape the tree had in the forest.

Quartersawn boards don't have cathedral figure. Their faces show bold straight lines, sometimes running off the edge. That shows the tree grew with some curve; the board will not remain straight at where the grain runs out.

Prized in large part for their dimensional stability, quartersawn boards of some species are spectacularly beautiful. Because of the cellular structure of the wood, quartersawn boards show ray fleck, the amount and style depending on the species (see the photo

◀ Ray fleck shows in the quartersawn boards of some species. This is quartersawn white oak.

above). Quartersawn oak surfaces have shimmering rays interspersed with the strong grain, and many other woods, such as maple, show a pleasing mottled appearance.

Look for abrupt color changes at the edges of a board that indicate the presence of **sapwood** (see the top photo p. 42). Some people reject sapwood because they don't like the look

▲ The sapwood near the edge of this cherry board is not only different in color but also less stable.

► Sight down a board to check it for crook, bow, and twist.

of it, but the real problem is that sapwood is more sensitive to changes in relative humidity. It's less stable than **heartwood.**

Knots occur where branches grew on the tree and are not necessarily grounds to reject a board. Sometimes a knot can be an interesting design element, but knots can cause localized problems. Knots are harder than the surrounding wood, so they can make it difficult to flatten a surface. Because they shrink differently than the surrounding wood, knots can crack and split, and if they're on the edge of a board, they can cause a severe localized kink.

Many boards have splits at the ends, termed **checks.** They're not a problem unless they extend far enough into the board to effect yield. Just cut them off.

Edges. When you've found a piece of wood that passes both the end-grain and face-grain inspections, turn it on edge. You're looking for three things here—crook along the edges, bow along the face, and twist.

A small amount of crook is normal and easy to remedy, but a severe case should be rejected. A severely bowed board should be ditched, but a small amount of bow is not a problem, especially if the board is crosscut into smaller pieces. Over a shorter length, the bow becomes negligible.

Twist is difficult to assess accurately in the yard, but you should be able to learn something by looking closely at the far end. If the bottom of the board is off to one side as you sight down it, you've got some twist. Like bow, it's not a problem if the twist is not severe and the board will be crosscut.

Where to buy solid-wood lumber

The projects in this book use standard sizes of lumber readily available at virtually any lumberyard or home center. You'll find a good selection of lumber that's been carefully graded, selected, and milled into standard dimensions so it's easy to ship, store, and sell. It's not difficult to find decent lumber. The hard part is knowing how it's sold, what to ask for, and how to talk to the sales staff.

Most of the wood sold at a lumberyard or home center is rough **structural lumber** for building houses and decks. Some of it is wet—not even kiln dried, and what has been kiln dried is often

How a Board Acts Depends on Where It Comes From

Boards flatsawn from the outer edges of a log shrink moderately in width and cup slightly, with the bowl away from the center of the tree. It's a useful fiction to think of the growth rings as trying to straighten out. Boards flatsawn from near the center of the tree shrink a little less in width but cup more; you could say the smaller-diameter growth rings have a stronger tendency to straighten out.

How Wood Dries

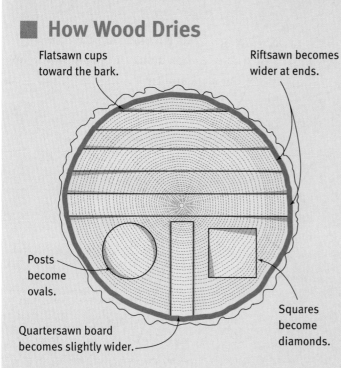

Flatsawn cups toward the bark.

Riftsawn becomes wider at ends.

Posts become ovals.

Quartersawn board becomes slightly wider.

Squares become diamonds.

When a board is cut through the center of the tree, the growth rings appear as vertical lines at the outer edges and curved lines near the pith, or center, of the tree. If you saw out the pith from the center, you end up with two boards with vertical growth rings, which are said to be quartersawn. These boards shrink a little in width, a little less in thickness, and won't cup. Every pile of flatsawn boards will contain a few that are quartersawn, but some sawyers cut to maximize the yield of quartersawn boards by sawing around the log. This requires more labor than flatsawing, but because quartersawn boards are so stable, they can be sold at a premium.

Quartersawn Boards

Quartersawn boards are prized for their dimensional stability. They are more costly to produce.

Sawing around a log is more time consuming. but it yields more premium quartersawm boards.

Flatsawing yields only a few quartersawn boards.

▲ Whereas structural lumber is piled outside in the weather, dimensional lumber is kept dry and out of the sun.

dried to only 19%. There's no reason to dry it any further, since many yards store the lumber in piles under the open sky. It's not worth the expense to dry the wood when in the course of building the house or deck, the lumber will be exposed to the elements.

In the sheds you'll find the **dimensional lumber,** hidden from the elements and kept warm and dry. This is where you'll find the woodworkers. Here you'll find neatly stacked piles of

pine, poplar, oak (usually red oak), fir, maple, cedar, mahogany, and sometimes cherry. The selection varies from region to region, but these are nearly universal.

Dimensional lumber is surfaced on four sides and is available in standard widths of 2", 3", 4", 6", 8", 10" and sometimes 12". Generally, these are nominal dimensions, meaning that the actual dimensions are less. A standard 1x6 starts out as a roughsawn 1x6. By the time it's been kiln dried, cleaned up, and made straight it ends up as ¾" x 5½". Boards that start out as 1x6 or narrower end up ¼" thinner and ½" narrower. Boards wider than 6" end up ¾" narrower.

If you go into a lumberyard and ask for "one-by" lumber, the salesperson typically assumes you mean nominal 1" lumber, which is ¾" thick. If you want lumber that is 1" thick, ask for ⁵⁄₄ lumber, pronounced "five quarter." A roughsawn ⁵⁄₄ board cleans up to 1" thick.

As if that weren't confusing enough, some places are now selling lumber from select species in which the boards are actually the dimensions on the label. When they say 1x4, they mean 1" thick and 4" wide.

The easiest way to get exactly what you want is to tell the yard staff the actual dimensions you need. If you ask for a "one by four" you could mean a board that's ¾" x 3½", or you could mean one that's 1" x 4". No one will be confused if you say, "I need a board that is actually 1" thick and 4" wide."

You can walk into the lumberyard with your nice tidy list, but chances are you won't be able to buy exactly what's on it. Say the list for your project specifies 4' 2x2s, but what if the yard has

Buying Rough Lumber

If you live near a woodworkers' store, a fine hardwoods dealer, or a local sawmill, you might choose to buy your wood roughsawn. The price will be lower, but you'll pay for the labor of milling and the wood it removes. A roughsawn board is harder to read, but at least you'll have expert assistance to help you pick out good ones.

Tell the staff what you need to end up with, and they'll help you select boards that will mill down to the correct dimensions. If you need a finished board that's 1" x 4", you may have to pay for a board that's 5/4 x 5½" or larger. You'll also pay an additional fee for the milling.

Whereas dimensioned lumber is typically sold as so many dollars per lineal foot, roughsawn lumber is sold by volume. It's an easy way to price lumber that's sold in irregular forms and of varying lengths, widths, and thicknesses. The unit is a board foot, which is equal to the amount of wood in a cube 1" x 12" x 12". Lumber dealers selling by the board foot needn't keep price lists for every possible combination of thickness and width. Three quick measurements are all you need.

To find the number of board feet in a piece of wood, multiply thickness, width, and length together (all in inches) and divide the result by 144. Multiply this figure by the price per board foot to get the cost of the board. This isn't easy to do in your head, but it's painless with a calculator.

only 8-footers or 3-footers? Before you can make a choice, you must know the approximate final lengths of the pieces used in each project. In the book you'll find that information in the "Notes" column in the materials lists.

Some yards are self-service, where you're free to pick through the lumber to select the best boards on your own, but most often you'll be under the protection of a yard employee. Keep in mind that it's not customary for contractors to be overly fussy, and you don't want to be branded as that woodworker who obsesses about the perfect board. Be firm about rejecting the worst boards, but don't make the yard guys work too hard. It's better to keep their goodwill. You'll need it in the long run. Once you've put a salesperson through the hassle of shifting piles of wood so you can get a closer look, help stack it back as neatly as it was when you arrived. Or neater.

■ Stacking Lumber While Conditioning

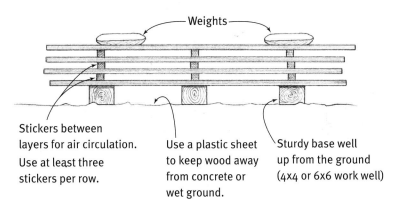

Weights

Stickers between layers for air circulation. Use at least three stickers per row.

Use a plastic sheet to keep wood away from concrete or wet ground.

Sturdy base well up from the ground (4x4 or 6x6 work well)

Storing lumber

Once you've selected the wood, take it to your shop and let it sit for a couple of weeks so its moisture content can reach equilibrium with its new environment. Don't stack the boards one atop the other—it's important that air circulate around each one. Put **stickers** that are at least ¾" thick between each layer.

► Sheet materials are dimensionally stable. Shown are a high-end plywood with many plies (top), MDF (right), and hardboard (bottom).

WORK SMART

Concrete is like a sponge for moisture, so never put your wood directly on a concrete floor. Use stickers or plastic sheeting to keep the wood dry.

You can also store your lumber vertically against the wall, which allows you to select it for best figure, or in racks against the wall in your shop.

Sheet Goods

After all the trouble solid wood can cause, it's sometimes a relief to deal with stable, man-made materials such as plywood and **MDF.** Uniformly flat, dimensionally stable, easy to machine, and virtually unaffected by changes in relative humidity, sheet goods can solve all kinds of woodworking problems.

Plywood

Plywood is made from thin pieces of wood (called **veneers**) layered with each **ply** perpendicular to those on either side of it. The veneers are well-glued together under high pressure and so thin that wood movement is impossible. Plywood is strong, waterproof, capable of bending around curves, and

is perfect where great strength and dimensional stability are required (see the illustration on the facing page).

Plywoods are specified by two different systems depending on whether they're **hardwoods** or **softwoods**. Softwood plywoods (such as pine and fir) are comparable to structural lumber and are too rough for most woodworking applications. Hardwood plywood is the woodworker's staple—it's used for shop jigs and fixtures, the backs and interiors of cabinets, and when made with handsome veneers, for furniture.

When buying hardwood plywood, first specify the quality of the faces, using letters:

- A faces use the best veneers matched for grain pattern and color.
- B faces are clear and matched for color but not grain pattern.
- C faces are not matched and may have plugs.
- D is a paint-grade finish that may have filled splits and holes.

- MDO face is covered with smooth paper; also called signboard because it paints so well.

Then specify the quality of the back:

- 1 is the highest quality, but it is not comparable to an A front.
- 2 has some wooden repairs.
- 3 has more repairs, sometimes filled with putty rather than wood and allows splits.
- 4 may have open splits and repairs that do not affect the strength of the panel.

Here's how it works. Let's say you want good-quality ¾"-thick plywood for making jigs, fixtures, and other general shop applications. You're not too concerned with appearance, but you don't want ugly scrap wood, either. Ask for ¾" B2 birch. Or you're going to build a lateral file and you want a handsome cherry veneer on the outside and a pretty good one on the inside. Ask for ¾" A2 cherry.

Although the outside dimensions of a sheet of plywood are a true 4' x 8', the specified thickness is nominal. The plies are laid up to yield, say, a ¾"-thick panel. After gluing it up at high pressure and heat, the panel is sanded flat. By the time both sides have been sanded, the ¾" has become ²³⁄₃₂" thick.

MDF

MDF stands for medium-density fiberboard, a homogenous material made from sawmill waste. Although it sounds a little like particleboard, MDF is a first-rate material. Sawdust, chips, and other wood debris are refined to a very small particle size, mixed with adhesive, and formed into sheets under extreme pressure. MDF machines beautifully, although cutting it makes a lot of dust. You can saw, plane, rout, and

Plywood Construction

Plywood is dimensionally stable because the plies are oriented with alternating grain direction.

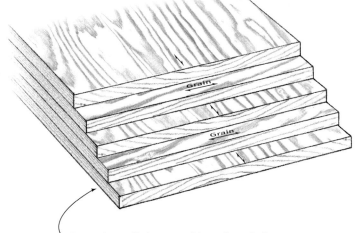

Plywood usually has an odd number of plies. More plies=higher strength and more uniform bending.

shape MDF, and it's easy to paint. It is more dimensionally stable than plywood, and unlike plywood, a ¾"-thick MDF panel is truly ¾" thick.

MDF has only two drawbacks to keep in mind. First, screws driven in its edges tend to split it, and second, it's heavy. A full sheet of ½" MDF is a handful, but some yards carry the lighter-colored, lighter-density version.

I like to use MDF around the shop for jigs and fixtures because of its even texture, good looks, and low price. A sheet of MDF costs about half as much as a sheet of plywood. Some yards offer "MDF lumber" in one-by sizes, primed and ready to paint. This is a great way to keep some ready-to-use MDF on hand.

Hardboard

You're probably familiar with hardboard in its pegboard incarnation—it also comes in a smooth-faced version. Similar to MDF in construction, hardboard is even denser and heavier. It's only sold in ⅛" and ¼" thicknesses. It's good to keep some ¼"-thick hardboard on hand because it's good for drawer bottoms, inserts, and for building things around the shop.

Beadboard

Take plywood or MDF and rout a series of lengthwise groove-and-bead profiles, and you have a stable, good-looking panel for walls, the backs of furniture, and cabinet doors. In this book, it's used for the back of the bookcase. I prefer MDF beadboard because it is easier to paint and often comes primed.

Where to buy sheet goods

You can usually get birch, luan, and oak plywood at home centers; lumberyards will likely have a wider variety of veneers, including cherry, maple, and luan. For rarer veneers, find a plywood specialty company that is accustomed to dealing with cabinet shops (see Resources on p. 198). MDF is readily available in lumberyards and home centers, and most places carry some type of beadboard.

You'll typically have to buy a full sheet—although some dealers offer half and even quarter sheets of their best sellers. If you must buy a full sheet, check to see if the yard is willing to make a cut or two to help you get it into your vehicle.

Fastenings

You can't always use glue—maybe you're in a hurry, or you may need to be able to take a joint apart. You need to know a little about metal fasteners to hold pieces of wood together.

Wood screws

Screws are the most useful fasteners in the woodworker's arsenal. They're stronger than nails, can pull a joint tight on their own without clamps, are removable, can be driven at almost any angle, and can be rendered invisible by using plugs (with clear finishes) or fillers (with paints).

The key to the screw's strength and usefulness lies in its threads, which wind around the root in a helix. As the screw turns, the helix bites into the wood, drawing the fastener through the piece of wood to be held and into the anchoring piece until the head of the screw is tight against the top piece, holding it in place. Within the anchoring piece, the threads cut through or crush some wood fibers, but most are simply shoved aside and end up molding themselves around the threads.

Dense hardwoods don't compress enough to allow the threads to mold, and the wood's resistance to the screw's passage can be enough to break the screw. If the screw doesn't break, something else must give, and the wood splits rather than allowing the thread to enter.

To prevent splitting, **bore** a **pilot hole** to remove some of the material in the anchoring piece to relieve the pressure. Drill the top part of the pilot hole at the shank wider so no threads engage the top piece and try to force it away from the piece below. Use a tapered countersink drill bit.

There are two basic types of wood screws on the market today: the traditional (made from a 500-year-old design) and modern production screws (see the photo on the facing page). The design of a traditional screw stems from having once been cut by hand. The shank is the same diameter as the outside of the threads, tapering slightly at the tip. The upper third of the screw is not threaded.

■ Ideal Proportions of a Wood Screwed Joint

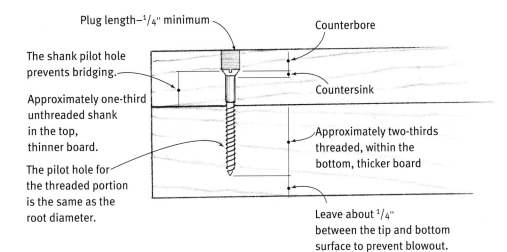

Plug length–1/4" minimum

Counterbore

The shank pilot hole prevents bridging.

Countersink

Approximately one-third unthreaded shank in the top, thinner board.

The pilot hole for the threaded portion is the same as the root diameter.

Approximately two-thirds threaded, within the bottom, thicker board

Leave about 1/4" between the tip and bottom surface to prevent blowout.

There are several proprietary production screw designs, and most have added a notch or extra thread or some similar feature at the tip that makes the screw into its own little pilot-hole bit. Except for very long screws, very hard woods, or fastening near the ends, you won't need to bore a pilot hole for these self-drilling screws. In addition, modern screws have aggressive thread designs that make them easier to drive by power.

I try to buy square-drive screws whenever possible. They're available with a countersinking head or with a wide washer-head for pocket hole screws or other applications where the load is spread over a greater area. The surface area between the bit and the screw is greater than with Phillips-head screws, and the bit stays in the slot at high torque. With a Phillips bit, high levels of torque often cause the bit to rise out of the slot enough to chew up the head as it rotates. You have to exert enormous pressure on a Phillips-head bit to keep it engaged. A square-drive screw is much easier to drive.

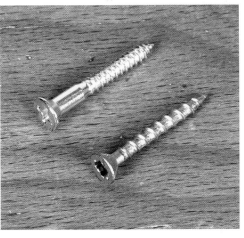

▲ Two #8 x 1 ¼" wood screws: an old-fashioned screw (left) and a modern rolled-thread wood screw (right).

Lag screws

A cross between a screw and a bolt, lag screws have large diameters, coarse threads, and big hex heads for driving with a wrench. They're the perfect solution for heavy-duty applications where the fastener is longer than about 3".

Lags need shank holes and pilot holes, just like traditional wood screws. Like bolts, lags also need a washer under the head to spread out the force so the head won't sink into the wood, crushing the wood fibers around it (see top photo on p. 50).

WORK SMART

Only wood screws have the correct characteristics and proportions for fastening wood. Self-tapping screws are designed for metal-to-metal applications, and drywall screws have special characteristics that make them wrong for fastening wood.

▶ Lag screws are like coarse, long wood screws installed with a wrench. Always use a washer under the head to keep the wood around it from being crushed.

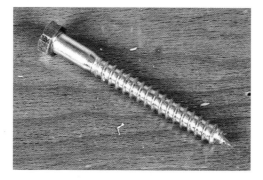

▶ When woodworkers use nails, the nails are typically thin, small brads, or finishing nails such as these.

Brads and finishing nails

If a woodworking project calls for nails, it'll likely be for small, thin finishing nails or brads. Similar in size and proportion, brads and nails have different characteristics.

Finishing nails have sharp points and slightly larger heads, whereas brads have smaller heads that are easier to conceal. Finishing nails tend to be used by home builders. Brads are a hardware store item. Either is appropriate for the projects in this book—simply use what is available to you.

Glues

Strength is seldom a factor with modern woodworking glues; they're all stronger than the wood they bond. Other properties are far more important, like whether they're water-resistant, fill gaps, or have a fast cure time. Although there are hundreds of glues, most woodworkers stick with just a few.

Yellow glue

This is the staple woodworkers' glue because it's easy to use and cures fast enough to remove the clamps in about an hour. Yellow glue is applied to both surfaces of the wood in an even coat just thick enough to obscure the grain pattern in the wood. A glue joint with the right amount of glue will squeeze out an even line of beads its whole length when clamped tightly. If there are no beads, you may have a glue-starved joint. On the other hand, if the glue runs out of the joint, you've used too much (see the photo below).

Once you've applied the glue, you've got about 10 to 15 minutes of open time, depending on the temperature and humidity. After that, the surface of the glue has started to cure, and you can't count on getting a good joint. Some companies make extended open time yellow glue, which can be a big help for complicated glue-ups and on hot days.

Yellow glue has no gap-filling qualities; for full strength the joints must fit very well and the clamps have to be cranked tight. Because yellow glue is a water-based product, it causes the

▲ If the glue runs out like this you've got too much. Don't try to clean it up—you'll just spread it around. Wait until it's dry and scrape it off.

wood to swell immediately adjacent to the joint. This is important to remember, for if you plane or sand the joint flat too soon after gluing, when moisture evaporates, the wood around the joint will shrink into a low spot around the joint.

Yellow glue cleans up easily with water, but be careful to remove all traces. A thin film left on the surface may be invisible but will seal the wood like a finish, preventing stain from penetrating. If you've applied the right amount of glue, there's not enough squeeze-out to be a problem. Just leave the beads of glue to dry, then scrape them off cleanly.

For gluing dark woods or for highlighting gluelines, try dark-tinted yellow glue. Although light brown in color when applied, it dries almost black. For applying moldings or working on vertical surfaces, you can get thickened yellow glue that is less runny. Outdoor projects require the water-resistant version of yellow glue.

Epoxy

Epoxy is the only glue that bridges gaps and makes poorly fitted joints as strong as perfect-fitting joints. Since epoxy dries clear, it's also great for filling flaws in wood, like wormholes and knots. Just fill the hole with a little epoxy (you can mix in sawdust, too, if you like) and sand it flush once fully cured.

Epoxies are two-part products that must be well mixed in the proper ratio or they don't cure. Exactly what the ratio should be between parts A and B depends on the formulation of your epoxy. For most home-use products, the ratio is simply 1:1, with a margin of error of about 10%.

Open time and cure time depend on the formulation and can be anywhere from five minutes to eight hours at room temperature. Epoxy cures much faster in warm weather—the cure time halves for each 10°F increase.

Uncured epoxy can be cleaned up with vinegar, denatured alcohol, or acetone. Once epoxy has cured, it's waterproof and impervious to pretty much everything except solar radiation.

Polyurethane

Honeylike in appearance, polyurethane glue cures in the presence of moisture. At room temperature you have about 20 minutes of open time, and the joints should remain in clamps for about two hours. You can speed the cure by moistening one surface with water before clamping. Polyurethanes are unique in that the squeeze-out turns to foam, which is easy to remove from the surface.

Polyurethanes are not gap-filling adhesives, but they are waterproof and can be stained.

Cyanoacrylate

Cyanoacrylate is the woodworker's version of Super Glue™. It cures very fast (30 seconds to five minutes depending on formulation) and is crystal clear, making it perfect for fixing splits, failed plugs, small holes, and other minor problems. It is not suitable for large jobs but keep a bottle around. Sometimes it can save the day by fixing a split or gluing back a busted corner.

Abrasives

Abrasives are used in woodworking for shaping, smoothing, and finishing wood, as well as for sharpening plane irons and chisels. Rough sandpaper with a low grit number is used for shaping and flattening or any time you

▲ Pick the right abrasive paper for the job: (left to right) silicon carbide, garnet, aluminum oxide, wetsanding paper.

want to remove material quickly (such as when getting rid of old finish or flattening the back of a plane iron). Once the surface is flat (or rounded if that's your goal), you switch to a finer-grit paper to smooth away the scratches left by shaping.

Getting a smooth surface is simply a matter of replacing the scratches left by the coarse sandpaper with finer ones. Sand the surface thoroughly (by hand or with power), brush it off to remove the dust and abrasive particles, and switch to the next finest grit. Repeat until the surface is as smooth as you want.

Sanding bare wood

Working wood, you'll use sandpaper ranging in grit from 36# (aggressive removal of material or finish) up to about 220#. Any finer grit than that and the surface becomes too smooth for stain to penetrate or for glue or a finish to adhere.

Of all the minerals used in making sandpapers, only two are suitable for sanding bare wood—aluminum oxide and garnet. It's an aggressive paper; it cuts fast and rather harshly. It's good all-around sandpaper for woodworking and is readily available in sheets and disks.

Garnet paper is harder to find, but many woodworkers prize it because

grit for grit it leaves a smoother surface than aluminum oxide. Garnet is a softer abrasive that tends to burnish the surface rather than cut it, leaving a lovely sheen. That burnishing can also be used to advantage when sanding woods like pine that tend to absorb stains unevenly. A surface sanded with garnet paper is less prone to blotching. It is available in sheets.

Sanding paint and other finishes

Finishes are harder to sand than bare wood and call for a more aggressive abrasive like **silicon carbide.** You'll use it in papers with grits ranging from 100# to 220# between coats and up to 2,000# for polishing.

You can get silicon carbide papers with special backing made for **wetsanding.** Once a couple of coats of finish are on and dry, many people prefer to sand with water or oil as a lubricant. Wetsanding is fast and efficient but best of all, it's dust free.

Synthetic steel wool

You've probably used these pads around the house—you can get synthetic steel wool scrubbers with a handle and sponges backed with a thin layer of it. Unlike steel wool, these pads won't shed little metal shards, and they're great for wetsanding.

They're long lasting and reusable, so get one of each color. The green is the coarsest, which makes it best suited for rough work—you'll use this the least. Maroon is great to use between finish coats when wetsanding. The gray pads are good for intermediate coats when using oils, and the white is the finest. Use the white ones for final coats of oil and for applying wax and oil/wax finishes.

Stains

You can use stains to change the color of wood, but they won't make one species look like another. Although it's unreasonable to think that you'll ever get pine to look like cherry, it's not unreasonable to try to get the color of your pine piece in the same tonal range as a cherry piece in the same room. Think color, not species. This frees you up to experiment with mixtures of color that yield surprising results, like the rich golden brown you get from putting a wash of lemon yellow beneath a brown mahogany stain, or the surprising results you get from a light wash of black on figured maple.

The range of effects is virtually limitless, and each finisher's taste so personal that I'm not even going to try to suggest color combinations. What you need to know are the qualities of the basic types of stain and how to apply them.

It's important to remember that staining merely colors the wood—it does not protect it. For that you need a clear top coat over the stain. Make sure the stain is completely dry before applying the top coat.

Prestain conditioners

Many common furniture woods are difficult to stain. Pine, cherry, and birch are notable for their tendency to blotch because of variations in the density of the wood. The porous areas take on more color. To even out absorption, you need to partially seal the porous areas so they take up less stain. Most stain manufacturers sell a compatible product for this purpose, but I've had better luck using a thin coat of shellac, which works well under an oil- or water-based stain.

Pigment stains

Made from colored powders (pigments) added to an oil or water base, pigment stains are commonly available in hardware stores and home centers. The pigments don't go into the wood as much

Oil- Vs. Water-Based Finishes

Oil-based finishes go on smoothly and cure when the volatile petrochemical solvents evaporate, leaving behind a tough film. This process typically takes about eight hours, and as a result, the surface settles and bubbles and brush marks usually disappear. It's much easier to get a glassy-smooth surface with an oil-based finish. However, the solvents are flammable and in high concentrations are proven to have a negative impact on health over the long term. Consequently, chemists have developed a number of water-based finishes that cure by the evaporation of water.

Because of their chemistry, water-based finishes are on the whole less shiny and durable (especially outdoors) than oil-based finishes. The other drawback of water-based finishes is that they cure quickly, so brush marks don't have a chance to settle out. But they clean up with water, and the fumes are safe. This makes them ideal for finishing jobs done indoors (especially in the winter when you might be using a heater) and when you need to build up your coats quickly.

When you're finishing a project, it makes sense to choose either oil-based or water-based products and go with the same type and brand throughout the finishing process. By using prestain conditioner, stain, and top coat of the same product line, you won't have any chemical incompatibilities that could cause your finish to fail long before its time.

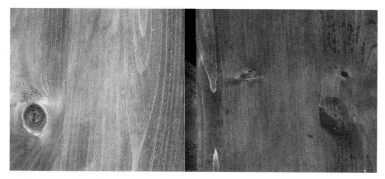

▲ Some woods such as pine soak up stain unevenly. Use a prestain conditioner to reduce blotchiness. The board shown at left got a light coat of thinned shellac before staining with a water-based pigment stain. The stain was applied directly to the board shown at right.

as they sit on top of it, so pigment stains obscure the grain somewhat. If applied too thickly they look muddy, but they have the advantage of being reversible if treated with the proper solvent before drying. That means that if you don't like the effect you get with a pigment stain, you can remove most (if not all) of it with a solvent-soaked rag and try again.

Pigment stains settle in the open pores, accentuating the grain. Use them to highlight open-grained woods like oak, but be careful with woods like pine and birch. Their uneven grains are intensified and can look blotchy.

Dye stains

Dye stains penetrate the wood and lend a more vivid, even color than pigment stains. When applied, dye stains soak right into the wood, often leaving nothing behind to wipe up. To control color, thin the dye with the appropriate solvent (usually alcohol) and apply multiple coats.

Because of their even penetration, dye stains don't call attention to grain or figure in wood. That makes them your best choice for hard-to-stain woods such as birch and pine. Dye stains are available at specialty finishing and woodworking suppliers.

Gel stains

These thickened, highly pigmented stains are a little easier to apply on vertical surfaces. They also offer more color control than standard pigment stains, making them a better choice on woods that tend to blotch. Some companies sell gel stains that are a combination pigment and dye stain and have the advantages of both.

Finishes

Most amateur woodworkers enjoy the process of finishing and consider it an important part of the process of building something by hand. You can get great results by learning to use only a few basic finishing methods.

Oil finishes

The most common oils used in wood finishing are boiled linseed oil, tung oil, and Danish oil. All take a long time to dry but provide an inexpensive, moderately durable finish that's suitable for interior use. Oil deepens the color and tends to "pop" or highlight the figure in wood and has a soft, natural look. Apply with a rag, let the oil soak into the wood for a while, and wipe off the excess. Two or three coats are typically sufficient.

Oil finishes are easy to maintain—simply clean and "sand" the surface with synthetic steel wool and apply another coat.

Oil/wax finishes

The old fashioned way to make this finish is to melt beeswax into linseed oil, then thin with a little turpentine. These days the recipe includes modern fast-drying and durable polymers, but the soft sheen remains. This finish

FINISHES AT A GLANCE

Type of Finish	Solvent	Durability	Best Uses	Maintenance
Oil (tung, boiled linseed,) or danish	Turpentine or mineral spirits	Good indoors but won't last more than a few weeks outdoors.	Any time you want to enhance the grain. For tables or other furniture that won't be used hard.	Recoat periodically using synthetic steel wool.
Oil/wax	Turpentine	Good	Decorative items that aren't subjected to everyday wear and tear—boxes, display cabinets, figured tabletops.	Recoat periodically using synthetic steel wool. Polish with a soft cloth.
Wax	Turpentine	Good	Tables and other furniture.	Recoat periodically using synthetic steel wool. Polish with a soft cloth.
Shellac	Denatured alcohol	Fair	Use alone or as a sealer before or after staining or under an oil/wax finish for color.	Sand and recoat.
Varnish	Turpentine or mineral spirits	Excellent	Outdoor furniture or dining tables, suitable anywhere.	Sand and recoat. When used outdoors, sand and apply two coats yearly.
Varnish/oil	Turpentine or mineral spirits	Excellent, but not as durable as straight varnish.	Outdoor furniture or dining tables, suitable anywhere.	Doesn't require sanding between coats. Just make sure the surface is clean.
Water-based clear coats	Water	Very good	Tables, cabinets, etc.—anything indoors that gets hard use.	Sand and recoat.
Latex paints	Water	Very good	Indoor and outdoor furniture.	Sand and recoat (every few years outdoors).
Oil-based paints	Mineral spirits	Excellent	For a hard, shiny, durable surface.	Sand and recoat every few years.

gives even new work an instant patina that is both rich and simple.

Apply the oil/wax finish in very thin coats with a rag or a piece of synthetic steel wool. Let it sit for 10 to 15 minutes, and rub out with a soft cloth. It takes about 24 hours to dry completely. Two or three coats are adequate for protection, adding more deepens the patina. An oil/wax finish is suitable for pieces that won't be subjected to much heat or moisture.

Waxes

Wax is a soft but forgiving finish. Many people feel it's not durable to stand on its own, but I've lived for years with an antique French country dining table that's finished with wax and it still looks lovely. Hot plates and dishes can dull the surface, but all it takes is a little more wax applied with a shoe-shine brush to bring it back.

Wax goes well over any other finish—be it paint, varnish, shellac, or oil—and gives it a warm luster and silky feel. You can also use tinted waxes to impart some interesting effects. For instance, a dark brown wax over shellac or paint makes a piece look instantly old, especially when it lodges in knots, end grain, or surface imperfections.

Apply two or three thin coats of wax with synthetic steel wool and rub out with a soft cloth. If the surface is large, use a shoe-shine brush or a car polisher.

Shellacs

Shellac is made from the shell casing of female lac bugs (indigenous to India) dissolved in denatured alcohol. You can buy ready-made shellac in cans (be sure to get the more durable dewaxed variety) or you can buy it as flakes and make your own.

Shellac can be used as a finish in its own right or as a sealer coat beneath other finishes. It's the pro finisher's secret weapon because it solves myriad finishing problems. A very thin wash coat of shellac soaks into porous areas that tend to get blotchy when stained, lightly sealing the wood. Shellac reduces but does not eliminate stain penetration, effectively evening the color. A moderately thinned coat of shellac sticks to oily wood and prevents knots from bleeding resin so that subsequent finish coats stay put and look good. And finally, several coats of shellac on its own build up to a deep, rich finish with a warm glow.

Shellac is easy to apply with a brush or rag and dries quickly, allowing you to recoat in an hour or two. Since the solvent for shellac is alcohol, you needn't worry about toxic or highly flammable fumes. The only downside to shellac is that it is only moderately durable—and is certainly not the finish to use on a bar, since a spilled alcoholic beverage will act as a solvent. A coat or two of wax over shellac offers a bit of protection.

Varnishes

These are the toughest clear finish and the only ones suitable for hard service and exterior use. They're also the most difficult to apply. The relatively thick film takes a long time to dry and tends to pick up dust in the air. It will drip and wrinkle if not applied properly.

To apply varnish, use a foam brush. Thin the first coat 50% with the solvent suggested by the manufacturer. Thin the second coat 25% and all subsequent coats 10%. Although you can get by with as few as three coats, serious varnishers apply eight or more for a deep, rich finish that has no equal.

Varnishes are made with a variety of resins; you'll most likely have a choice between phenolic, alkyd, and polyurethane. The alkyd is the least durable; polyurethane is the most durable.

Gel varnishes

A gel varnish is a slightly thickened varnish, typically polyurethane, that is meant to be applied with a rag. It's less messy than a regular varnish (which you can also apply with a rag) and slightly less durable. Apply thin coats.

Oil/varnish mixtures

Available in a variety of formulations with various degrees of sheen, pigment, and durability, these finishes combine the durability of varnish with oil's ease of use. Whereas you must sand varnish between coats, you can build up multiple coats of oil/varnish mixture without sanding.

Apply with a brush or rag, and put on a few coats for a natural oiled look. Or you can apply several coats to approach the thick, rich look of varnish.

Water-based clear-coat finishes

You can't beat these finishes for ease of use. They dry quickly, emit no noxious fumes, and clean up with water. They're quite durable, too—only polyurethane varnishes are more resistant to daily wear and tear.

Perfectly clear, these finishes lack the rich glow of varnishes and oils, and many people feel they have a cold, plastic look. You can minimize that effect by applying water-based clear coats over shellac or by putting a few drops of amber tint (available at woodworking suppliers and paint stores) into the mixture.

Apply with a nylon bristle brush, and sand between coats.

Fine Paint Finishes

Paint is tougher and more durable than clear finishes and makes good sense for furniture used outdoors or in high-traffic areas. Paint also has a place in high-quality construction. A fine paint job is as handsome as natural wood.

The key to an awe-inspiring paint finish is to start with high-quality paint. You want one that's high in solids, with finely ground pigments and a hard, shiny surface.

It's easier to get a smooth painted finish with an oil-based paint, such as an alkyd or polyurethane enamel. Because of their longer drying times, oil-based paints self-level better than quick-drying water-based paints. Brush marks disappear as they dry. Lower-priced water-based paints, like common latex house paint, are designed to go on in a thick film and will almost

▲ Properly sanded filler (right) shows a sharp delineation between the filled spot and surrounding wood. The hole on the left hasn't been sanded at all; the one in the middle hasn't been sanded enough.

always show brush marks. For painting furniture, look for an acrylic latex enamel or a waterborne polyurethane.

No paint looks good when applied over an ill-prepared surface. You've got to sand the surface smooth of all machine marks, make it flat and free of waves and ripples, and it must be smooth and free from rough grain, pinholes, dents, dings, and knots.

So start your fine paint job when you sand your project, and work hard to keep the surface flat. Keep your sander moving and use hand-sanding blocks. As you sand the surface, keep your eyes open for surface imperfections and circle them with pencil so you can fill them later with putty (see p. 58).

Once the filler is dry, sand carefully until with your eyes closed, you can't tell when your fingertips are running over the putty.

A coat or two of primer under your top coat seals the surface and smoothes out the wood grain. Look for a primer labeled "grain filling" or "high build." They're formulated to sand smooth in a short time and form a good chemical bond with paint. After priming, you may need to fill in a few places and sand again.

Finally, apply the paint in thin coats either by brush or from an aerosol spray can. The surface will end up smoother and dry more quickly than if the paint is caked on.

Putties and fillers

Many beginning woodworkers make the mistake of thinking that wood putty can hide a multitude of sins. Small holes and cracks filled with putty tinted to match the wood end up pretty well camouflaged, but large flaws will remain evident.

If you're not using stain, you can make a thick paste of fine dust from hand-sanding and shellac or epoxy to fill the holes. These fillers don't stain well, but they are almost invisible under a clear finish. If you're staining the wood, use a putty that's near the wood's color before staining, and apply the stain to the wood and the filler. Even so, the repair will probably not stain in the same way as the wood.

If you're painting, you have a wider selection of fillers, since color is not important. The best fillers to use for a fine paint job come from an auto body-supply shop. Fill large areas with two-part polyester filler—it dries fast and is easy to sand. Once you've done the initial filling and are touching up pin-holes, rough grain, and other small flaws, use an acrylic glazing putty (another autobody product). These putties are light, smooth, easy to apply, and dry quickly and sand out beautifully.

Brushes

Four kinds of inexpensive brushes will serve most of your woodworking needs. Three of them are disposable. When using oil-based finishes, it's usually cheaper and easier to use disposable brushes than to buy, store, and properly dispose of the harmful solvents used to clean a higher-quality brush.

Acid brushes

These coarse brushes are only ½" wide and make great applicators for glue. If you're using epoxy or polyurethane, just throw them away. But if you're laying down yellow glue, you can clean the brushes in soap and water and use them repeatedly.

Inexpensive natural bristle brushes

These brushes are pretty thin and they always lose bristles in the finish, but the price is right. They're not good enough to apply a film finish, but they're fine for applying stain that you're going to wipe off anyway or for an oil/varnish mixture. These are available in sizes from 1" to 4".

Foam brushes

Foam brushes produce a wonderful finish when used with oil-based paints and varnishes. Their smooth surface promotes self-leveling, and they don't hold too much finish to produce runs or drips. However, they're not a good choice for thicker water-based finishes.

Nylon bristle brushes

Water-based finishes make natural bristle brushes splay out and lose their shape, so you need to apply them with a synthetic bristle brush. Look for a thick nylon brush with smooth, feathered ends. It's worth it to spend around $8 for a brush for water-based paints, since you can clean it with soap and water and use it again and again.

Other Finishing Supplies

In addition to paint and brushes, you need a few other items to achieve a fine painted finish.

Tack cloths

These sticky swatches of cheesecloth make it easy to get a smooth oil-based finish. After sanding and vacuuming the surface, wipe it down with a tack cloth to pick up any lingering dust and grit that could rough up your paint job. Be sure to buy compatible tack rags when using water-based fishishes.

Paper towels and rags

There's always something to wipe up when finishing—if it's not part of the prescribed application process, then you're cleaning up. Most of the time I use a premium brand of paper towel for wiping up during finishing. Bargain brands are too flimsy and full of fine lint and dust. Just about the only time a rag is necessary is when rubbing out a wax finish—the friction is often too much for any paper towel. When rags are called for, they must be clean, lint-free cotton rags, which are sold by the pound in most home centers and paint stores.

Solvents

Whenever you buy a finishing product, make sure you buy the solvent recommended by the manufacturer. That's the only way to ensure it has the right chemistry to do what it's supposed to do. In addition, it's a good idea to keep a can of denatured alcohol on hand. It's a good all-around cleaning agent. You can use alcohol for cleaning off pencil

◀ To start woodworking, you need only four types of brushes: (bottom to top) disposable acid brush, foam brush, cheap bristle brush, and moderate-quality nylon bristle brush.

marks, price tags, oil, uncured epoxy, and most unspecified goo. It's powerful but not dangerous.

Tapes

For most woodworkers, tape is a legitimate tool. Of course, every shop has a roll of duct tape, but it won't work in every situation.

Masking tape

Aside from its proper purpose of protecting adjoining surfaces from unwanted paint, masking tape has a variety of uses around the shop. I use it to label parts (no pencil lines to sand off), to serve as light-duty clamps, to help hold clamping pads in place, and sometimes to protect surfaces from dirt and scrapes. I don't like the old-fashioned brown kind; it tears too easily when trying to get it off the roll or the project. I keep rolls of 1½" and ¾" bright blue tape at strategic locations in my shop.

Double-sided tape

Sometimes you can't beat double-sided tape as a light-duty clamp. It's the preferred way to hold a pair of workpieces together when routing or sawing, and you'll find other uses as well. For woodworking applications, you need tape that's at least ¾" wide. For added strength, choose a vinyl tape.

Simple Handmade Box

This is a simple box, its joints exposed for all to see. Displayed on a coffee table or sideboard, it will be noticed and admired. But a box is a private place, full of mystery and promise. It's a place for hopes, memories, and dreams come true: a ticket stub from a long-ago concert, a photo of your childhood best friend, the cork from the wine served the night you got engaged, or a fountain pen reserved for finally inking that big deal.

Handmade boxes epitomize woodworking for many people. Building a simple box doesn't require a large space or expensive tools, just some time to practice and enough materials to get it right. Each one will be better than the last, but even your first effort will be a treasure.

The easy joinery of this box, which is made from dimensioned lumber, teaches lessons you'll use in all your woodworking projects. Making this box will give you a firm foundation of hand skills to deal with those little glitches that woodworking throws at you. By the time you've built it, you'll know how to use clamps, chisels, and planes, as well as how to make a square crosscut and keep your tools sharp.

In the end, you'll have a beautiful box for display. But only you will know the most valuable treasure it contains—your initiation as a successful woodworker. ◼

What You'll Learn

- Handsawing
- Crosscutting to length
- Marking face side and face edge
- Using a sliding square
- Laying out and marking joints with a knife
- Paring with a chisel
- Flattening and smoothing with a block plane
- How to keep your tools sharp
- Strategies for planing end grain
- Applying an oil or oil/wax for a smooth finish

You don't need a sustained effort to build this project. You can accomplish a lot in an hour or two fit into a busy work week, although it'll take you a few such sessions to complete the box. Take it easy and learn as you go. And don't be hard on yourself if something doesn't end up as well as you hoped. Just like dancing or playing tennis, learning to do woodworking takes practice and experience.

A sharp chisel can cut a tissue-paper-thin slice with ease.

No matter how much skill and practice you have, you can't do good work with dull tools. They'll make hash of your project, tearing out the **grain** and making it nearly impossible to work with any degree of accuracy. Time spent learning to sharpen now is time well spent. Put a good edge on all of your chisels and plane irons before you start (refer to Skill Builder: Sharpening on p. 66), and things will go much easier for you.

Planing is another foundation skill, and one that many machine-oriented woodworkers lack. I've taught pro cabinetmakers to plane, and they say it changes their lives. A handplane is the fastest, most accurate way to true up uneven joints, flatten a surface, and smooth it to a burnished glow. You can take a hair off the edge of a joint with a handplane in less time than it takes to set up a machine, with no danger of messing up the workpiece. Get that skill now, and you'll use a plane at some point in almost every project you build.

Simple Handmade Box

Top from the Side

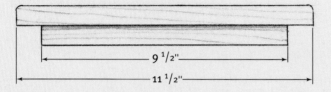

9 1/2"

11 1/2"

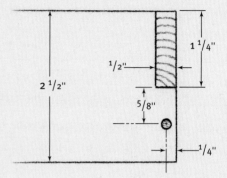

2 1/2"

1 1/4"

1/2"

5/8"

1/4"

Top from Below

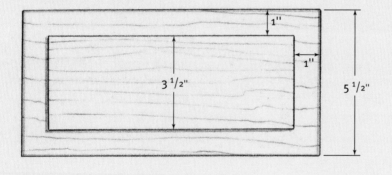

1"

1"

3 1/2"

5 1/2"

Side

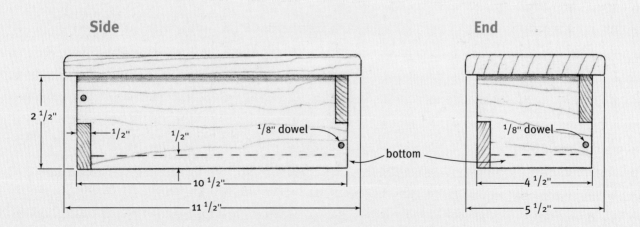

2 1/2"

1/2"

1/2"

1/8" dowel

bottom

10 1/2"

11 1/2"

End

1/8" dowel

bottom

4 1/2"

5 1/2"

MATERIALS for three boxes

Quantity	Actual Dimension*	Length	Description	Notes
1	½" x 2½"	8'	Sides and ends	Buy 1x3. One at 8' or any combination to make up 8'. Longest piece is 10½".
1	½" x 3½"	6'	Bottom and inner top	Buy 1x4. One at 6' or any combination to make up 6'. Longest piece is 9½".
1	½" x 5½"	3'	Top	Buy 1x6. Finished length is 11½".
1	⅛" dowel	3'	Corner pins Glue Masking tape Double-sided tape Acid brush 220-grit sandpaper White and gray synthetic steel wool pads Danish oil or oil/wax mixture Lint-free rags or paper towels Mineral spirits, turpentine, or alcohol	 For finishing. For cleaning up when finishing.

*See p. 44–45 for a discussion of actual vs. nominal dimensions.

Tools

- Tape measure
- Miter saw or miter box
- Sliding square
- Layout knife or knives
- Fine-toothed backsaw, English or Japanese style
- ¾" or 1" chisel
- Block plane
- Panel clamps (two)
- Bar clamps (eight, at least three should be 12" or longer)
- ⅛" brad-point drill bit
- Cordless drill/driver
- Hammer
- Ruler
- Hand-sanding block

You can't do much in the shop without clamps, and you'll get right up to speed with this first project. Small though it is, the box requires a lot of clamps to hold it together while the glue dries, as shown in photo Q. on p. 78. The very first step in building the box requires clamps, so have a look at "Skill Builder: Clamping" on p. 68 before you begin.

Building the Box

Your choice of materials for this project will be limited by what's available in ½" thickness. Select a wood that's soft and easy to work, such as pine, aspen, basswood, or butternut. Most home centers will have pine, but you might be able to choose from other regional species as well. I built the box shown in the photos from aspen I bought at my local home center.

Whatever variety you choose, pick the boards carefully, and get the flattest ones you can find. Try for quartersawn or riftsawn pieces (for more on this, see "Solid-Wood Lumber" beginning on p. 39. At this thickness, most woods will cup and even warp into S-curves across their width, so pick well and make sure the wood you choose has a chance to acclimate to your shop environment before you start building.

◄ Knowing how to plane is a fundamental woodworking skill. You'll use it in just about every project you undertake. Here, a block plane is being used to shape the edges of the box lid.

Crosscut to Length

1 Using a miter box or miter saw, crosscut two pieces of ½" x 3½" to 16" in length, using the techniques shown in "Skill Builder: Accurate Crosscuts" on p. 71.

2 Clamp or tape the pieces together with double-sided tape so the left ends and top edges are flush to ensure that each pair is identical. Make the end pieces by first marking and cutting 4½" from the left side, and then cut 10½" in from the end you just cut to yield the two sides.

3 To make the inside piece of the top and the bottom identical, first cut one piece of the ½" x 3½" a little long at about 9¾". Place the offcut on the remaining piece of wood with the ends and top aligned and clamp or tape them together. Then cut the inside top and bottom at once to the proper length at 9½".

4 Crosscut the ½" x 5½" piece to 11½" long for the outside top piece. These are all the parts of the box, as shown in photo A.

Mark the Face Side and the Face Edge

Starting all marks and measurements from the same side or edge ensures that the box will go together as planned. Any slight variations in the thickness or width will show up on the outside of the box and not interfere with the way the bottom and top fit into it. This is not terribly important in a simple piece like this, but as your projects get more complicated, this kind of thing matters a lot. Practice it while the stakes are low, so that when you build something more complex good technique is second nature.

■ **WORK SMART**

A small amount of cup in the boards for the top and bottom is okay. Most of it will straighten out in clamping, and a little leftover cup actually gives a nice-looking domed effect to box.

A

SKILL BUILDER Sharpening

What You'll Need

- Wet/dry sandpaper in the following grits: 150, 220, 320, 400, 600, 1,000, 1,200, 2,000
- Two sheets of ¼" plate (or float) glass, about 12" x 12"
- Spray adhesive
- Honing guide
- Spray bottle of water

Many beginning woodworkers have never held a sharp tool and are unaware that many woodworking frustrations would vanish if they knew how to sharpen. Dull tools fight every step of the way. Sharp tools make you feel talented.

The easiest and most cost-effective way to sharpen is on sheets of wet/dry sandpaper glued to a piece of glass with spray adhesive (put two grits on each sheet of glass, one on either side). The glass provides a perfectly flat surface and the sandpaper an aggressive abrasive to remove metal fast. To keep the metal dust from filling the sandpaper and reducing its effectiveness, spray the surface with water from time to time.

With all that water and metal dust, sharpening can be a messy operation. Put the glass on a piece of scrap plywood or plastic laminate, and keep lots of paper towels handy to soak up the mess. You might also want to wear rubber or latex gloves—the fine slurry gets under and around your fingernails and can be hard to scrub out.

Flattening the Back

A sharp edge results from the intersection of two smooth surfaces at the proper angle. The normal process of honing an edge takes care of both the angle and the smoothing of the bevel side, but you'll have to flatten and smooth the back of the blade in a separate step. It's a time-consuming process, but you'll only have to do it once in the life of the blade.

1 Keeping the blade absolutely flat, rub it back and forth on the 150-grit sandpaper (see photo B). You needn't flatten the entire blade; the lower 1" or so is enough.

2 Work the blade until that inch of the back is uniformly dull. This means that every point on the surface is being abraded, and the back is flat (it's okay if there's a small hollow in the middle of the back). Flattening may take more than half an hour (and more than one sheet of sandpaper), depending on the blade. Keep the surface wet so the paper won't clog.

3 Switch to 220-grit sandpaper, and work the blade until the surface is uniformly abraded with the finer scratch pattern. Continue working your way through the grits. By the time you get to 2,000 grit, the part of the back you've worked on will begin to shine.

Sharpening the Bevel

The critical aspect of honing a blade is to keep it from wobbling as you move it over the abrasive. For best results, use a honing guide with a roller to keep the blade steady (see photo C).

Most blades come from the factory with a 25-degree bevel, but that's too low for general woodworking. It makes for a very fragile edge, likely to chip out the first time you hit a pin knot. Sharpen your blades to 30 degrees for longer life and better cutting characteristics.

1 Sharpen the blade at a 30-degree angle, starting with the 1,000-grit paper. Hone for a minute or so, or until you feel a burr on the back side. You've sharpened enough when this burr is along the whole length of the edge.

2 Switch to 1,500-grit paper, hone for a couple of minutes, then switch to 2,000 grit. Mist the paper often. It's not necessary to sharpen the whole bevel—the part right at the edge is all that matters.

3 After the 2,000 grit, remove the blade from the guide and rub the back flat on the finest sandpaper to remove the burr.

4 Test for sharpness by lightly holding the blade and touching it to your thumbnail (see photo D). A sharp blade catches immediately; a dull one skids across your nail. If it's not sharp, rub the back on the finest grit again. If that doesn't work, you'll have to go back and spend more time on the coarser grit, and then work your way up to the fine grit again.

5 Resharpen often. If you've been using the tool steadily for more than 15 minutes, it's probably time to sharpen.

SKILL BUILDER   Clamping

What You'll Need

- Three bar clamps (or C-clamps)
- Pieces of scrap wood to clamp, about 12" long
- Small pads of scrap wood, about 2" x 3"

The secret to getting your clamps to grab without fumbling is to make certain the pads on both jaws are perfectly aligned before tightening the hand-screw. If they're not, you'll have a hard time getting them to tighten. If they do close, they'll try to align themselves by skewing the wood they're supposed to be holding steady, a problem made worse by a slippery layer of glue.

The locking mechanisms on the lower jaws of bar clamps differ among manufacturers, but they all move readily toward the head when released. In most cases, the handscrew must be loose for the jaw to slide. Before starting a clamping operation, open your clamps so the jaws are plenty wide to give you room to maneuver. On bar clamps, screw the **handscrew** back as far as it will go, and slide the jaw back far enough so it's well out of the way. On C-clamps, unscrew the pad so it's well out of the way.

1 Place the head of the clamp squarely on the wood and hold it in place with one hand. The lower jaw will naturally align with the head.

2 Slide the lower jaw upward until the pad touches the clamping surface as shown in photo A.

3 Tighten the handscrew, making sure the work-piece doesn't shift. In general, you want to make your clamps **hand-tight**, meaning that you screw them down as tightly as you can without straining.

4 Use a piece of scrap wood to protect soft surfaces from being dented, as shown in photo B. Sometimes you'll need pads on both top and bottom, and it can be hard to hold the clamp, the work, and two pads in place with only two hands.

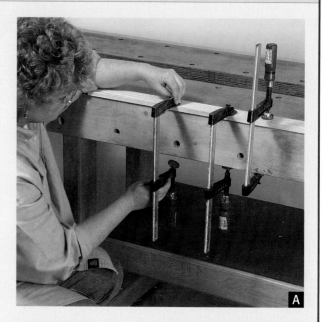

A

A bit of tape is a big help. If your clamps have rubber or plastic pads on the jaws, that's enough padding for all but the most delicate surfaces.

You can clamp with the hand screws up or down, depending on the circumstances. Since gravity is against you, it can be a little awkward to hold the work and tighten at the same time when the screws are down, especially if pads are involved. Learn versatility—practice both ways.

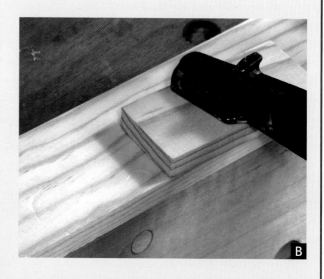

B

1 Decide which side of each piece you want facing out—usually the best-looking surface. Label the inside as such. The traditional way to do this is with the mark shown in photo B on the face, with the bottom of the mark going off one edge as shown. Think of this mark as the top part of a perfect third-grade cursive capital F. This is called the **face side.**

2 On the edge where the face mark trails off, make a V. This is the **face edge.** All subsequent measurements will be made from one or the other of these surfaces.

Lay Out and Cut the Finger Joints

When using hand tools, you don't try to work to a level of machinelike precision that ensures interchangeable joints. In real life, it's not always possible to get everything perfectly square and true. Instead, you'll cut the joints of each corner one at a time, working your way around the box. Cut one side of the joint, then cut the other to match—in the end, the pieces will fit properly in only one arrangement, so mark them carefully.

When laying out these or any other handmade joints, use a marking knife rather than a pencil. The knife scores a line into the wood, leaving a mark you can feel as well as see. When it comes to making the last paring cut with a chisel, you can feel the line with the blade. Place the chisel on/in the line, pare lightly and vertically, and you'll get a good, tight fit.

WORK SMART

Mark your lines lightly so they don't crush the wood and are easy to remove. If they don't erase, try removing them by wiping with some denatured alcohol on a paper towel. If that won't do, sand lightly with 220-grit paper.

Squaring around the ends

Start by squaring a line around both ends of all four side pieces.

1 Loosen the blade-locking screw on your sliding square and hold the base against the face side of the workpiece. Slide the blade until its end is flush with the back side of the board, as shown in photo C, and extend it just a hair (about ¹⁄₃₂") beyond the back.

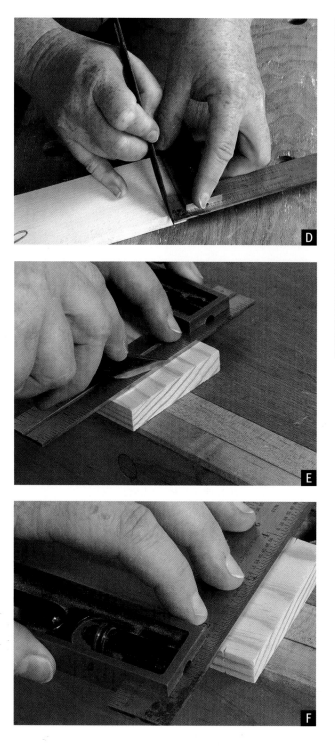

and score a line along the blade and across the face of the board as shown in photo E.

4 Put the piece on the bench with the face side down and the face edge toward you. Place the base of the square against the face edge and slide up to the notch. If you squared around properly, the notches should be right at the edge of the blade. Score this line as well, as shown in photo F.

Laying out the finger joints

From this point on, you'll work one joint at a time.

1 Set the sliding square to 1¼" (half the width of the sides and ends). With the base on the face edge, make a mark at each end from the end of the board to the scored line, as shown in photo G. Do this on both the face side and on the back side of the workpiece.

2 Make your first joint on a side piece with the waste on the top half of the board. Mark the waste with an X to

2 Place the base against the end of the workpiece, with the top of the blade along the edge. Using a marking knife, make a notch on the edge as shown in photo D.

3 Place the knife in the notch, and put the base of the square on the face edge. Slide the blade gently up to the knife,

SKILL BUILDER | Accurate Crosscuts

What You'll Need
- Miter box or miter saw
- Small bar clamps
- Scrap wood to crosscut

An accurate miter box, either hand or electric powered, can only make square cuts if the workpiece does not move, so clamp the workpiece in place before any critical cut, no matter what kind of saw you're using.

1 Start by making sure your saw is screwed, bolted, or clamped down to the bench so the whole thing doesn't move when sawing.

2 Clamp the workpiece to the fence so it won't shift during the cut, as shown in the photo at right. Clamping the waste part, called the **falling board**, is only necessary when it's so long and heavy that it might cause the whole board to shift during the cut. Some saws have their own hold-down clamps; if yours does, these are usually more efficient than using the bar clamps shown.

3 If you're using a handsaw, see "Skill Builder: Using a Handsaw" on p. 76 for tips on stance and hand position.

You can use these same setups for angled cuts, properly called **miters.**

---

prevent confusion later. This may not seem important now, but as you proceed around the box, you'll see it becomes more significant.

Removing the waste

Use a backsaw to remove the waste as discussed in "Skill Builder: Using a Handsaw" on p. 76.

Paring to the line

Using the skills you learned in "Skill Builder: Paring with a Chisel" on p. 74, pare down to the line, being careful to keep the cuts square and perpendicular, as shown in photo H.

H

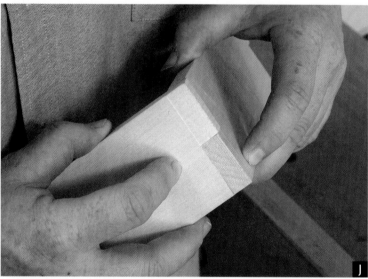

Marking and cutting the mating joint

1 Clamp a piece of scrap in your vise, then clamp the piece you just cut to it, as shown in photo I. This arrangement ensures that the piece is steady and vertical. Make sure your face mark is on the inside.

2 Hold an end piece up against the finger you've just cut. Make sure it's vertical, that the face side is on the inside, and that its outside face is flush with the end of the side piece.

3 Using a layout knife, carefully mark across the top of the finger so the score line shows on the end grain of the end piece. Pencil an X on the lower part of the end, the part that will be waste.

4 Place your knife in the notch on the edge and the base of the sliding square on the end grain. Moving the square up to the knife, score a line right up to the scored line you made ½" in from the end. Turn the board over and do the same to the other side.

5 Saw out the waste.

6 Pare to the line. Take very light cuts as you near the line, checking often with your square.

7 Check the fit as shown in photo J. Pencil an A on the top edge of each piece near the corners so you'll know how the pieces go together.

Cutting the remaining joints

1 Cut the remaining joints in matched pairs, going right around the box, as shown in photo K. Be careful to label the mating joints (B, C, and D), and double-check that you've marked the waste correctly before cutting.

Repairing Joint Gaps

If you pare so much that there's a gap in the joint, you can make a nearly invisible repair by putting a sliver of the same wood into the joint when you glue it up (see the photo at left). Trim the sliver to fit after the glue is dry.

If you need to make some slivers, you can split off a piece of the waste the you cut out with a backsaw. Place the chisel on the end grain of the waste and push down firmly to split away a sliver of the right thickness. The first paring cuts sometimes yield pieces that are suitable for making this kind of repair.

WORK SMART

Don't mark beyond the scored lines squared around the ends in step 4 on the facing page, or they'll show after the joint is made.

2 Once you've cut all your finger joints, test the fit to see how the pieces go together to make the box, as shown in photo L. Put the bottom piece in place inside.

Clamp the Box Together

This box takes a surprising number of clamps—it must be clamped across both its length and width, as well as from top to bottom on the corners. You'll use both **panel clamps** and **bar clamps** to keep all the mating surfaces in close contact while the glue dries. Make a trial run before you apply the glue to figure out your clamping strategy.

Working out your clamping strategy

1 Place two panel clamps on the bench, then lay the box bottom on the bars and put the sides in place next to it. Check to make sure the pieces are flat on the bars. The clamps should be about 1" in from each end of the box.

WORK SMART

The joints won't be flush along their outside faces until later in the process. To ensure the clamp presses on the face grain and not a protruding bit of end grain at a joint, use a piece of scrap as a clamping pad. The waste from the finger joints works well. Slide it right up next to the end grain to get the clamping pressure across the joint.

2 Add two or three bar clamps the long way over the top of the box as shown in photo M. But keep the clamping pressure near the bottom of the box to keep the sides vertical. Use small pads

SKILL BUILDER   Paring with a Chisel

What You'll Need

- Sharpened ¾" or 1" chisel
- Mock finger such as you made practicing joints using a backsaw
- Vise

Wherever a small area needs fine-tuning for a perfect fit, the surest way to get it right is by paring with a chisel. With a little practice, you'll be able to take a slice that's so thin it's translucent.

Hold the chisel with the bevel up and the back against the face to be cut—you'll have complete control to balance the downward and forward forces.

There are two basic grips for paring: the vertical and the horizontal. Generally, you'll use the vertical orientation on hardwoods and end grain when you need a lot of pressure, and the horizontal for moderate pressures. Horizontal paring is a little more comfortable and easier to control, so you'll want to use it for larger areas, when you have more material to remove, and for delicate cuts and fine-tuning.

Vertical Paring

1 Hold the work in a vise so the paring action will be perpendicular to the ground (you'll be paring down to the lines you marked prior to sawing).

A

B

2 Hold the chisel like an ice pick and lock your elbow with the chisel roughly at jaw height. Bend over the work, using your upper body to push down on the chisel, as shown in photo A.

3 Press the back of the chisel against the workpiece with the fingers of your other hand. Start with a moderate amount of pressure. If the blade skips over the surface, increase the pressure until the downward motion is slow and controlled. You can wiggle the blade side-to-side a little to get the cut started.

4 Vary the pressure moment by moment to maintain a slow, controlled, and very thin cut.

5 Every cut or two, clear the bottom of the cut by scoring the corner with the face of the chisel on the horizontal.

Horizontal Paring

1 Secure the workpiece in the vise horizontally or at a slight angle if it's more comfortable.

2 Hold the chisel with your forefinger extended toward the blade. Use the thumb or fingers of your opposite hand to control downward pressure (see photo B).

3 If you have a large amount of material to remove, use a three-step procedure. First, angle the chisel to pare one side to the line, leaving the middle high, as shown in photo C. Do the same on the other side. Then, hold the chisel flat and make the middle flush with the sides, as shown in photo D.

4 Clean out the corners as in step 5 for vertical paring.

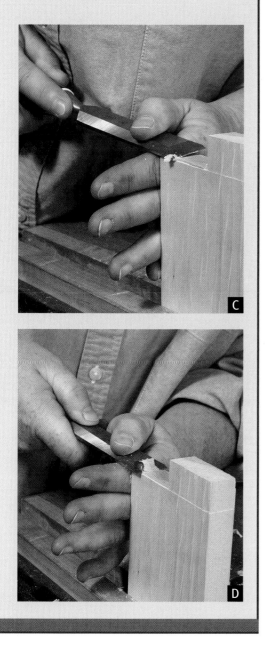

between the clamp and the box (you can see these pads clearly in photo N).

3 Clamp the corners from top to bottom to close the joints as shown in photo O.

4 Check the joints all around the box to make sure they're tight. If they're not, add more clamps to adjust for your situation. For instance, some bow in one of the side pieces may require a clamp across the middle of the box, or a little cup may call for another clamp

WORK SMART

It's hard to hold the pads in place while clamping to the box. Make it easier by letting one end of a pad rest on the benchtop, or hold the pad in place with a small piece of double-sided tape.

SKILL BUILDER Using a Handsaw

What You'll Need

- Backsaw
- Square
- Vise or clamps
- ¾" scrap wood for practice cuts

Body position is critical when using any handsaw. Your hand, wrist, elbow, and shoulder must be oriented correctly to prevent any twisting that makes the saw bind in the cut. Incorrect orientation to the work makes sawing a nasty, uncomfortable affair. Get it right, and the cut is smooth and almost effortless.

1 Since you can't saw a true line unless you have a reference, use a square and square lines around the top and near side of the workpiece. Always hold the work perfectly steady, using a vise or clamps as necessary. You can't make a smooth, accurate cut if the work is moving around. Orient your work so you're always sawing perpendicular to the floor.

2 Put your feet shoulder width apart, with your knees bent comfortably for a solid stance. Step forward with the foot opposite the hand that holds the saw to open your body and for stability. Stand far enough away from the work so you're not cramped or leaning down over it. Your arms and upper body should be loose and free to move.

3 Hold the saw lightly but firmly with your forefinger pointed along the blade, as shown in photo A. Note that my finger, wrist, forearm, elbow, and shoulder are aligned. Make sure your wrist is not cocked out to the side, or the saw will bind.

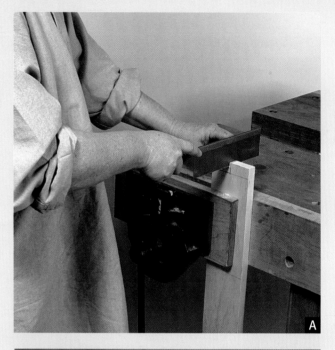

across the ends. Sometimes you'll have to loosen adjoining clamps to draw the joint tight. Once the joint closes, retighten all of the clamps.

5 Remember your clamping arrangement, taking notes if necessary, and remove the clamps.

Applying glue and clamping up

Once the glue goes on, you've got to work efficiently. At 70°F you have about 15 minutes to get the clamps settled before the glue gets too tacky to

■ Sawing to the Line

1. With the piece clamped in the vise so the line is parallel to the floor and holding the saw at an angle, saw the front side almost to the line.

2. Using the curf as a guide, hold the saw parallel to the floor and sawing gently down, almost to the line.

4 Start your cut by drawing the saw backward lightly, using the finger of your other hand to guide it, as shown in photo B. Once the saw has bit in and established a kerf, you can start sawing in earnest. Don't push the saw or force it in any way; let the teeth do the work. If the saw binds, is hard to push, or fights you in any way, stop cutting and regain your alignment.

Don't try to cut to the line. Cut near it and parallel to it, as shown in photo C; you'll use a chisel to pare back to the line. As your skill grows, you can get closer to the line, but for maximum accuracy, always follow up with a chisel.

Short cuts can be made with the saw parallel to the bottom of the cut, but if it's more than about 1¼" long, use the three-step approach as shown in the illustration at right.

make corrections. When the temperature is higher, you have less time. If it's cooler, you have a little more.

1 Using a ½"-wide acid brush, apply glue around the edges of the bottom piece. Rest the bottom piece on the bars of sash clamps.

2 Apply glue along the bottom ½" of each side piece and the mating surfaces of the fingers. Put the sides in place against the bottom, check that they're flush, and clamp lightly.

▲ Clamps hold pieces together for gluing, keep your work steady, and serve as an extra pair of hands. Here, the inner piece of the box lid is being clamped in place with several small bar clamps.

3 Likewise, apply glue to the end pieces, as shown in photo O, and pop them in place.

4 Apply the rest of the clamps and clamping blocks, and check to make sure all joints are tight. Let the box sit for at least one hour before removing the clamps.

Make the Top

The top is made by gluing a narrow piece onto a wider one. The narrow piece fits down inside the box, holding the lid in place.

Fitting the inside piece

1 When the glue is dry, check to see if the other ½" x 3½" piece slips inside the box. If it doesn't, use a block plane to remove a little from the edge, then try again. When it fits, set it aside. For information on how to use a block plane, see "Skill Builder: Using a Block Plane" on p. 80.

2 Take a close look at the ½" x 5½" piece that will be the lid; chances are, it has a little cup. Mark the concave side the inside. It will give the top a little dome.

3 With the inside of the piece facing up and the sliding square set at 1", pencil a line around the edge by running the base of the square along each side with the pencil against the end of the blade.

4 Glue the narrower inside piece in place within these lines, as shown in photo P.

5 If your lid has a lot of cup, you may need as many as eight clamps to hold the pieces together, as shown in photo Q. Instead of a pad for each clamp, use long pads that don't obscure your view of the pencil lines. Start by clamping two opposing corners to lock the inner piece in position, then apply the other clamps. Before you leave it to dry, be certain the inner piece hasn't slipped from its lines.

Pin the Joints

Finger joints aren't one of woodworking's strongest joints; the problem is the large proportion of end grain involved. End grain doesn't glue well because its open structure doesn't provide enough surface for the glue to grab. You can increase the gluing surface by drilling a relatively long hole through the finger that shows face grain into the end grain of the adjoining piece, and inserting a pin (screws or nails could serve the same function, but they aren't nearly as elegant).

Drilling the holes

1 Chuck a ⅛" brad-point drill bit into a drill and set the drill speed, direction, and torque as described in "Skill Builder: Drilling Holes" on p. 83.

2 Using the sliding square, draw a light line ¼" in from the end of each face-grain finger.

3 Reset the sliding square to ⅝", and use it to make a light mark on the previous line that distance from the edge.

4 Wrap a piece of masking tape around the drill bit so its bottom edge is 1" from the tip, as shown in photo R. You'll stop drilling when the tape reaches the surface of the wood.

Cutting and installing the pins

1 Put the dowel on a piece of scrap, then use your handsaw to cut eight pieces each 1⅛" long.

2 Take a leftover piece of dowel about 4" long, and hold it at a slight angle with one end on the scrap. Use a chisel or knife to sharpen it to a long point for getting glue down into the holes.

WORK SMART

Once you plane the edge of the inside top piece, it may fit only one way. Mark how it goes in for easy reassembly later.

WORK SMART

If the piece slips when clamping, either you've used too much glue or your clamping technique is off. Perhaps both. Making sure the clamp head is flat against the wood when the lower jaw is tightened usually solves the problem.

3 Apply glue to the holes, and hammer the 1⅛" dowel into place, as shown in photo S.

4 Repeat this procedure in each finger that shows face grain (as opposed to end grain).

5 Let the glue dry for at least an hour.

Trimming the pins

Use a sharp chisel with the bevel up to pare the pins flush with the surface. Keep the back flat on the surface to prevent the corners from marring the surface.

SKILL BUILDER   Using a Block Plane

What You'll Need
- Block plane
- Softwood scraps at least 14" long to plane
- Vise

Many people, myself included, think planing is one of the best things about woodworking. More than merely fun or satisfying, planing is the one surefire way to get things flat and smooth. No machine can equal its results. The instructions below work just as well with a two-handed bench plane.

1 Make sure your plane iron is sharp, and use a vise to hold the workpiece. Start by planing the edge of the wood, rather than the face. See p. 19 for more information on the parts of a plane and how they go together.

2 Hold the plane with the heel on the benchtop and look down the sole of the plane. Extend the blade until it appears as a dark line sticking out of the mouth. Photo A shows the blade extended too far, and it's not parallel. Adjust the blade so the line is parallel to the sole, then retract the blade so it is just about to disappear through the mouth. This ensures your first cut isn't too deep.

3 Standing about 12" away from the bench, face your work. The starting end of the workpiece should be roughly in line with a spot between your navel and your hip on the dominant side. Place your feet shoulder width apart and knees slightly

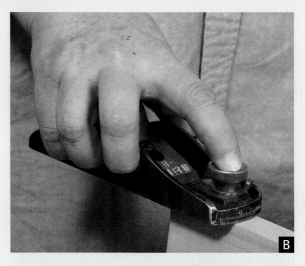

B

C

bent for stability. Turn your body slightly so the foot on your nondominant side rotates to point in the direction of the end of the board. Let your back foot rotate a little for comfort.

4 Since block planes are primarily a one-handed tool, grip it as shown in photo B. Make sure all of your fingers are safely on the side of the plane. Sometimes a two-handed grip gives more power and control, as shown in photo C.

5 Start the cut by putting the forward ¾" or so on the wood. (Make sure the blade is not on the wood.) Press down firmly on the front of the plane so the heel doesn't sag. Moving forward, keep the momentum up when the plane starts cutting.

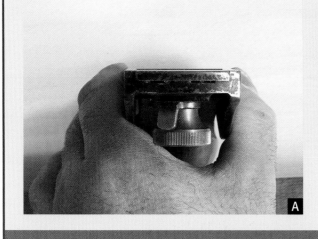

A

6 Once the whole plane is on the surface, ease up on your front hand and concentrate on forward motion.

7 As you reach the end of the board, lighten up on your front hand and press down firmly with your back hand so the front of the plane doesn't sag and cut too deeply at the end. Your first cut should be very light, or it may not cut at all. Turn the depth adjuster clockwise an eighth of a revolution and try again. It may take more than one adjustment to get a thin shaving.

8 Follow through, continuing the planing motion beyond the end of the board.

9 If the planing is difficult and the surface of the wood becomes rough, you're planing against the grain. Turn the board end for end and plane in the other direction. In photo D, the board on the right was planed against the grain.

10 Take care of the blade when you set your plane down on the bench. Set it with the front on a scrap of wood so the blade is off the bench, or lay it on its side.

Plane to Flatten and Smooth

When it comes time to flatten and smooth, most people think of a sander, but a plane is usually the best tool for either job. Make sure your plane iron is sharp before you begin.

Planing the corners, then the sides

When planing the sides of this box, you'll also be planing the two bits of end grain where the adjoining fingers show through. If you don't handle that end grain as described below, the corners of the box can be damaged, as shown in photo T.

Do this operation with the box in the vise with the side or end up, rotating as necessary.

1 Plane from both edges inward, so that the edge of the end grain is not an issue. Just plane the corners for several strokes, as shown in photo U, then go the full length with a light cut, taking care at the end-grain corners, as shown in photo V. It's sometimes easier to plane if you skew the plane as shown.

2 If grain in the side pieces won't plane smoothly enough to allow you to work inward from both ends, figure out which way the grain allows you to plane smoothly, and support the end

Planing the bottom

Plane the bottom of the box so the sides are perfectly flush with the bottom piece. If all went well with the clamping, this should be a simple process. If your wood is bowed or something went wrong, the box won't lie flat and you'll have to follow the steps shown in the illustration on p. 84.

Planing the top edge

Depending on how well your joint cutting and gluing went, you may have some small discrepancies in the top edge. To get them level to one another, plane them in pairs.

1 Place the heel of the plane on one side of the box, skewing it so the blade can cut the other corner, as shown in photo W. Plane the corner flush.

2 Move the plane to the corner you just completed, and place the heel of the plane on it. Use this planed surface as a starting point to plane the adjoining edge.

3 Place the heel on that surface and plane it as in step 1.

4 Plane the length of the side, starting on the just completed corner, and continue around the box following steps 1 through 3.

Planing the top

If your top piece has no cup, all you have to do is plane the outside smooth. If your top has a slight dome to it, fit the sides to match the dome.

1 Make a vertical tick mark at the midpoint of the top edge of each end. Place the top on the box and hold or clamp it down so it won't wobble. The top will touch at the corners, with a gap in the middle of the end.

grain at the end of the cut with a piece of scrap clamped over it with its top edge flush to the end grain. That way, if any end grain blows out, it'll be in the scrap.

3 Plane all four sides of the box.

SKILL BUILDER | Drilling Holes

What You'll Need
- Cordless drill/driver
- ⅛" brad-point drill bit
- Scrap wood to drill
- Vise or clamps
- Square

There are three points to remember whenever you drill (or bore) a hole in wood: Run the drill as fast as it goes, clear the chips often, and keep the drill aligned with the axis of the center line of the hole (usually vertically).

Setting Up the Drill

To serve its two different but complementary functions, a drill has several controls. If they're not adjusted properly, you'll have trouble drilling. (See p. 25 for a description of the drill and its parts.)

1 Set the clutch to the pictograph of a drill bit to operate at full torque.

2 Set the forward/reverse switch to forward. You'll know it's in forward when the chuck turns clockwise while sighting down the barrel.

3 Set the high/low speed switch to high.

Drilling a Hole

Make sure your work is clamped down and be careful not to drill through to your benchtop. If you want to drill holes straight through, hold the workpiece in the vise or clamp it overhanging the bench.

1 Chuck the bit into the drill and tighten. Hold the lower part of the chuck steady and tighten the upper part near the bit. Make sure the bit is centered in the jaws, or it will wobble. Check before drilling by running the drill. You'll instantly know if it's not centered.

2 Keep the drill vertical both front to back and side to side, as shown in the illustration below.

3 Using a one- or two-handed grip, depress the trigger fully so the drill runs at its highest speed. Don't force the drill and be sure to keep it aligned, or a small-diameter bit might snap. Pushing too hard as the drill comes through the back can break an irregular chip from around the edge of the hole; just push firmly and let it draw itself in.

4 About halfway down, clear the chips by pulling the still-turning drill partway out of the hole. On larger-diameter holes, you may need to clear the chips two or three times.

5 To remove the bit from the finished hole, keep it turning and draw it out. You don't need to use the reverse unless the bit is jammed in the hole.

Drilling a Vertical Hole

Imagine a line from the tip of the drill bit through the drill. Keep this line vertical both side-to-side and front-to-back.

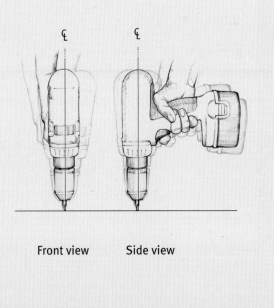

Front view   Side view

■ Adjusting for Uneven Joints

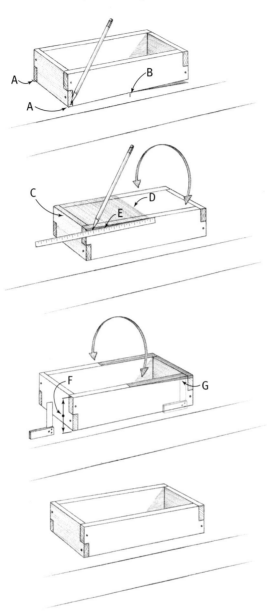

1. Hold or clamp the box so it can't rock.

2. Using a pencil, make a mark on the corner that sits flat at distance A from the benchtop.

3. Make mark B where the bottom edge stops touching the bench.

4. Repeat on the other side at A' and B'. These marks may not be exactly the same as on the first side. Make sure the box doesn't shift in the process.

5. Turn the box over and draw lines C, D, and E, using a ruler as a straightedge.

6. Plane away the hatched area, leaving half the thickness of the penciled line. Don't plane anything that's not hatched.

7. With its base against the box bottom, slide the blade of your sliding square to get height F.

8. Move the square along the bottom edge and draw line G all the way around the box.

9. Remove the high areas by planing down to the line as in step 6. Your box is now flat with the top and bottom edges parallel, though it's not as tall as when you began.

2 Put a mark on each corner down from the edge the same distance as the gap between the end and the top at the center. Sketch in the curve you should follow, using the top as a guide. Repeat at the other end.

3 Draw a line down each side of the box connecting the marks on the ends.

4 Plane to the lines all around. The slightly curved parts on the ends are hard to smooth with a plane. Get as close as you can, and smooth it later when hand-sanding.

Sand the Box

Once everything is flush, straight, flat, and smooth, sand the whole box inside and out with a hand-sanding block and 220-grit paper.

Breaking the edges

Square corners can be dangerous—you can actually cut yourself on the edge of a freshly planed piece of hardwood. Woodworkers always soften them slightly by running along the edge with a plane or sandpaper. Take care not to actually round the edges. A very light touch keeps the box looking fresh and crisp.

1 Using a hand-sanding block and 220-grit sandpaper, break the edges, top and bottom, around the box, as shown in photo X.

2 Break the vertical corners in the same way.

3 Round the upper edges of the top a little more aggressively to soften its appearance, as shown in photo Y.

Finishing

This box looks best with a simple finish to protect the wood and heighten the grain pattern without adding much luster. My two favorite such finishes are Danish oil and an oil/wax mixture. They both leave a silky smooth surface that brings out the contrasts in the grain, and the oil/wax mixture also gives the patina of a well-kept antique. (For more information on these finishes, see p. 55.) You can apply these finishes in the same manner, although it's worth noting that any manufacturer's instructions supersede those found here.

1 Start by brushing away the sanding dust, and wipe the surface with a rag moistened with turpentine, mineral spirits, or alcohol to clean it.

2 Apply a thin coat of finish with a rag or brush, paying attention to the end grain. The end grain soaks up the finish and will need more than the rest of the box. Don't put finish on the inside of the box, or else anything you keep in it will end up smelling like the finish.

3 Using a gray synthetic steel wool pad, "sand" the surface. This produces a slurry of sanding dust and finish, which you should then wipe off with a clean, lint-free rag or paper towel.

4 Let the finish dry according to the manufacturer's directions, typically overnight.

5 Apply another coat or two as you desire (up to a total of four coats), and sand with a white synthetic steel wool pad, as shown in photo AA.

6 After the final coat has dried, polish the box with a soft cloth.

Outdoor Easy Chair

This is an outdoor easy chair with attitude. It evokes the sobriety of Shaker furniture, the honest simplicity of the Arts and Crafts movement, and the easy-living sloth of an Adirondack chair. Every line is straight and square, yet the chair feels funky and relaxed. Even though it's easy to construct from several small pieces of wood, it has a self-confident presence that works in almost any setting, from watching TV or playing video games in the family room or kid's bedroom to lounging by the pool with a book.

This funky chair has a lofty pedigree. It's based on the Red Blue Chair, designed by Gerrit T. Reitveld in 1917. Much has been written about it, from learned discussions of its form and meaning to studies of the spiritual significance of its geometry. The original chair garners high praise, even to the point of being called one of the pivotal designs in the history of architecture.

Reitveld, a cabinetmaker turned designer, was surprised by the praise. He had no intention of changing design sensibilities; he simply set out to design a good-looking and functional chair that could be made quickly and economically using simple joinery and off-the-shelf lumber.

Beginning woodworkers should take heart in the fact that such a simple premise could create a chair that turned the art world on its ear. It proves that building great furniture doesn't require a complex design or a master craftsman's skills. ∎

What You'll Learn

- Measuring techniques that don't require a ruler
- Cutting multiples to exact length
- The essentials of glue-and-screw construction
- Using wooden plugs to cover screw heads
- Making and using simple jigs to increase speed and accuracy
- Working with epoxy
- Applying and maintaining an oil/varnish finish

▲ Glue-and-screw joints are easy to construct and make this chair redundantly strong.

▼ A simple jig made from leftover 2x2s (on the right) accurately positions the uprights (on the left) and holds them in place while driving the screws.

With its straight lines and right angles, the Outdoor Easy Chair is an excellent project for learning the essential skills of getting and keeping things square. If your uprights vary in length, or if your horizontals aren't perfectly horizontal, you'll find that your chair wobbles. Perhaps worse, it'll lack the uplifting crispness that makes you want to sit down.

Since reading and remembering fractions is a source of trouble for many, I'll show you some simple tricks that can eliminate measuring. You'll learn how to use clamps and stop blocks to cut multiples to the exact same length, the essentials of glue-and-screw construction, how to make and use simple jigs to accurately locate joints, and how to apply and maintain an oil/varnish blend finish.

This chair features screwed joints reinforced with adhesive. The screws provide the joints' founda-tion of strength and act as clamps to hold the joints together while the adhesive dries (you can continue working without all those clamps in the way). This chair is best built with epoxy, a tough waterproof adhesive that's very forgiving. It bridges gaps between imperfect joints, making a powerful, water-tight connection that's stronger than the wood itself.

The versatile glue-and-screw joint is an important addition to your reper-toire; it works well in a variety of situa-tions. You can leave the screw heads visible for quick-and-dirty utilitarian construction (such as jigs), fill them with putty, or (as in this project) you can cover them with elegant wooden plugs set flush to the surface.

A strong joint is only part of what makes this chair last. Redundant strength is built into the design.

Outdoor Easy Chair

Scale 1 ½" = 1'- 0"

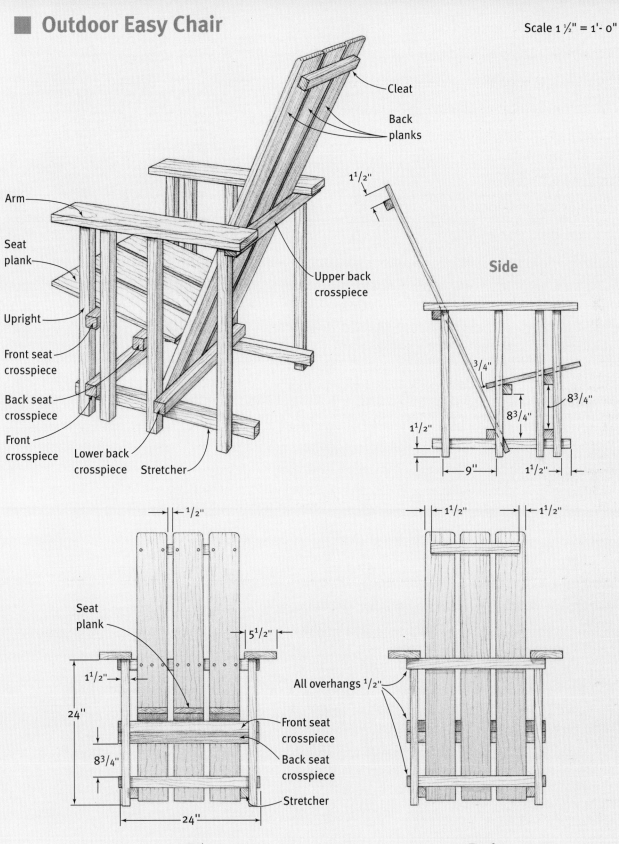

Cleat

Back planks

Arm

Seat plank

Upright

Front seat crosspiece

Back seat crosspiece

Front crosspiece

Lower back crosspiece

Stretcher

Upper back crosspiece

1½"

Side

¾"

8¾"

8¾"

1½"

9"

1½"

½"

Seat plank

5½"

1½"

24"

8¾"

Front seat crosspiece

Back seat crosspiece

Stretcher

24"

Front

1½"

1½"

All overhangs ½"

Back

MATERIALS

Quantity	Actual Dimension	Length	Description	Notes
9 or 5	1½" x 1½"	4' 8'	Base materials. 9 pieces of 4' long. 5 pieces of 8'.	Buy 2x2 baluster stock. Final length 24".
3	¾" x 5½"	8'	Planks for back, seat, and arms	Buy 1x6. Back length 48", seat 18", arms 27".
1 box	#8	2"	Flat-head wood screws	Self-drilling tip, square drive preferred.
1 box	#8	1¼"	Flat-head wood screws	Self-drilling tip, square drive preferred.
2	½" x 3"	12"	Spacers for back planks	Plywood or solid wood; use scrap; length is approximate.
1	¾"	12"	Spacer between seat and back	Any width is fine. Use plywood or solid wood; use scrap.
1 package	⅜"		Tapered plugs	Face grain if possible.
2 tubes			15-minute-cure epoxy	Self-mixing gun if possible. If not available, use polyurethane adhesive. Five-minute cures too quickly.
5			150-grit sandpaper	Sheets and disks
3			100-grit sandpaper	Sheets and disks
3			220-grit sandpaper	Sheets and disks
2 quarts			Exterior oil/varnish finish	
1			Tack cloth	
4			1½" disposable foam brushes	
2			Maroon synthetic steel wool pads	

*See pp. 44–45 for a discussion of actual vs. nominal dimensions.

Tools

- Tape measure
- 4" or 6" square
- Miter box and saw (hand or power)
- Two Light-duty bar clamps with 4" opening
- Two Quick-grip clamps with 12" opening
- 2 medium-duty bar clamps with 12" opening
- Cordless drill/driver (variable speed, reverse, clutch)
- #2 square-drive bits , 3" long (or Phillips head. Either way, get a few spares)
- #8 countersink drill bit (with stop collar)
- Flexible drive shaft for drill/driver
- 12" metal ruler
- 3/4" or 1" bench chisel
- Light mallet or flat-faced hammer
- Random-orbit sander
- Hand-sanding block (felt, cork, plastic, or made from scrap wood)
- Jig for positioning uprights (make as per directions on p. 98)

Multiple joints share the loads, and the structural members support one another to keep all the pieces aligned. No single joint deals with stresses beyond its comfortable limit.

Each side assembly has four uprights, so the chair has in effect eight legs. **Stretchers** span the uprights near the bottom of each side assembly, tying the uprights together structurally. Each upright is glued and screwed to the stretcher at two points to prevent racking. The side assemblies are connected by five crosspieces, which likewise share the loads and stresses. The arms fasten to the uprights as well as to the upper back crosspiece, providing additional strength and rigidity.

Building the Chair

When I'm teaching, I often put up a big sign that reads, "A pleasing result supersedes all measurements." I find myself pointing to the sign often. Most beginning woodworkers obsess about measurements, worrying far too much about whether their project exactly matches the specifications in the drawing. All that really matters is that parts go together square and true to one another. The actual final measurements don't matter.

To make this point forcefully, you won't do much measuring in this project. Instead of referring to a ruler, most of the time you'll use 2x2 offcuts to use as your measuring guide. This way, you can't focus on the minute markings on the tape measure or ruler; I want to encourage you to step back and look at the big picture. Even an untrained eye is surprisingly accurate about relative distances and can see if something is out of place. Before you drive any screws, see if it looks right.

The illustration on p. 89 shows dimensions, but your results may be different, since 2x2s can vary in width and thickness depending on what kind of wood they're made from. The actual dimensions are typically close to 1½" x 1½" but range to 1⅜" and 1⁹⁄₁₆" (see pp. 44–45 for information on nominal vs. actual dimensions).

Before you start, remember to condition the wood by stickering it for a couple of weeks as described in chapter 2. This is especially important for 2x2s sold for decking (meranti, ipe, some cedars). Decking lumber is often stored outside, giving it a higher moisture

Which Wood for Your Chair?

When you go to a home center or lumberyard and ask for balusters and matching one-by material, you'll have a selection of woods to choose from, depending on the local market.

- **Red cedar**—The lightest in weight, the least expensive, and the least strong of the choices. Tends to split, but works very well outdoors unfinished. Light pink to brown color. Paints well.

- **Redwood**—Great weathering characteristics, light, strong, fragrant. Light reddish-brown color; when untreated, it weathers to a silvery gray. Expensive.

- **Port Orford (or white) cedar**—Moderate cost, moderate strength, paints well, takes exterior stains well. Light golden color, also weathers to a silvery gray.

- **Meranti**—Similar in appearance to mahogany, substantially heavier than red or white cedar. Moderate in cost, weight, and strength. Looks good with a clear finish, and takes paint well. Often sold as decking lumber, it's sometimes called mahogany, though it's not a true mahogany. Sometimes sold prefinished.

- **Oak**—Hard, strong, heavy. Paints well. Looks good with clear finish. It quickly turns black when exposed to water, so it's not suitable for clear finish outdoors. Moderately expensive.

- **Ipé (or Brazilian walnut)**—Dense tropical hardwood often used for outdoor decks and railings. Dark in color, very heavy, very strong. Can be left to weather, or looks great with a clear finish. Moderately expensive.

- **Pine**—Soft, light in color, not very strong. Doesn't stain well, knots may bleed sap. Expensive

- **Poplar**—Moderately strong, easy to work. Sometimes has a greenish-purple cast that doesn't look well with clear finish or stain, but it paints very well. Moderate price.

content. Without proper storage and conditioning, the wood might twist and bow during or immediately after building. Better to condition the wood to your shop, and discard any pieces that get too crooked in the process.

Build the Side Assemblies

Once your lumber has been conditioned, you're ready to get started. The first step is to crosscut all the 2x2s to the proper length.

Crosscutting and sanding base parts

1 Using the technique described in "Skill Builder: Crosscutting Multiples to the Same Length" on p. 94, cut the 2x2 into 17 identical pieces about 24" long (you need 14 for the chair and the other three are extras for mistakes and jigs).

If you're using a miter saw, your pieces will end up just a hair less than 24". A chopsaw has a thicker blade and makes a wider **kerf**; your pieces will be

more like 23¹⁵⁄₁₆". It doesn't matter exactly how long the pieces are as long as they're identical.

Don't assume you can cut all your 4' 2x2s exactly in half with one cut. If they vary in length at all, the chair won't come out right. To be safe, position the stop block to cut a little less than 24". Cut the first piece to length, and then put the other piece against the stop block and cut a sliver from it.

2 Sand all four sides of each piece using a random-orbit sander and 150-grit sandpaper (see photo A).

Laying out the stretchers

1 Start by crosscutting one of the extra (or one cut too short) 2x2s to get two identical pieces 8¾" long for measuring blocks to use instead of a tape measure for several "measuring" operations.

2 Lay two 24" pieces on the bench, and get the ends flush by pushing them against one of the measuring blocks (see photo B which shows the operation to flush 5 pieces). Clamp them together to prevent shifting while laying out the positions of the uprights.

3 Holding a measuring block as shown in photo C, make a mark on the inside edge. Keep the block in position, and place the other block alongside it,

toward the center of the stretchers. Make a mark along the inside edge of the block as shown in photo C. Lift off that block, and make **hatch marks** between the two lines. This is where the back upright crosses the stretcher. Mark this end of the stretchers "Back."

4 Using a ruler, make a mark at the back edge of the third upright toward the middle of the stretcher 9" from the line that represents the back edge of the back upright (the first line you drew in the previous step). Using the measuring block to mark the overlap, make the hatch marks and label it "#3."

5 Mark the location of the first upright back from the front of the stretcher, using the measuring block and hatch marks as in step 2.

6 Next, mark the position of the second upright exactly one block width inward from the first upright. To make the marks, put the block back in place over the marks made in step 5, and put the second block along the inside of the

first. Hold it in place and mark the inside edge. Don't let go of it yet.

7 Lift the first block, leapfrog it over the second, and put it down snug against the inside of the second block (see photo D). Let go of the leapfrogged block, hold this one firmly, and mark the inside edge. Then lift it off to put hatch marks under it.

Laying out the uprights

The uprights extend below the stretchers by the width of one measuring block.

1 Align four of the uprights flush at the ends and clamp them as you did with the stretchers. (It's a little easier to get everything aligned doing four at a time rather than all eight at once.)

2 Lay the measuring block flush with one end of the uprights, and make a mark on the inside end of the block across all four uprights.

3 Without moving this measuring block, hold the other measuring block against it and mark along its edge. The area under this block is where the

SKILL BUILDER   Crosscutting Multiples to the Same Length

What You'll Need

- Crosscut saw
- Clamps
- Small scrap blocks with at least one square end

Crosscutting one or two identical pieces is typically done using clamps or double-sided tape. Once you're cutting more than a few, it makes sense to use a **stop block,** as shown in photo A.

A stop block is simply a piece of wood with a square end clamped in place to position pieces for identical cuts. If the workpieces are longer than the saw's fence, rig up an extension table to support long pieces, as shown in the photo at right and the drawing below. Whether built for a miter saw or a chopsaw, the principles are the same.

1 Measure the first piece and put a mark where you want to make the cut. Square it across the face you intend to cut, as shown in photo B.

2 Clamp the piece in place on the saw table so the blade will cut on the line. Use the built-in hold-downs or small bar clamps.

3 Clamp a block to the fence so it's snug against the workpiece. Since you don't want the stop block to wriggle out of position during the course of many cuts, use two clamps.

4 Make the cut, remove the workpiece, and put another in place. Repeat until all are cut.

A

B

■ A Shop-Built Crosscut Extension Table

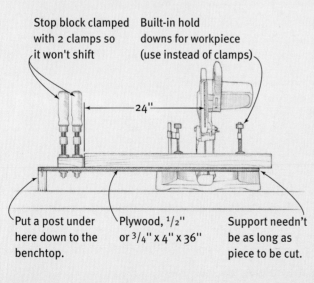

Stop block clamped with 2 clamps so it won't shift

Built-in hold downs for workpiece (use instead of clamps)

24"

Put a post under here down to the benchtop.

Plywood, ¹/₂" or ³/₄" x 4" x 36"

Support needn't be as long as piece to be cut.

screws go through the upright and into the stretcher. Make hatch marks, and label each piece as "Upright."

Countersinking the uprights for plugs

A **countersink** is nothing more than a funnel-shaped hole that matches the contour of the underside of a screw head. The countersunk hole allows the screw to nestle down flush with the surface of the wood. If you countersink deeply enough, the hole is far enough below the surface to contain a tapered wooden plug. It's an elegant way to hide unsightly screw heads in fine work.

1 Start by hanging the end of the workpiece off the edge of the bench so you don't drill into the bench (see photo E).

2 Drill and countersink just a little less than ¼" deep (about ⁷⁄₃₂") in the area that you hatch-marked. Locate the holes so they're catty-corner from each other using the methods shown in "Skill Builder: Countersinking for Screws and Plugs" on p. 96.

Fastening the uprights to the stretchers

To keep the chair from wobbling, the uprights must sit squarely on the floor, and the distance from the floor to the stretcher must be exactly the same on each. A simple jig made from a 2x2 makes it easy to position the uprights and hold them in place while fastening. (For more on this, see the sidebar on p. 98).

1 Lay one stretcher on the bench and clamp it down with the front to your right. This is important. The side assemblies are not interchangeable; they're mirror images of one another as shown in photo F. When you follow these steps for the other side, you'll place its front to the left. Put an extra piece of 2x2 about 20" above the stretcher to support the tops of the uprights while you work.

2 Apply glue to the hatched surface on the stretcher as well as on the back side of the upright at the countersunk holes (see photo G).

3 Position the front upright on top of the stretcher with the glued surfaces together. Use the jig to locate it properly, clamping as necessary. (See the photo on p. 98 for details.)

WORK SMART

If your 2x2s are narrower than 1½", 2½" screws will be too long. Use 2" screws instead.

E

F

SKILL BUILDER — Countersinking for Screws and Plugs

What You'll Need

- Cordless drill/driver
- #8 countersink/counterbore (stop collar optional)
- Scrap wood: ¾" pine and ¾" oak, two or three pieces about 4" x 14"

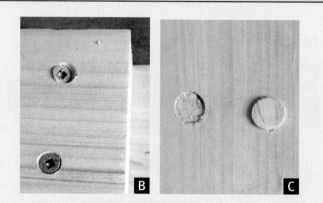

Countersinking for a Screw

A countersink is made by slipping a cone-shaped cutter onto the shank of a drill bit. The cutter makes a cone-shaped hole at the top of the shank hole to allow the head of a flathead screw to lie flush with the surface. In harder materials such as oak or MDF, a drilled countersink is necessary. When you're driving a screw near the edge of a board, a countersunk pilot hole will help prevent splitting.

1 Position the countersink for a 1¼" screw. Line up the tips of the screw and the bit, and slide the countersink so the top of the V that cuts the countersink is at the same level as the head of the screw, as shown in photo A.

2 If your bit came with a stop collar, set the stop collar right where the cutter changes from a V to straight sided. If you don't have a depth collar, you can use a piece of masking tape or go by eye.

3 Chuck the bit into the drill and drill the hole. Make sure the drill is set to high gear, full torque, and high speed. Alignment relative to the surface is important when countersinking. If you're not perpendicular to the surface, the screw will sit at a slight angle and won't be flush, as shown in photo B.

Countersinking for a Plug

If you drill the countersink deep enough, you can fill the hole with a wooden plug. If you have a stop collar, slide it into position about ¼" from the top of the funnel. Otherwise, use a piece of tape.

1 Drill a couple of holes, then insert the plugs using a hammer. If the hole is the correct depth, the plug will go in until it's about 1⁄16" above the surface. This makes it easy to trim flush. Find the correct depth by trial and error, as shown in photo C.

2 Once the depth is correct, drill several holes you can fill with plugs as discussed in "Skill Builder: Installing and Trimming Plugs" on p. 106. Keep the stop collar in position for countersinking the screw holes in the chair.

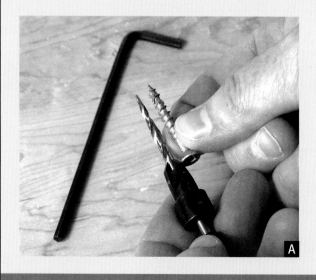

4 Drive two 2½" screws into the countersunk holes. Be careful not to drive the screw too deep—if necessary adjust the clutch to get it right. Watch the joint to make sure the screw goes in all the way and the two pieces draw together so the excess epoxy squeezes out.

5 Repeat steps 1 to 4 for the second, third, and the back uprights.

6 Place the other stretcher on the bench with the front pointing toward your left. Fasten the uprights as described above.

Connect the Side Assemblies with the Lower Crosspieces

Once you've built the two side assemblies, it's time to join them together with the lower crosspieces. They connect the stretchers at the bottom of the structure.

Laying out the crosspieces

The two sides are fastened together with a total of five crosspieces. These crosspieces extend ½" beyond the face of the uprights, giving the chair some visual texture.

1 Align the ends of the five crosspieces flush, and clamp them together. Use your sliding square to mark lines down both ends of all five that are ½" in from the ends.

2 Look at the crosspieces. Two of them fasten the stretchers together at a point two measuring blocks back from the line drawn in step 1. Let's call these crosspieces Type A. Two other crosspieces have their joints one measuring block back from the mark. These I'll call Type B. One crosspiece, Type C, needs no other mark. Use the blocks to "measure" out these distances as you did for the stretchers and upright, and make hatch marks in the joint areas (see photo H).

Upright Jig

This simple jig takes all the fight out of locating the uprights (see photo A). It keeps the bottoms of the uprights in line and assures perpendicularity. It also makes it easy to get the correct spacing between the first and second uprights.

Clamp the jig to the stretcher as shown in photo B. In most cases you'll be able to drive the screws as shown, but you may have to hold the upright to the jig or even clamp them together.

■ Jig for Positioning Uprights

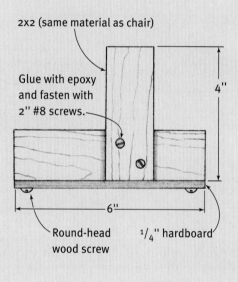

2x2 (same material as chair)

Glue with epoxy and fasten with 2" #8 screws.

4"

6"

Round-head wood screw

¹/₄" hardboard

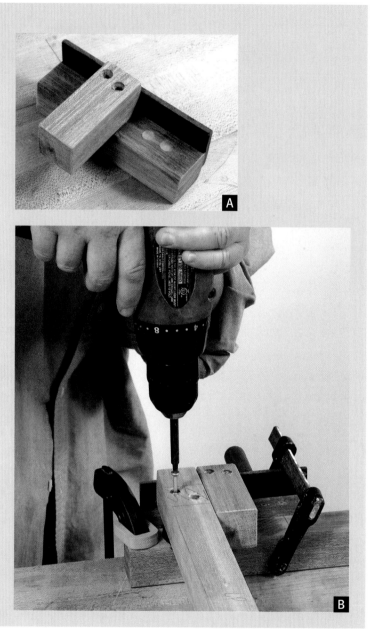

Countersinking the crosspieces

Just as you drilled countersinks in the hatched areas on the uprights, do like-wise in the hatched areas of four of the five crosspieces. The fifth crosspiece gets no holes at this time.

Connecting three crosspieces to one side

1 Put one side assembly on the bench so the stretcher sits on the top, with the extended bottom of the legs clearing the edge of the bench. Hold it in a vise or with clamps. Lay the scrap or extra crosspieces on the bench to support the far end of the crosspieces, as shown in photo I.

2 Select one Type A crosspiece to fasten between the two front uprights, positioned with the countersinks up. Apply glue to the bottom and both sides in the hatched area on the cross-piece and to the mating surfaces on the

side assembly. Make sure the crosspiece extends beyond the upright by ½" (see photo J). Clamp it in place while you drive two 2½" screws.

3 Do likewise with the lower back crosspiece (Type A), gluing and screwing it to the back edge of the third upright.

4 Lift the assembly out of the vise and place it on the benchtop, then clamp the other side assembly to the stretchers. Make sure everything fits, the ½" overhang is correct, and that the assembly is square. Then clamp the upper back crosspiece (Type B) in place.

5 Remove the crosspieces one at a time, and apply epoxy to the mating surfaces on the crosspieces, stretchers, and uprights. Clamp in place once more (double-check the ½" overhang), and drive the screws. Then move on to the lower back crosspiece (Type A). Finally, fasten the upper back crosspiece (Type B).

Install the Seat Supports

The seat supports connect the side assemblies near the middle of the structure.

Installing the back seat support

1 Place a measuring block vertically on the stretcher, along the front side of the third upright. Use one per side, and clamp them in place (only one clamp is necessary).

2 Position the remaining Type B crosspiece atop the measuring blocks while fastening. Apply epoxy to the mating surfaces and screw the crosspiece in place, carefully maintaining the ½" overhang (see photo K).

3 Remove the measuring blocks and clean them with alcohol, then clean up any squeeze-out at the joint.

Installing the front seat support

1 Position a measure block vertically atop the lower front crosspiece, between the first and second uprights. Clamp in place (see photo L).

2 Place the only Type C crosspiece atop the blocks. Clamp in place and countersink two holes on each side through the front upright and into the crosspieces (see photo M).

3 Remove the front seat crosspiece to clear away the dust from between the joint, and apply epoxy to all mating surfaces.

4 Replace the front seat crosspiece, carefully aligning the ½" overhangs. This is hard to do without spreading a bit of epoxy around, but do your best to keep the mess to a minimum. Drive the screws, remove the blocks, and clean up.

Install the Back and Seat Planks

A ½" gap between the planks provides ventilation and prevents water and leaves from gathering in the seat. Install the center plank first, then the

two sides using a piece of ½"-thick scrap (a piece of plywood or some leftovers from the Simple Handmade Box project).

Cutting the back and seat planks

1 Crosscut the three back planks from 1x6 stock to 48" long.

2 Crosscut the three seat planks from 1x6 stock to 17½" long.

3 Using a random-orbit sander and 150-grit disks, smooth all surfaces of the planks before assembly.

Installing the center back plank

If your workspace has low ceilings, you may have to move your chair to the floor for the following steps. If you have 50" above your workbench, keep the work on the bench and save your back.

1 Using a tape measure, find and mark the midpoints of the upper and lower back crosspieces as well as the front and rear seat crosspieces.

2 Using a ruler, mark a line half the width of a 1x6 (that's 2¾") out from the centerline on each side. The edges of the center planks will align with these marks.

3 Place two pieces of scrap 2x2 under the chair so the lower edge of the plank can rest on them. Use clamps to lightly hold the plank to the upper back crosspiece. Photo N shows the markings in step 2, as well as the extra pieces running fore and aft between the bottom of the plank and the bench.

4 On the back of the plank, draw lines along the upper and lower edges of the upper back support crosspiece, thus showing where the glue will go. Do the same on the lower back support crosspiece.

5 Next, determine the locations of the screws that will fasten the planks to the upper and lower back support crosspieces. Stand in front of the chair and bend or kneel so the upper back support crosspiece is at eye level. Draw a light horizontal line with a pencil on the plank along what appears to be the top of the crosspiece (see photo O). You'll drill and countersink for screws just below along this line. Do the same with the lower back support (if your chair is on the floor, this will be awkward).

6 Remove the plank and use a square to draw perpendicular lines about ⅛" below the lines you drew by eye. This extra depth is insurance against the angled screw missing or coming out through the edge of the crosspieces.

7 Mark the locations of three holes: one in the center of the plank and a hole 1" in from each edge. Drill and countersink for screws on both the upper and lower crosspieces.

8 Apply epoxy to the mating surfaces and replace the center plank, using your lines to get it positioned. Clamp lightly. Drive the first screw in the upper right countersink, and check the position of the plank. Is it still square? Did it shift? Reposition as necessary, then drive the second screw in the lower left countersink. Now the plank cannot shift, and you can drive the remaining screws in any order.

Installing the side planks

1 Slide the scrap 2x2s from beneath the center plank so they'll support the bottom of the right plank. Place a ½"

spacer about 12" long between the two planks near the middle of the back, then put a clamp across all three pieces—the two planks and the spacer. Slip another spacer at the bottom and clamp there, too. Make lines on the upper back crosspiece at each edge of the plank so you can quickly reposition it later (see photo P).

2 Remove the plank, apply epoxy to the mating surfaces, reclamp, and fasten in place.

3 Now that you've had a bit of practice, you can save a step when installing the left side plank. Just apply epoxy, clamp in place with the spacers, and drive the fasteners.

Installing the seat planks

To install the seats, follow the same procedure as with the backs, but with one difference. Whereas you used the measuring blocks to hold the back planks off the floor, now you'll use a piece of ¾"-thick scrap as a spacer between the seat planks and the back planks.

1 Position the center plank on the marks 2¾" from the center with the ¾" spacer between the seat plank and the back.

2 Gauging by eye, draw a light pencil line along the center of the crosspiece. Also mark screw holes in the center and 1" from each edge.

3 Use the ½" spacers to position the side planks the correct distance from the center plank and the ¾" spacer to position them relative to the back.

4 Glue and fasten in the same manner as the back planks.

Install the Back Cleat

If you stand behind the chair and look down at the tops of the back planks, they probably don't lie in a nice straight line. That's not because of anything you did as a builder, but because the wood is not perfectly flat. It may have some bow along its length or some twist. It may even be cupped a little. For a crisp, refined appearance, fasten a **cleat** near the top of the back

to hold the planks in alignment (see photo Q).

1 Measure the width of the back planks, then crosscut a leftover 2x2 to a length that is two block widths less and sand it smooth using a random-orbit sander and 150-grit paper.

2 Clamp the cleat in place so it's one measuring block down from the top and one measuring block in from each end (see photo R).

3 Draw around the edges of the cleat with a pencil to show where the glue will go. Unclamp the cleat to reveal the rectangle so drawn on the back side of the back. The screws that hold the cleat to the back planks will be on the centerline of the rectangle. The center

plank has three holes—one on center and one hole 1" in from each edge. The side planks have only two holes each—one on center and one 1" from the inside edge.

4 On the back of the planks, mark the locations of the screws that will hold the cleat in place.

5 Using only the drill portion of your countersink bit, drill a pilot hole for each screw through the planks from back to front. Don't let the countersink cut the wood; just bore a hole (see photo S).

6 Go around to the front of the chair, and using the pilot holes as guides, countersink proper holes for plugs.

7 Apply epoxy to the back of the cleat and to the rectangles on the back planks, and clamp it in place. If your seat back planks are much out of alignment, it may take your most powerful clamps to get them in place. Drive 1¼" screws from the front—through the planks and into the cleat.

Install the Arms

If you are both lucky and careful, all your uprights will be perfectly aligned. More likely, a couple of uprights are slightly bowed, or maybe one didn't get installed quite right. The arms are

designed to camouflage such discrepancies.

1 Crosscut a 1x6 into two pieces, each 27" long, and sand the planks using 150-grit paper and a random-orbit sander.

2 Clamp the ½"-thick plank spacer to the inside of the uprights with clamps at the front and back. Make sure the spacer doesn't extend above the tops of the uprights. Use another clamp to try and pull any misaligned uprights into place, but don't worry if they're not perfect. Photo T on p. 104 shows this clearly.

3 Mark the edges of each upright on the face of the spacer to show you where to drill later, when the arm will obscure your view up the uprights.

4 Set your sliding square so the base is on the spacer and the end of the blade is flush with the outside of the upright. Then set the arm on top of the uprights so that the inside edge is flush with the spacer and the back edge overhangs the upper back crosspiece by the width of one measuring block. Clamp front and back.

5 Even though you can't see the tops of the uprights, you can use your sliding square to mark their locations. The spacers already have marks on them showing the front and back sides of the uprights, and your square is now set to the outside edge. Mark these on the top of the arm, and reset your sliding square to ½" to get the inside edge. You don't need to be overly fussy about this—all you need is to locate the screw at or close to the center of the upright.

6 Mark the locations of the screws by eye in the middle of the square you've drawn to represent the upright. At the

WORK SMART

Be careful when driving the long screws into the narrow upright. If the screw gets much off the vertical, it could come out the side of the upright.

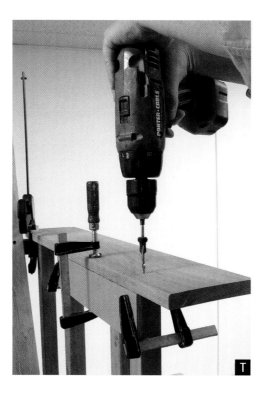

back of each arm, mark the locations of two countersinks for screws to go through the arms and into the upper back support crosspiece. Drill and countersink the holes (see photo T).

7 Put epoxy on the tops of the uprights and around the holes on the underside of the arms (just make it about the same size as the upright by eye). This being end grain, most of the strength comes from the screws, but the epoxy does add a little extra strength and, more important, seals the end grain against absorbing moisture.

8 Drive a 2½" screw into each of the uprights and two 1¼" screws into the back crosspiece.

Your chair is now structurally sound; before you do anything else, have a seat. You've earned it!

Install the Plugs

You'll have more choices in wood for your chair than you'll have for the plugs. If you can't get the same species

of wood for the plugs, consider a contrasting color. The chair shown is made from meranti with oak plugs. Try to get face-grain plugs—they're more stable and easier to cut than end-grain plugs.

Install all of the plugs in your chair according to the method described in "Skill Builder: Installing and Trimming Plugs" on p. 106, except that you'll put a little epoxy in the hole to keep the plugs in place. Allow the epoxy to fully cure before cutting the plugs.

Final Smoothing and Shaping

You did the lion's share of the sanding before assembly. Now all you have to do is clean up any errant epoxy, flatten the plugs, round the ends of the boards, and smooth the whole piece.

1 Lightly chamfer the ends of all the pieces with a block plane or sanding block. Pay special attention to the areas that come in contact with your body when you sit in the chair—the fronts of the arms and the front of the seat.

2 Also chamfer the ends of the back planks and arms, the ends of the crosspieces, and the ends of the stretchers. Cut light chamfers, slightly less than ⅛" wide, then smooth them over using 150-grit sandpaper and a hand-sanding block.

3 Give the bottoms of the uprights a slightly stronger chamfer (a hair more than ⅛") that's not rounded. This will make the chair appear lighter on its feet, almost as though it floats.

4 Hand-sand the entire surface of the chair using 220-grit paper. Go with the grain, and pay attention to the areas around the joints where you might have glue squeeze-out and to the area

around the plugs. You might need to use the chisel—bevel up—to remove a blob of epoxy.

Sealing the bottoms of the uprights

End grain soaks up water, which will tend to lift whatever finish you put on your chair. To prevent this, seal the bottom of the uprights with epoxy. It'll soak into the grain, so be prepared to put on a couple of thin coats to thoroughly seal it (see photo U). (If yours will be an indoor chair, you can skip this step.)

Finishing

The best easy-to-maintain clear finish for exterior use is a mixture of natural oils and modern varnish resins. This finish also looks good on chairs intended to be used inside. I've chosen not to stain this project, but if you want to change the color of the wood, be sure to use a stain intended for exterior use (see chapter 2 for more information on stains and staining).

Oil finish alone is easy to apply and visually enhances the grain, but it doesn't hold up to ultraviolet light and can take days to dry. Varnish provides a smooth, durable finish but requires 8 to 10 coats to look its best and can be fussy to apply. Mix them together, and you get the best of both worlds—a finish that looks great, is easy to apply,

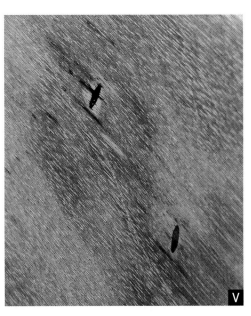

dries quickly, and is durable. (See chapter 2 for more information on oil/varnish blends.

1 Before applying the finish, repair minor divots, imperfectly fitting plugs, cracks, and other blemishes with epoxy. Simply fill a divot or crack with epoxy, or flow it into the space around an imperfectly drilled or cut plug. Cured epoxy dries clear, much like the finish, and the repairs will be hardly noticeable (see photo V). Sand it flush by hand.

2 After sanding, vacuum the chair and the surrounding area thoroughly to remove all sanding dust.

3 Wipe everything down with a tack cloth to get the last of the dust.

4 Apply a thin coat of oil/varnish mixture using an inexpensive natural bristle or foam brush. You can apply a second coat after eight hours (see photo W).

5 When that coat is thoroughly dry, you can apply another coat or two without sanding. In theory you needn't sand between each coat of oil/varnish mixture, but in practice you'll get a

SKILL BUILDER | Installing and Trimming Plugs

What You'll Need

- ⅜" flat-grain plugs (also called face-grain plugs)
- ¾" or 1" bench chisel
- Small flat-faced mallet or hammer
- Fast-cure epoxy (a self-mixing applicator is neater and easier)
- 150-grit sandpaper (if sanding end-grain plugs, use 100 grit first)
- Hand-sanding block

Practice setting and trimming plugs in scrap wood before you start on your chair. And when you do plug your chair, begin with plugs in hidden locations until you hit your stride. Save the most visible plugs (in the back and arms) for last. Make sure your chisel's sharp before you begin (see "Skill Builder: Sharpening" on p. 66).

1 Drill pilot holes and countersinks, then put a little glue in the hole and insert the plug. Align the grain of the plug with that of the surrounding wood. Set the plug with a small flat-headed mallet or hammer, as shown in photo A, but don't hit the plug too hard or it'll split. Be sure to listen: When the plug is snug against the screw head, the sound of the hammer blow changes to a clear, ringing thunk.

2 Once the glue has cured, cut the plug flush using a sharp chisel. It's a two-step process. First, use the hammer and the bevel of the chisel down to cut perpendicular to the grain to remove most of the plug, as shown in photo B. Then ditch the hammer and switch to paring with the bevel up (see "Skill Builder: Paring with a Chisel" on p. 74).

3 Start the cut at the back of the plug. Don't try to cut much off the plug, never more than about 1/32". Tap lightly using the hammer, tilting the chisel to control depth as you go. Make very light cuts to produce paper-thin shavings, as shown in photo C. If you cut too deep, you'll lose control and possibly mar the surface.

A

B

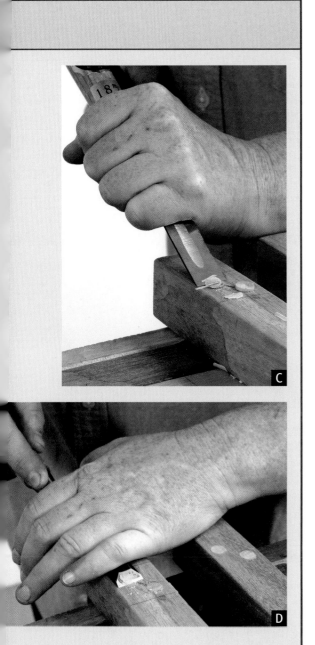

smoother finish if you do. I handle this by applying two or three coats and then sanding before applying another two coats. If I want a really rich, smooth finish, I'll sand once more and apply another coat.

6 Once you've got some finish on your chair, you can eliminate all the hassles of dust by **wetsanding.** Rather than making dust, wetsanding makes a slurry that you simply wipe down or hose away. Just make sure you get the slurry off your chair before it dries, or it will be harder to remove. Wetsand using a maroon synthetic steel wool pad.

7 Maintain your chair's finish by repeating step 6. If the chair lives outdoors, reapply once a year, twice a year in particularly sunny climes. If it's an indoor chair, you may go years before recoating.

4 Turn the chisel over and put the back flat on the wood. Press the back firmly with your hand to keep it flat on the surface, and move the chisel back and forth to pare away the last slivers, as shown in photo D.

5 Finally, sand the plugs smooth using 150-grit sandpaper and a random-orbit sander or a hand-sanding block. If you're using a machine, keep it moving and don't concentrate on the area around the plug.

Rustic Old-World Coffee Table

This table speaks of a simpler life, of Old-World farmhouses, bountiful harvests, golden sunlight, and long Sunday afternoons with friends and family. Old-fashioned, sturdy, and unpretentious, it's a piece of furniture you can live with for years.

The ready-made legs, with their big curves and generous proportions, provide a firm foundation for the table. They're connected by wide aprons featuring a beaded bottom edge. The top is made from a panel glued up from four narrower boards; its edge is a simple and graceful roundover.

Coffee tables are one of the hardest-working pieces of furniture in the modern home, and this rustic-looking table is designed to handle all the rigors of modern life—yards of Super Bowl snacks, a squirming child, impromptu dinner for the family, mountains of books, or a pack of roughhousing kids. It's engineered to be strong enough to handle the load, stiff enough to bear it without bending, and so well put together that a variety of stresses won't loosen its joints.

By the time you've finished this table, you'll have a solid grasp on some important woodworking skills: how to glue and clamp up boards to form a wide panel, how to make a decorative bead and use the tool to do it, how to round over an edge using a plane, and an effective method for preventing your stained finishes from looking blotchy. You're not only building a great coffee table but also increasing your skills. ■

What You'll Learn

- Making a pocket-hole screwed joint
- Making and using a hand-beading tool
- Gluing up wide panels
- Using a circular saw and fence for accurate cuts
- Rounding corners with a plane
- Using an orbital sander for flattening and smoothing
- Getting a blotch-free stain on pine
- Using colored waxes as a finish

There are good reasons for making a table like this early in your woodworking career. Its fashionable rusticity transforms "problems" or "mistakes" into charm. The top needn't be absolutely flat; in fact it won't look right if it is. The big legs draw the eye away from small problems, and the offset at the joints hides any misalignments. Dents or dings that might occur during construction just give it character, and if the bead isn't straight and true, it's just proof the table was made by hand. No matter how the table comes out, once it's in your home, you'll see that the outcome needn't be perfect for the result to be wonderful.

Although the pocket-hole screwed joint has been around for a long time, it is enjoying a new surge in popularity. Suddenly, every woodworking-supply outlet offers at least a couple of kinds of angled jigs for making the joints efficiently and accurately (see p. 28 for more information on pocket-hole jigs and screws). It's an ideal method for fastening corner joints where end grain meets side grain, as between the **aprons** and legs of this table, or between the **rails** and **stiles** of a face frame.

But pocket-hole joinery is more versatile than that. You can also use it to fasten the corners of boxes, cabinets, and drawers (just locate the screws so they don't show), to fasten edging, and even to make curves. Building this coffee table will get you started in pocket-hole joinery; once you know how it works, you'll find plenty of applications on your own.

Long before there were routers and other machines to mold edges, woodworkers used simple details to add visual appeal to a design. The beaded

▼ A pocket-hole screwed joint is easy to make, self-squaring, and strong.

Rustic Old-World Coffee Table

Scale 1" =1'- 0"

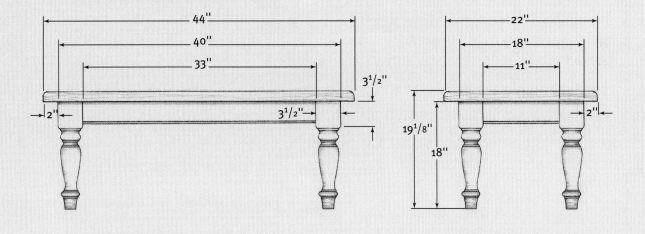

Front View

Side View

Construction Detail

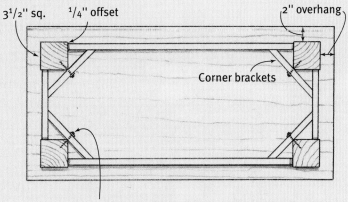

3½" sq. ¼" offset

2" overhang

Corner brackets

³/8" x 3½" lag screw with washer

MATERIALS

Quantity	Actual Dimension*	Length	Description	Notes
2	1⅛" x 5½"	8'	Pine lumber	Sold as 5/4 x 6". B or better select pine. If you choose #2 common, you may need three to yield four good boards each 44" long.
2	1⅛" x 3½"	8'	Pine lumber	Sold as 5/4 x 4" #2 common pine. Longest piece 33".
4		18"	Jumbo English country legs	Pine. From Osborne Wood Products, Inc. (see Resources on p. 198 for contact info).
3	¼" x about 3"	About 3"	Hardboard scraps to shim offsets	Use offcuts from shopmade circular saw guide).
8			Figure 8 table clip	
4	⅜"	3½"	Lag screws	
4	⅜"		Flat washers	
16 (approx.)		2½"	#8 washer-head pocket-hole screws, square drive	
16 (approx.)		1¼"	#8 washer-head pocket-hole screws, square drive	
1		1½"	#10 steel flat-head wood screw	For beading tool.
2 each			80-, 120-, 180-, 220-grit sanding disks	
2 sheets			220-grit sandpaper	
1 sheet			320-grit sandpaper	
			Glue	
			Dewaxed shellac	
			Denatured alcohol	For thinning shellac.
			Water-based stain	
			Inexpensive natural bristle brush	
			Dark-tinted wax	

*See p. 44–45 for information on actual vs. nominal dimensions.

Tools

- Tape measure
- Crosscut saw
- Beading tool (shopmade)
- Cordless drill/driver
- Pocket-hole jig
- ⅜" step drill for pocket holes
- 6"-long #2 square-drive bit
- Flexible shaft (optional)
- 1½" #2 square-drive bit
- #2 square-drive hand driver
- Straight screwdriver or Phillips screwdriver (depends on screws)
- Five panel clamps
- Six bar clamps
- Scraper
- Socket or other wrench to fit lag screws
- Block plane or bench plane
- 12" combination square
- Circular saw
- Saw guide (shopmade)
- ⅛" brad-point bit
- 5/64" drill bit
- Random-orbit sander
- ¾" Forstner drill bit

edge is a perfect example—fun and easy to make, it livens up an otherwise bland edge. In this project, you'll learn to make and use a beading tool, thus adding to both your woodworking and your design skills (see photo A). You'll also learn more about planes; they're not just for making things flat. In building this table, you'll see how you can use a plane to make a rounded edge.

Gluing narrow boards into wide panels is a critical skill you'll use again and again in your projects, and you'll learn how to do it right. Using the methods and tools described here, you'll learn to get flat panels with a minimum of trouble.

The skills you learn in building this simple project apply to all kinds of tables, from teacup-sized end tables to dining tables that seat 12. Your newfound skills in making panels and putting together pocket-hole screwed joints can be put to use making everything from jigs and shop furniture to kitchen cabinets to beds.

Building the Coffee Table

Make the aprons and build the support structure for your table, then make the top to fit.

Make the Aprons

1 Start by going through the 1⅛" x 3½" apron material and figuring out how to cut it to avoid major defects such as ugly knots, knots at the end of an apron, damaged edges, and swirling grain. Lay out the boards so you can comfortably ponder the best use of material. Figure out where each piece should be cut, label the pieces, then crosscut them an inch or so too long.

 A simple shopmade beading tool makes a decorative detail on the lower edge of the aprons.

2 Remember that the two short end aprons must be identical in length, as must the two long side aprons. If not, the corners won't go together at 90 degrees. Clamp or tape them in pairs so they come out alike, as shown in photo B. The actual length is not critical.

3 To get a firm idea of how your table goes together, put the four legs upside down on the bench and lay the approx-

Coffee Table Variations

This basic design is all you need to know to fill your house with tables of all kinds. Just change the dimensions, and most tables are within your capabilities.

For instance, a narrow end table with tapered legs is built the same way. It just needs narrower aprons and a smaller top. You can forgo the corner bracing on such a small table, as shown at right below. A dining table needs everything bigger—wider aprons, wider corner bracing, and depending on its length a cross brace or two across the middle, as shown at left below.

Determining the size of the aprons is something you can readily do by eye. Size the apron so it looks well with the leg and it will be strong enough. Sketch the leg full size and simply try out a few widths until you hit upon something that looks right. Just remember to leave a little bit of the square part of the leg showing beneath the apron.

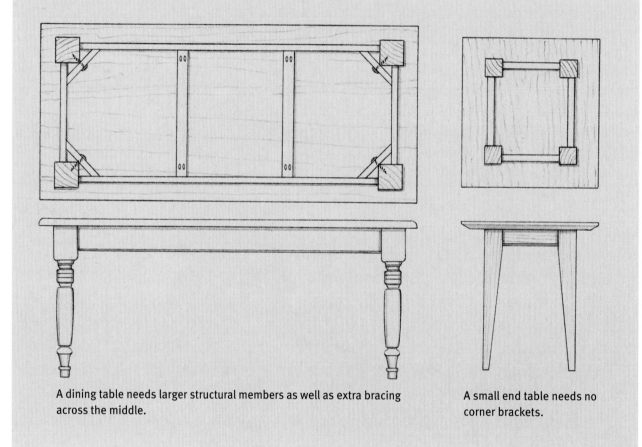

A dining table needs larger structural members as well as extra bracing across the middle.

A small end table needs no corner brackets.

imate-length aprons in place. Check the legs for knots and keep any big ones out of the way of the screws (knots are sometimes significantly harder than the surrounding wood). If there are any defects in the edges of the aprons, orient them so they won't get in the way of the beading and place them at the top of the base so they'll be under the tabletop where you can't see them (with the defect down on the benchtop in this orientation) as shown in photo C. Mark the pieces so you can reassemble them the same way later.

Selecting Pine

Rustic furniture has been made of pine for centuries because it's light in weight and color, easy to work, and readily available. Most lumberyards and home centers have pine in all shapes and sizes, although the exact type of pine differs from region to region.

Unlike most other species of wood, dealers typically carry more than one grade of pine. Boards are graded by strength and appearance according to specifications laid down by lumber industry associations. Most lumberyards and home centers offer both **common** and **select** grades. Common grades of pine (#1 through #5) are structurally sound but contain knots—#1 has the fewest, #5 has the most. The select grades (A through D) have fewer knots and a higher price. At my local yard, a B Select board costs three times as much as a #2 common board with the same dimensions.

For the base of the table, #2 common gives an appropriate rusticity, but keep in mind that knots near the edges can cause boards to twist. Try to pick boards that are straight and don't have too many knots. For the top, you might want to go with select, but the highest grades are too bland. I look for B Select boards with a few pin knots to give character.

Bead the Edge and Cut to Length

1 Use the beading tool and the method described in "Skill Builder: Making and Using a Beading Tool" on p. 116. Beading is similar to planing in that it's crucial the workpiece be held firmly, so use a vise or clamp the workpiece to the benchtop. If you use clamps, you'll have to figure out how to keep them out of the way. As the illustration on p. 116 shows, clamp thin pieces of wood tight up against the workpiece, using two clamps so nothing will shift.

2 Hold the tool as shown in photo A (on p. 113), and make several passes so the screw head slightly rounds over the wood, forming the bead. Do this for all four aprons. Don't press down too hard or go too quickly, or the bead will get

WORK SMART

Make the beads on the edges where the grain is straightest and where there are no knots.

C

SKILL BUILDER | Making and Using a Beading Tool

What You'll Need

- 4"-long piece of scrap 2x2 or similar hardwood
- One #10 x 1" flat-head wood screw (the old-fashioned kind, length is not critical, 1¼" is okay)
- Cordless drill
- Sandpaper
- ⅛" brad-point bit
- Hand screwdriver for the screw
- Scrap wood for beading, ⅝ or ¾" (any width, at least 12" long)

The decorative bead along the bottom edge of the aprons is distinctive and easy to make using a simple shopmade beading tool, as shown in photo A and the illustration at right.

A

1 Find a nicely rounded piece of hardwood that fits in your hand (a 4"-long piece of scrap 2x2 from your Outdoor Easy Chair is perfect). Sand it smooth.

2 Drill a ⅛" pilot hole in one face about 1½" in from the end and about ½" in from one edge. Drive a #10 steel wood screw into the hole until the underside of the head is about ¼" from the surface of the block.

3 Start the bead at whichever end is comfortable by pressing the block firmly against the side of the board and pulling the tool toward you. It's easier if you hold the opposite edge of the board with the other hand.

■ A Shopmade Beading Tool

Cut good-looking rustic-style beads with this simple tool which you can make from any scrap to fit your hand. The only dimension of importance is the ½" between the screw and the edge of the tool. Rounded corners are comfortable in the hand.

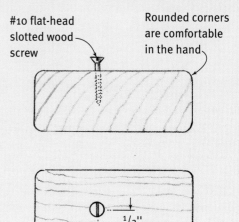

#10 flat-head slotted wood screw

Rounded corners are comfortable in the hand

½"

1½"

4 Run the tool the length of the board, pressing downward while pulling. Go slowly and be sure to keep the tool against the edge.

5 Take several passes, and stop when the underside of the screw starts rounding over the bead adjacent to the cut. Photo B shows only a few passes to the left of the black line. More passes were made with the tool on the portion to the right of the line—the bead is more defined. You can adjust the size of the bead by changing the distance between the head of the screw and the surface of the block. A greater distance makes a wider bead.

B

■ Alternate Clamping Arrangement for Beading

If you don't have a vise to hold aprons for beading, you can use this arrangement to get the clamps out of the way. Be sure the pieces of scrap are clamped tight against the ends. Right-handers will prefer to bead the inner edge, left-handers the outer.

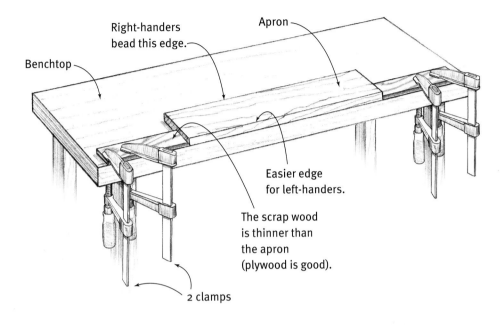

Right-handers bead this edge.

Apron

Benchtop

Easier edge for left-handers.

The scrap wood is thinner than the apron (plywood is good).

2 clamps

wavy as the edge of the screw head tends to follow the grain (rather than remaining parallel to the edge).

Mark and Drill the Pocket Holes

1 Once more, set the legs and base upside down on the benchtop. Make sure all of the beads are oriented properly (up and facing out in this orientation). Clearly mark the location of each pocket hole so you'll know where to drill.

2 Set up your pocket-hole jig as described in "Skill Builder: The Pocket-Hole Screwed Joint" on p. 118, drilling a test hole in a piece of leftover apron stock to make sure the stop collar depth is correct.

3 Drill two pocket holes on the inside of each end of each apron. Use a double-barreled jig to locate the holes, or place

D

them about ½" in from each edge, as shown in photo D. The exact location isn't critical. Make sure you don't drill through the beaded side; the jig goes against the back of the aprons so the pocket holes will show on the underside.

SKILL BUILDER The Pocket-Hole Screwed Joint

What You'll Need
- Cordless drill/driver
- Pocket-hole jig (see p. 28)
- Step drill with stop collar
- 6" #2 square-drive bit
- 1¼" pocket-hole screws (washer head #8)
- Scrap wood, ¾" thick and some ⁵⁄₄ stock
- Glue

1 Before setting up the jig or chucking the step drill into your cordless drill/driver, check that the stop collar is in the correct location on the step drill. Insert the bit into the guide bushing on the pocket-hole jig, and position the collar so that the tip is about ⅛" back from the bottom of the jig, as shown in the photos A and B.

2 If you have a bench-mounted jig, simply clamp a piece of ¾" scrap in it and drill the pocket holes, as shown in photo D on p. 117. If you're using a portable jig, align the bottom of the jig with the end of the workpiece. Clamp it in place with the supplied clamp (or use a small bar clamp), as shown in photo C. Orient your work so you drill and screw downward.

3 Chuck the step drill bit into your drill/driver and set the clutch and speed for drilling. Put the tip in the guide bushing and hold the drill lightly so that when you press the trigger, the drill will self-center in the bushing. Drill pushing downward until the collar hits the bushing

4 Remove the jig and check that there's no hole in the end of the workpiece. If you see any more than a tiny pinprick, set the collar a little lower on the bit to reduce the depth of cut. Try it again, and keep adjusting the collar until the step drill makes no hole in the end grain, as the nearest hole shown in photo D.

5 A pocket-hole joint needs two screws (it will pivot around one), so for maximum strength, get them as far apart as possible—about ½" in from each edge. On narrow pieces of wood, they will be quite close together, whereas on a wider piece, they'll be farther apart. A very wide piece could have two sets of two.

6 Switch the drill speed to low, and set the clutch about halfway. Change the step drill bit for a 6"-long #2 square-drive bit. Pocket-hole screws are easier to drive with long bits because of the angle.

7 Make a test by driving a screw into one of the pocket holes without fastening it to another piece of wood, as shown in photo E. Hold this up to the other ¾"-thick piece you intend to fasten to it.

D

E

F

Make sure the screw will be entirely within the wood and won't poke out the back. If it looks like the screw might be too long, use shorter screws or clamp the jig back slightly from the edge. Remove the screw.

8 Apply glue to the end grain of the piece with the drilled pocket holes, then lay it on the bench with the pocket holes facing upward. Butt the side grain of the other piece against it, as shown in photo F. Drive the screws, adjusting the clutch to get them all the way in. Be careful of overdriving the screw or it may break out the bottom of the drilled piece, as shown in photo G.

You can also use pocket-hole screws to join the edge of one piece to the face of the other, as shown in photo H.

G

H

Fasten the Short Aprons to the Legs

1 Clamp a leg at the edge of the bench with the top end near the edge, as shown in photo E. Make sure the inside of the leg is facing up, and use two clamps so it won't shift. Place a piece of ¼" hardboard against the inside edge of the leg and another about 8" farther away from the leg.

2 Apply glue to the end of a short apron, then lay it on the shims, using your thumb to align the top of the apron with the top of the leg.

3 Place a screw in one of the pocket holes, double-check the alignment, hold the apron steady, and drive a 2½" screw into the leg.

4 Drive the second screw.

5 Remove the clamps from the leg and use them to clamp another leg to the bench (don't forget to position it so the leg's best face shows outward in the finished table). Apply the glue, align the apron with the top, and fasten in place, as shown in photo F.

6 Repeat steps 2 through 4 and fasten the other short apron between the remaining legs.

Fasten the Long Aprons to the Ends

1 Clamp one end assembly on the right side of the bench so that the apron is vertical. Lay down the ¼" hardboard shims as for the short apron, apply glue, and fasten one long apron to it. Make sure the bead is oriented correctly.

E

F

2 Unclamp the leg and put glue on the end grain of the long apron. Position the remaining end assembly and clamp it in place as before, then position the long apron and fasten it in place.

3 Carefully flip the base and apply glue to both ends of the other long apron. Place the shims, slide the apron in place, and fasten both ends of the apron, as shown in photo G.

Make and Install the Corner Brackets

1 Select clear leftover pieces of apron stock and cut four brackets, each 8⅜" long. They will span the corner between the two aprons (behind the leg). They provide additional support for the corners, keeping the table square even when it's used hard (see the illustration on p. 111).

2 Cut two pocket holes in each end of each bracket.

3 Roughly mark each bracket on both edges as shown in the illustration at right so that you won't have to think about what angle to saw.

4 Set your crosscut saw for a 45-degree angle, and clamp the block in place. Make the cut so that the block is no shorter (or at worst a very tiny bit shorter). Unclamp, flip the piece end-for-end, and make another 45-degree cut, as shown in photo H.

■ Marking the Brackets

Mark the 45-degree angles on all four ends of the brackets. When you cut the angles with a miter saw, you'll have to flip them end for end. The marks must appear on both sides.

Roughly 45 degrees

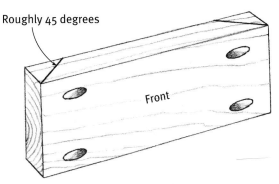

Front

Remember: The bracket is longest on the pocket-hole side.

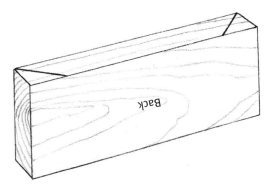

Back

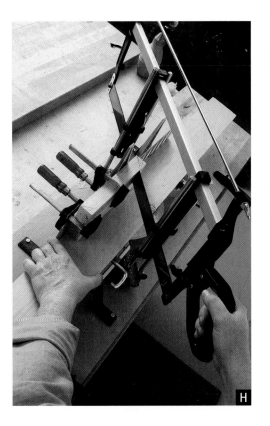

■ WORK SMART

If the bracket is too short to touch both aprons when you hold it against the leg, use a block plane or chisel to remove the corner of the leg behind the bracket so it can slip into place. It's okay if the bracket is as much as ⅛" away from the leg.

■ WORK SMART

You might need to put a clamp or two on the base to hold it to the bench while you work.

■ WORK SMART

Driving screws in this order ensures that the bracket is positioned correctly and that it is socked down tight without twisting or breaking it.

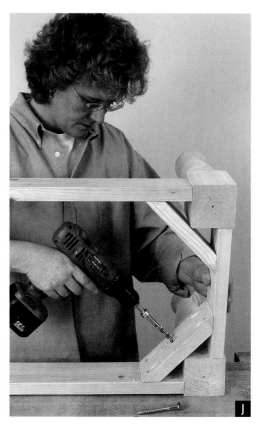

5 Repeat for all four blocks.

6 Hold one bracket in the corner so that the angles touch both aprons and the back touches the leg. Make pencil marks at the top and bottom of the bracket so you can reposition it.

7 Remove the bracket, apply glue to both ends, and put it back in place on the lines.

8 Holding the bracket, drive a screw in one hole but not fully, as shown in photo I. Driving the screw to full depth at this point might misalign the bracket.

9 Since the next screw goes in the bracket hole diagonally opposite the one you just drove, flip the assembly so the other end of the bracket is down on the bench. It will be much easier to work pushing downward.

10 Check to make sure the bracket is still on its lines, then drive the screw but, again, not to full depth.

11 Drive the other two screws to a similar depth, flipping the piece as necessary.

12 Once all the screws are in place, tighten them in the order in which you placed them.

13 Repeat for the other three brackets.

14 For added strength, drive a 3½" lag screw through the center of the bracket and into the leg. To make the pilot hole, use the pocket-hole step drill. Make the depth about ⅛" less than the length of the lag screw. Set the depth by adjusting the collar or by using a piece of masking tape. Change the drill speed to high, set the clutch for drilling, and drill the hole, as shown in photo J.

15 Place the lag screw (with a washer under the head) in the hole, and drive with a socket wrench. Drive so it's

tight, as shown in photo J, but not so tight the wood crushes around the washer.

Level the Aprons and Install Tabletop Fasteners

If all went according to plan, the tops of the aprons are flush with the tops of the legs, but in real life there are always some irregularities.

Planing the tops of the aprons

1 If the aprons are above the legs, plane them flush. If they're below the legs, just leave them. Set the plane for a very light cut; you won't have much to remove. Set the table on the floor and butt it against your bench or a wall, then kneel down to plane. Or if you have something firm to stand upon such as a step stool or box, you can clamp your table to the bench and plane standing up, as shown in photo L.

2 To keep the tops of the aprons perfectly flat, use the heel of your plane as a reference. You can use a block plane for this or a larger bench plane if you

have one. Rest the heel on the apron near the middle, and plane toward one end, carefully holding the plane level. Skew the plane if required. Don't plane the end grain of the tops. This process is similar to that used in leveling the top of the Simple Handmade Box.

3 Run the plane over the bracket, and continue along the adjoining apron. Continue in this fashion around the tops of the aprons until they're all flush.

Installing the tabletop fasteners

A wide tabletop shrinks and swells with changes in ambient moisture and must be fastened to take this into account (see the materials chapter for more information on moisture and wood). Use figure 8-style tabletop fasteners; they rotate slightly to accommodate the movement differential between the tops and the base.

1 Using a Forstner bit, drill ¾" holes in the aprons, as shown in the illustration location and photo M.

2 Fasten the wide end of the figure 8 in the apron using the screws that came with the clips. Use a ⁵⁄₆₄" bit and drill a pilot hole slightly shallower than the depth of the screw to ensure it drives tightly. Drive the screw by hand.

M

■ Locating the Figure 8 Clips

Drill ³/₄" holes just slightly deeper than the thickness of the clip. They should be right on the edge of the apron.

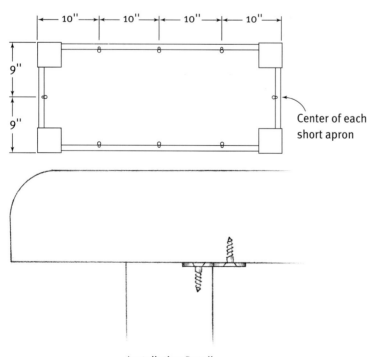

Center of each short apron

Installation Detail

Make the Tabletop

The wide tabletop is glued up from narrower boards. With careful gluing and clamping they'll be nearly flat—a little sanding will smooth the joints and add some character.

Selecting the boards

1 Start by taking the time to look at the wood you've selected for the top, and figure out how to orient the pieces so they look best. Choose the most likely boards and crosscut them to about 45", which is the finished length plus 1".

2 Place these boards on the bench and look at the color and grain pattern, paying attention to the color at the edges of the boards. Try to get the colors at the edges to match as shown in photo N, or at least orient them so there are no

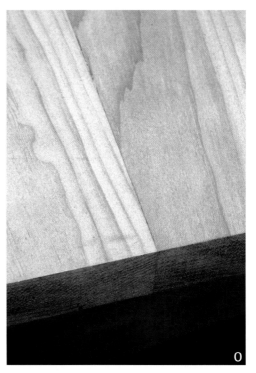

WORK SMART

Don't try to clean up the glue; wiping it will only spread it thinly over the surface of the wood. If you stain your piece, the glue smears will show because the glue prevents the stain from soaking in. Leave the glue to dry, and remove it with a scraper later.

abrupt changes in color across a glue-line, as shown in photo O. Also look at knots or defects and decide whether to place them artfully in the top or hide them on the underside.

3 Once the boards are laid out in a pleasing arrangement, draw a triangle across the joints so you don't have to figure it out all over when gluing and clamping.

Gluing up the panel

1 Before gluing up the panel, make a dry run to practice clamping according to the techniques shown in "Skill Builder: Clamping Up a Wide Panel" on p. 126. Lay out your clamps and see how this particular set of boards is going to act.

2 Disassemble the dry run, and apply glue to both edges of each joint by using a glue roller. Be sure to apply enough glue so that both edges look wet and coated, as shown in photo P.

A Triangle Keeps Glue-Ups in Order

Once you've arranged your boards for the nicest-looking panel, draw a triangle that crosses all the joints.

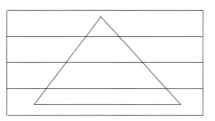

It's easy to see if a board gets out of sequence.

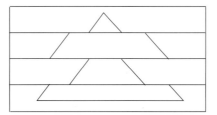

SKILL BUILDER | Clamping Up a Wide Panel

What You'll Need

- Five panel clamps that open to at least 30"
- Two clamping pads about 1" x 2" x 48" (or as long as your panel)
- Six or more 12" bar clamps
- Four stout pieces of scrap about 24" long (2x2s are good for this)

Clamping a wide panel is a complex dance between force and geometry. Too much pressure in the wrong place can distort the panel, as shown in photo D, but by the same token you can sometimes force recalcitrant pieces into place with the right clamps in the right locations. That's why it's always a good idea to make a dry run of any clamping setup before the glue goes on. You'll have time to find any problems and work out solutions without the dangling sword of curing glue over your head.

1 Lay out three panel clamps on the bench—one in the middle and one about 2" in from each end. Open the sliding jaw wider than the panel and unwind the handscrew so it's back as far as it can go. If your clamps aren't new, use a scraper to clean up any old glue from the bars so it won't interfere with the leveling or dent your tabletop.

2 Place a long clamping pad against the fixed jaw, and lay the boards on top of the bar. Bring up the sliding jaw with the other clamping pad between it and the wood, as shown in photo A.

3 Press down on the center of the panel, and take up on the middle clamp until it's only moderately tight. Next, move to one of the end clamps. Push downward, concentrating your force on the places where the boards don't align. Tighten the end clamp lightly, as shown in photo B.

4 Clamp across the end of the panel with two stout pieces of scrap and three bar clamps to force the ends of the boards into alignment. When you're clamping up for real, you'll want to put waxed paper between the scrap and your tabletop so the squeeze-out won't glue the scrap in place. Tighten these clamps only moderately, as shown in photo C.

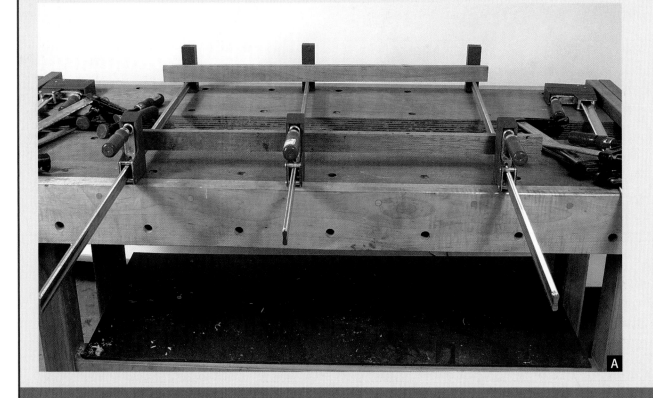

A

clamps, push the panel downward, and take up on the top two. You'll have to try various combinations to see what works. Lift up the assembly and check the underside, too.

8 When the panel is as flat as you can get it, crank all of the clamps as tightly as you can by hand. Start with the middle clamp, and then move one to the right. Then go one to the left of the middle, then on to the next clamp on the right. Always work from the center to the ends, alternating sides.

9 Note how the clamps were set (writing it down if need be), and take everything apart to apply the glue. Then reclamp.

5 Follow steps 3 and 4 for the other end.

6 Next, place two panel clamps with their bars across the top of the panel, and take them up to the same degree as the others.

7 Check the alignment of the boards in the panel. The joints should be flush or very nearly so. Use a straightedge to check for bowing across the width. If the panel is bowed, ease up on the bottom three

When the panel is clamped up, the glue will squeeze out of the joint in even beads all along its length, as shown in photo Q.

3 Leave the panel in the clamps for at least an hour (at 70°F). Keep it clamped longer if it's cool or damp.

Cutting the top to length

1 Using a 12" combination square, square from one edge across one end of the tabletop. Make your mark about ⅛" inside the end of the shortest board, as shown in photo R.

2 Place your saw guide along this line, clamp at the bottom, and square up the top edge, as shown in photo S (see "Skill Builder: Making an Accurate Circular Saw Guide" on the facing page).

SKILL BUILDER | Making an Accurate Circular Saw Guide

What You'll Need

- ¼" hardboard about 12" wide and as long as you want the guide to be
- ¾" plywood or MDF about 6" wide and as long as the hardboard
- ¾" screws
- Countersink drill bit
- Cordless drill/driver

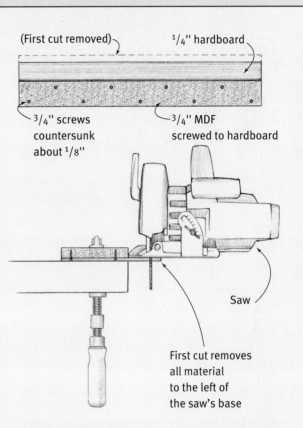

(First cut removed)　　　　　¼" hardboard

¾" screws countersunk about ⅛"　　　　　¾" MDF screwed to hardboard

Saw

First cut removes all material to the left of the saw's base

This guide makes it easy to use a circular saw to make accurate rips and crosscuts. You won't have to measure any offsets; the edge of the guide is the cutline. Just put a mark on the workpiece at both ends of your cutline. Clamp the guide so the ¼"-thick edge is on the line and the saw and guide rests on the part you want to keep. When you run the saw with its right edge along the MDF, it'll cut right on the line, as shown in the photo below.

This is such a versatile tool you'll want to make several sizes. I have 24", 38", and 50" guides, plus one that's 8' 4" long for cutting sheets of plywood lengthwise.

These dimensions work for my saw; check to make sure they work with yours.

1 Countersink and screw the ¾" MDF to the hardboard, aligning the edges.

2 Clamp the guide to a bench with the hardboard overhanging the edge.

3 Place the right edge of the saw base against the MDF and turn on the saw. Run the saw the length of the guide, being careful to keep the base pushed hard against the MDF. The newly cut edge is the cut line.

WORK SMART

Make sure the glue is fully cured before flattening the top. Wet glue expands the wood around the joints, and if you flatten too soon, the joint won't be smooth when it's dry. Wait at least eight hours to get the best result.

3 Clamp the top edge of the guide in place.

4 Run the saw along the guide, and cut the edge square.

5 Hook the end of your tape over the freshly cut edge and measure 44" along each edge. Align the guide with these marks, clamp, and saw. If the arrangement of the boards doesn't allow for a full 44", simply cut the top as large as possible. If the overhang ends up a little less than intended, no one will notice.

Rounding the edges

1 Use a block plane or a bench plane to round over the edges according to the method described in "Skill Builder: Rounding Edges with a Plane" on p. 132.

2 Start with the ends of the table. When planing end grain, the far corners sometimes blow out, as with the box. By planing the ends first, you can fix any blowout in the next step, as shown in photo T.

3 Once the ends are done, plane the sides to match, paying careful attention to getting the corners even.

4 When all your planing is done, switch to sandpaper. Don't use a block, cup your hand over the edge so the sandpaper smoothes away the plane marks and completes the rounding. Pay close attention to the transitions at the corners, both on the edge and at the top. Shape them by eye to a pleasing contour, as shown in photo U.

Sanding the top

You'll likely find that despite all your care in gluing up, the top is not perfectly flat. Pine tends to move around a lot with changes in moisture levels; it may not be possible to get flat. No matter, you can make it flat enough for this piece by using a random-orbit sander, as shown in photo V.

1 Starting with 80-grit paper, move the sander constantly over the surface. Go back and forth, diagonally, in circles; just keep it moving. Pay attention to the high spots, but don't let the sander sit in one spot or you'll quickly make a hollow. Get the top as flat as you can, and make all of the joints smooth, but don't make it perfect or the table will be out of character. Some high and low spots are good for this piece, but they shouldn't be extreme. This step will take 10 to 20 minutes depending on how uneven the joints were.

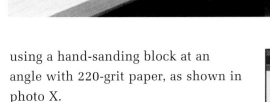

2 To remove the random pattern of swirls the sander put in the surface of the wood, replace them with lighter ones by using finer-grit sandpaper. If you don't do this, the swirls will become even more visible, as shown in photo W, when you apply stain or finish. Switch to 120-grit sandpaper, and sand the surface thoroughly to get rid of the 80-grit swirls. Be sure to brush the surface to clean away the coarser grit before sanding with finer paper.

3 Use 180-grit paper and sand again, then sand with 220 grit. These steps will take only 3 to 5 minutes each.

4 Finally, finish by sanding back and forth along the grain by hand. Use a block and 220-grit paper until there are no swirl marks.

5 Brush off the bench, flip the top, and smooth the underside of the top using a random-orbit sander. Start at 120 grit and work up to 220 grit, following the sequence above.

6 Break the sharp edge on the underside of the tabletop by sanding lightly using a hand-sanding block at an angle with 220-grit paper, as shown in photo X.

Sand the Base

Now is the time to sand the rest of the table and clean it prior to putting on the finish. Once the top goes on, it'll be a lot harder to get at the inside and underside of the table.

1 Sand the aprons and legs by hand, smoothing the surfaces and breaking all of the edges. Start with 120 grit on the aprons and 220 grit on the legs. If the surface of the aprons is particularly rough or dirty, you can use a random-orbit sander, but don't let the edges of the disk hit the legs—they'll cut a groove.

2 Take some time working on the inside of the base, breaking all of the corners and smoothing the surfaces.

WORK SMART

Always plane before sanding. Once you've sanded, don't use a plane—little bits of grit left by the sandpaper will quickly dull your plane iron.

SKILL BUILDER | Rounding Edges with a Plane

What You'll Need
- Sharp block plane or bench plane
- 5/4 pine at least 12" long
- Vise
- Sandpaper

Even though a block plane is used mostly to make things flat, smooth, and square, you can also use it to make a roundover. It's only a matter of planing a series of flats and then breaking the corners with sandpaper, as shown in the illustration on the facing page.

B

A

1 Plane a chamfer at 45 degrees. The first few cuts will produce a very narrow shaving that gets wider with each cut.

2 Plane until the chamfer is about ½" wide, as shown in photo A. You can check the evenness of your planing by making sure the chamfer is ½" all along its length.

3 Move down to the lower edge of the chamfer and hold the plane at about 45 degrees to it. Plane away the shoulder of the chamfer until it's about ⅛" wide. Then move to the upper corner of the chamfer and do the same, but make the new chamfer narrower, as shown in photo B.

4 Next, plane the shoulders made in step 3, then plane the shoulders that result from that cut. Finally, you'll be planing very narrow chamfers and the edge will be nearly round.

5 Finish rounding the edge using a piece of sandpaper. This time, don't use a hand-sanding block—cup the sandpaper around the edge to get it round.

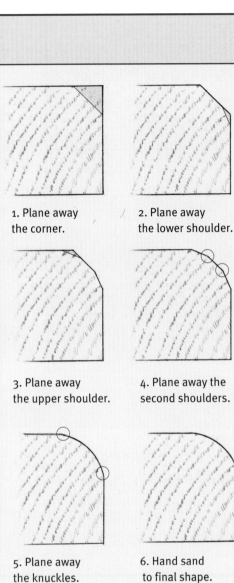

1. Plane away
the corner.

2. Plane away
the lower shoulder.

3. Plane away
the upper shoulder.

4. Plane away the
second shoulders.

5. Plane away
the knuckles.

6. Hand sand
to final shape.

3 Pay attention to the corners of the legs, rounding them slightly. Be careful not to let the sandpaper scratch the aprons while doing this.

Cleaning

1 Before applying any finish, vacuum the table with a brush attachment and clean up your work area, too. Dust left on the bench, floor, and surrounding surfaces will swirl into your finish as you move around.

2 Wipe the entire coffee table with a loosely wadded tack rag.

Finishing

No matter what finish you plan to put on pine, for a fine finish, the first step after sanding is to "condition" the surface with shellac. Since pine is a difficult wood to finish well, a light sealer coat of shellac solves problems such as blotchy stain, knots bleeding through paint, dull natural color, and resin beading out. In photo Y, the board on the left has been shellacked; on the right, the same stain was applied to the bare wood.

Y

WORK SMART

Always test your stain on an offcut from your project that's been sealed and prepared in exactly the same way as the project. Color charts are approximate. The only way you'll know what the finish will look like is to test it on the same wood, let it dry properly, and look at it in the sunlight.

Prestain conditioning

1 Thin dewaxed shellac with alcohol about 50%. If you're making your own, make up a mixture that's proportional to ½# of shellac to a gallon of alcohol (see p. 56 for more info on shellac).

2 Using a brush, apply a thin coat to the top, as shown in photo Z. I prefer to leave the legs and the aprons unshellacked to save time and trouble. The end grain in the legs will stain a deeper color, giving more character, and the blotchiness won't really show on the aprons. Let dry at least ½ hour.

3 After applying the sealer coat, the surface seems rougher than when you began because the finish raises the grain, so sand very lightly using 320-grit paper and a sanding block. Remove the nibs without sanding through to the bare wood, and vacuum up the dust when you're done.

Applying the stain

Using a water-based stain and following the manufacturer's directions, stain the entire table, inside and out, top and bottom. Work only a small area at a time, and keep plenty of paper towels on hand to wipe up.

Applying the wax

To make new furniture look like it's had good care for generations, use a dark-colored wax over the stain.

1 Apply the wax with a square of a white synthetic steel wool pad, rubbing in circles.

2 Wipe down using cotton rags or lint-free paper towels, as shown in photo AA.

3 Apply two coats to the base and the underside of the top. Apply three coats to the top.

Affix the Top

1 Put a piece of clean carpet, a blanket, or a towel down on the bench, and place the tabletop on it upside down.

2 Set your sliding square to 2" and make light marks in from both the ends

and the edges at each corner, as shown in photo BB.

3 Place the base on the tabletop so the corners of the legs align with these marks.

4 Make light marks to record this alignment, in case the table gets bumped while you're working.

5 Drill a ⁵⁄₆₄" pilot hole, and drive one of the screws that came with the figure 8 clips into the tabletop. Use a hand driver, as shown in photo CC.

6 Check the opposing corner to make sure the base is still aligned to the marks. If it isn't, rotate the base a little to get it in place. When aligned, drive a screw into a nearby clip.

7 With the base locked in position, drive the rest of the screws.

8 Apply one more coat of wax to the tabletop before using it.

9 Maintain your coffee table by keeping it clean and applying a new coat of wax once or twice a year.

Classic Bookcase

"A room without books is a body without a soul," wrote Cicero more than 2,000 years ago. A great scholar, he also understood the pleasures of building bookshelves, although a noble statesman of ancient Rome couldn't be expected to do handwork. He wrote to a friend, "Your men have made my library gay with their carpentry work. . . . Now that [we have] arranged my books, a new spirit has been infused into my house. . . . Nothing could look neater than those shelves."

Things haven't changed much—even in the Information Age you still can't have too many bookcases, and this classic design will instill new spirit into any room. Its simple good looks work just about anywhere—the kitchen, the kids' rooms, the office, the living room, or filled with towels and soaps in the bath. With a neat finished back, it can serve as a simple room divider, or it can go against the sofa or wall. Paint it white, use bright primary colors for the kids, distress it or use crackle paint to make it look old, or dress it up with fancy moldings.

This bookcase is designed to get you up to speed with one of woodworking's most valuable tools—the router. While building this project, you'll learn two fundamental ways to guide a router, how to make a nearly foolproof jig that keeps the router in check, and how to use four different router bits. You'll learn how to make grooves across the middle of a board (called dadoes), make a shoulder in the edge of a board (a rabbet), rout edge profiles, and use straightedges and templates to put a smooth edge on a piece of wood—even one with curved edges.

As Cicero knew, building a bookcase is an ideal complement to the life of the mind. ■

What You'll Learn

- Setting up and using a router
- Routing rabbets
- Template routing
- Making dadoes with a router
- Squaring the ends of a routed dado or groove
- Routing edge treatments
- The elements of mitering a molding
- Filling and smoothing using putty
- Prepping for and applying a high-quality paint job

Everyone's heard Murphy's Law–if anything can go wrong, it will. It's not a bad motto for woodworkers—if you interpret it the right way. Though often cited as a curmudgeonly joke, the real meaning of Murphy's Law is that with experience and forethought you can get the outcome you want.

Murphy's Law was developed in 1949 by scientists and engineers of the U.S. Air Force researching the effects of rapid deceleration on the human body. The tests were technically complex and brutal on the subjects. Every time a technician plugged an electrode into the wrong receptacle or made an ambiguous note, the whole operation had to be repeated at great expense and a fair bit of human suffering. The team (led by Capt. Edward A. Murphy) soon developed a methodology that required analyzing every aspect of the test to find everything that could possibly go wrong. Then, they redesigned the whole system so nothing could go wrong and the tests could be conducted quickly and safely.

Successful woodworking is all about adopting the true spirit of Murphy's Law—that you can plan ahead and prevent problems before they occur. With a little experience gained from time in the shop and from reading and talking with other woodworkers, you'll soon learn the kinds of things that can go wrong and how to prevent them. You'll get lots of practice with this when you're using a router.

Routers are one of the most versatile tools in the shop, but I suspect more woodworking projects have been messed up by routers than any other means. It's not that routers are particularly dangerous or malignant; they are so fast and efficient that a moment's inattention can mess up hours of previous work.

This bookcase gives you a good grounding on using a router with complete control. You'll learn to guide the router with fences, bearing-mounted bits, and jigs so that the machine cuts along the path you want.

Classic Bookcase

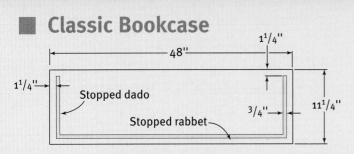

48"

1¹/₄"

1¹/₄"

Stopped dado

Stopped rabbet

³/₄"

11¹/₄"

Top as seen from underside

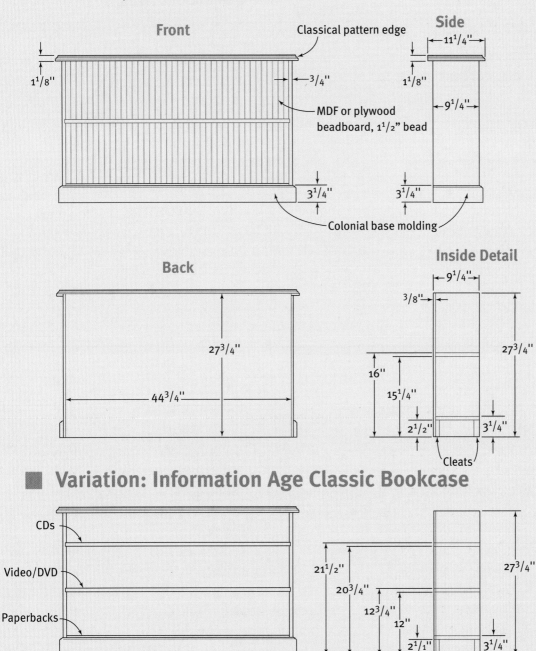

Front

Classical pattern edge

1¹/₈"

³/₄"

MDF or plywood
beadboard, 1¹/₂" bead

3¹/₄"

Colonial base molding

Side

11¹/₄"

1¹/₈"

9¹/₄"

3¹/₄"

Back

27³/₄"

44³/₄"

Inside Detail

9¹/₄"

³/₈"

27³/₄"

16"

15¹/₄"

2¹/₂"

3¹/₄"

Cleats

Variation: Information Age Classic Bookcase

CDs

Video/DVD

Paperbacks

Front

21¹/₂"

20³/₄"

12³/₄"

12"

27³/₄"

2¹/₁"

3¹/₄"

Cleats

Side

MATERIALS

Quantity	Actual Dimension*	Length	Description	Notes
1	1⅛" x 11¼"	4'	Top	5/4 x 12" poplar. Finishes at 48".
1	¾" x 9¼"	6'	Sides	1x10 poplar. Yields two sides, finished at 28".
2	¾" x 9¼"	8'	Shelves	1x10 poplar. Yields two shelves, finished at about 44".
1	½" x 3¼"	8'	Colonial base molding	Any material; primed is nice.
1	¾" x 2½"	10'	Aprons and cleats	1x3 poplar. Two pieces finish to 44".
1	¼" x 4' x 4' (half sheet)		Back	MDF (primed is easiest to paint) or plywood beadboard, 1½" beads. Or plain MDF or plywood.
1	¾ x ¾"	18"	Molding stock	Used for converting jig for stopped moldings.
			Yellow glue	
		1¼"	#7 or #8 flat-head wood screws	Self-drilling, square drive preferred.
		2"	#7 or #8 flat-head wood screws	Self-drilling, square drive preferred.
		1"	Brads	
			Double-sided tape	
			Quick-dry, easy-to-sand filler	
			Paintable caulk	
			Random-orbit sanding disks	150 and 220 grit
			Sandpaper	120, 180, 220 grit
1			Tack cloth	For use with oil-based paint only.
1 quart			Primer	Optional, gives the best finish.
1 quart			Paint	Oil or water based.
			Solvents	As per paint label.
			Denatured alcohol	For general cleanup.
			Paintbrushes	Five disposables or one moderate-quality bristle brush if using water-based paint.

*See p. 44–45 for information on actual vs. nominal dimensions.

Tools

- Cross cut saw capable of cutting an 11¼"-wide board
- Router
- ½"-diameter x 1" cutting depth template bit
- ½"-diameter x ¾" cutting depth template bit
- ⅜" rabbet width x ½" cutting depth rabbeting bit
- Router depth gauge or small sliding square
- Tape measure
- Several small bar clamps, two 24" panel clamps and two 48" panel clamps
- Plywood straightedge
- Steel ruler
- 6" sliding square
- 12" sliding square
- Classical pattern edge-trimming bit
- Corner chisel
- Mallet
- #8 countersink drill bit
- Square-drive bit
- Cordless drill/driver
- Warrington hammer
- Circular saw and 50" guide
- Nail set
- Random-orbit sander
- Hand-sanding block

▲ Knowing how to cut and fit mitered moldings is useful for all kinds of woodworking, from furniture making to picture framing, or for putting up moldings and trimming windows in your living room.

You'll use the router to make dadoes and rabbets to build a bookcase that uses standard dimensional lumber, goes together square, is nearly impossible to rack, and with its complex profile routed on the top edge is classically good looking.

You'll also learn the basic elements of a high-quality paint job, mitering corners, and applying molding—all skills you can use around the house, from refinishing furniture to building picture frames or trimming a window.

Building the Bookcase

Take the time when selecting your materials for this project to get wood that has very little cup. A cupped ¾"-thick board simply will not slide into a ¾" dado.

▲ You'll need four router bits to build the bookcase. From left: a ¼"-shank template-cutting bit with a 1" cutting depth and a ½" diameter; a classical pattern bit with a ½" shank; a ¼"-shank template-cutting bit with a ¾" cutting depth and a ½" diameter; and a ½"-shank rabbet-cutting bit with a ⅜"-wide cut.

Cut the Parts to Length

1 Check your material for knots, gouges, and other flaws. Orient flaws on the inside or back edge whenever possible.

2 Crosscut two ¾" x 9¼" sides to 27¾". Cut the 1⅛" x 11¼" piece for the top to 48".

3 For ease of handling, rough-cut the ¾" x 9¼" shelves to 48".

Lay Out the Dadoes and Rabbets

To avoid confusion later and to understand the bookcase-building process, start by drawing directly on the wood all the various cuts you'll make with the router. This way you'll see clearly on the wood just what you're supposed to do, and it's apparent immediately if the router is set up wrong or if you're about to rout in the wrong place.

Laying out the sides

The shelves slip into **dadoes** cut into the sides. For the shelves to be parallel to the floor and to one another, the dadoes in each side piece must be exactly the same distance from the floor. To make sure this happens, you'll mark and cut them together, with the bottom edges of the side pieces aligned. You'll also mark the locations of the cleats that will be fastened beneath the lower dado to give extra support to the bottom shelf and provide a firmer footing for the bookcase.

Each side piece also has a **rabbet** on the inside back edge, running the full height to conceal the edges of the MDF back. Building it this way gives the bookcase a more polished appearance, as well as providing solid bearing surfaces for the back to prevent racking.

1 Lay the side pieces on the bench side by side with the ends flush. Clamp them together and down to the bench so they can't shift.

2 Hook the tape measure from the bottom, and lay out the locations and widths of the cleats and the dadoes according to the measurements in the illustration on p. 139. Put hatch marks where the dado will be cut to make it clear where material will be removed, as shown in photo A.

3 Unclamp the side pieces and draw a line ⅜" in from the back edge of each piece. The side pieces are mirror images of one another, so the back edges are the edges that are touching in the middle. Put hatch marks in this area to represent the rabbet.

A

Laying out the top

The top of the bookcase is wider than the side pieces, and it overhangs all around—1¼" on the sides and front and ¾" at the back. The side pieces slip into stopped dadoes in the top so that the groove won't show at the front of the case. The back edge of the top is also rabbeted to accept the MDF back, but unlike the sides, it has a stopped rabbet. A rabbet that went the full length of the back would mar the bookcase's appearance from the side.

1 Use a sliding square to set out the stopped dadoes according to the measurements in the illustration on p. 139. Draw hatch marks in what will be the dado.

2 Draw the stopped rabbet along the back edge, with hatch marks to show the material that will be removed.

Rout the Rabbets

Now that you know exactly where the rabbet is cut, you can use your router and rabbeting bit to remove some wood.

Cutting rabbets for the sides

Set up your router as described in "Skill Builder: Router 101—Rabbeting" on p. 144, and cut ⅜"-wide x ⅜"-deep rabbets in the back edges of the side pieces.

Cutting rabbets for the top

The stopped rabbet in the top is ¾" wide x ⅜" deep—wider than the rabbets in the sides. This is to allow for the fact that the top overhangs in the back. You'll need two setups to cut it.

1 Clamp the top to the workbench with the hatch marks up. The edge to be rabbeted should overhang the bench. Make sure the clamps are out of the router's way.

2 Don't try to start the rabbet perfectly at the left corner of the stopped dado on the left side of the top. Simply start the rabbet within the hatch marks of the stopped dado—the left edge will be cut cleanly in the course of a later step when you route the stopped dado. Continue routing until you reach the other stopped dado. Stop when the rabbeting cutter is within the hatched area that will be removed when routing the other stopped dado.

3 Widen the rabbet to ¾" by making a second cut with a ¾"-long template routing bit according to the method described in "Skill Builder: Template Routing with a Straightedge" on p. 148, as shown in photo B. Set the depth to ⅜". Once more, the stopped dadoes will clean up the ends of the rabbet.

B

Rout the Dadoes

Dadoes are a great way to support bookshelves. They're good looking and strong, and when the fit is good, the square corners lock the shelves in place to prevent racking. There are many ways to cut dadoes, but using a router jig that takes Murphy's Law into account makes the operation safe and quick. Since the jig uses a template routing bit and has guides on both sides of the cut, the bit is under control at all times (see the sidebar on p. 150 for how to make this jig).

Cutting dadoes for the sides

1 Clamp the two side pieces together with the penciled dadoes aligned and the rabbets in the middle. Clamp them to the bench with the penciled dado about 8" from the end and one of the rabbets slightly overhanging the front edge.

WORK SMART

Both ends of these rabbets will be hidden from view, so don't worry if they aren't perfect.

WORK SAFE

Keep the router base on the workpiece until the bit stops turning.

SKILL BUILDER | Router 101—Rabbeting

What You'll Need

- Router
- Rabbeting bit, ⅜" rabbet depth and a ½" cutting length
- Scrap wood for practice, 1" x 5" x 3'
- Two clamps
- Combination square or router-bit depth gauge
- Dust mask
- Hearing protection
- Safety glasses

Rabbeting is a great application to start learning to use the router because it's a simple cut that's easy to set up and guide. With the bearing on the tip of the rabbeting bit, the router is docile and easy to control as long as you remember the rule: Rout against the turning of the bit. The easiest way to figure out just which way to rout is by making an L with your right thumb and forefinger. Point to the surface you want to rout with your thumb. Your right forefinger points in the direction the machine should travel.

If you rout in the other direction (called climb cutting), the router tends to pull itself along buy the turning of the bit, making it difficult to control. Climb cutting is used in some circumstances, but

■ Routing Rule of Thumb and Forefinger

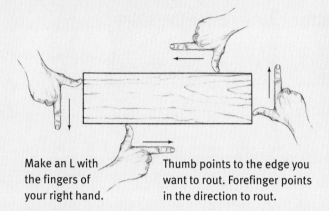

Make an L with the fingers of your right hand.

Thumb points to the edge you want to rout. Forefinger points in the direction to rout.

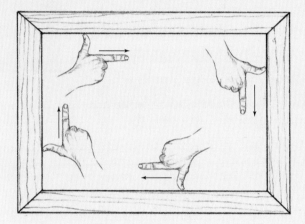

most of your routing should be done using the above rule.

The key to router success is keeping the base flat on the surface. If the router tips just a little off vertical, it can rout a perfectly molded divot in the edge before you know what has happened. Concentrate on keeping the router flat on the work, with the bearing pressed against its guiding surface. Keep your work area clean, your clamps out of the way, and make sure the router cord runs free before you start. That moment of inattention when you look down to step over an obstruction could be enough to mess up a perfect edge. Whenever you run a router, you should wear hearing protection, eye protection, and a dust mask.

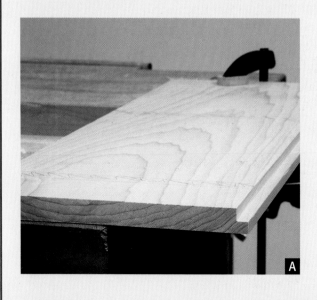

A

Setting Up the Router

Before working with the collet or bit, be certain the router is unplugged.

1 Move the base plate away from the body of the router to give you room to work. Loosen the collet lock nut by holding the shaft steady with one of the two wrenches that came with your router, as shown in photo B, or by using the shaft-lock button if your router has one.

2 Insert the shank into the collet as far as it can go, then back it out about $1/16$" and hand-tighten the collet.

3 Using the wrench or wrenches, crank the lock nut as tightly as you can.

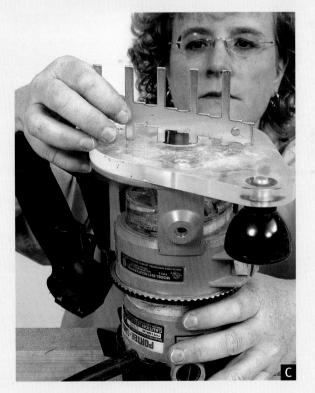

4 Put the router upside down on the bench. Hold the $3/8$" step on a router-bit depth gauge over the side of the bit and raise or lower the cutter until the end of the cutter just touches the gauge, as shown in photo C. You can also use a sliding square. Set the blade at $3/8$" and put the end of the blade on the router base, with the base of the square as a height gauge for the bit. Make sure the end of the blade is within the square's base so that it can rest flat on the router base plate so the base of the square is perpendicular.

5 Check that your workspace is clear, make sure the on/off switch is set to off, and plug in the router.

continued on next page

SKILL BUILDER   Router 101—Rabbeting — *continued*

Routing the Rabbet

1 Clamp the workpiece with the edge to be rabbeted overhanging the edge of the bench (this prevents the bearing from scoring your benchtop). Position the clamps so the router base won't run into them when making the rabbet.

2 Start your first test cut anywhere in the middle of the piece. Put the router base on the workpiece, but make sure the bit is about 1" away from the edge. The seemingly great distance from the work is because many routers give a little twitch when switched on, and you don't want the bit to accidentally touch the wood before you're ready to cut.

3 When you're routing, you need to be in a strong and stable position that lets you see what's going on at the bit. Stand well back from the work, and bend at the knees to see the cutter, as shown in photo D.

4 Once the router comes up to speed, push it directly inward. It'll make a lot of noise and dust at first, but as soon as the bearing touches the edge, it'll quiet down. Push the router from left to right, at the same time exerting a steady inward pressure to keep the bearing against the edge. Don't push too hard, or the bearing will dent the wood.

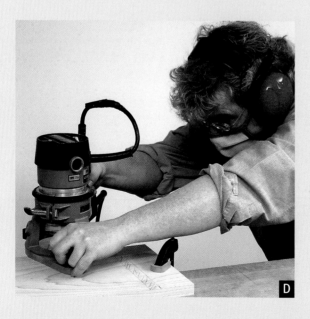

D

5 Make a cut several inches long, move the bit about 1" away from the edge (as in your starting position), and turn off the router. When the bit has stopped spinning, remove the router and check the depth of cut with a sliding square. Adjust by trial and error until the depth is correct.

Rabbeting the Ends

It takes some practice to get the rabbet perfect at the ends of the board. The most common mistake is taking a little chunk out of the end by running around the corner. This happens when you are trying too hard to keep the bearing in contact with the edge of the workpiece. With a little practice, you can get perfect corners. The secret is an inch of climb cutting at each end.

1 Clamp a board as described above, and start the router about 2" to the right of the left end of the edge to be rabbeted.

2 Turn on the router, push it against the edge, and slowly bring it to your left. You're making a climb cut in the opposite direction of the rule of thumb and forefinger. You'll find the router doesn't want to stay against the edge as it does when you rout in the other direction. Be prepared for the router to pull toward you a little, but don't worry if it does. Go slowly and you'll be in control. Watch the bit, and you'll see that before the bearing reaches the left end of the board, the wider diameter cuts a rabbet right to the end.

3 When you reach this point, stop your motion to the left, and push the router inward so the bearing contacts the edge. Then you can start cutting from left to right in the normal fashion.

4 When you get to the far end, slow down and watch what's happening. In a similar fashion, you'll stop when the cut goes to the end, but before the bearing runs off the edge. The biggest mistake people make when routing is to assume they have to rush just because the router is so fast and noisy.

2 Place the jig on the workpiece so the left edge of the slot aligns with the left side of the dado. The hatch marks should be visible in the slot. The right side of the slot should be parallel to the right side of the penciled dado but slightly wider. If the slot isn't parallel, either the jig's vertical fence isn't square to the slot or the dado was drawn wrong. Figure out which is the case and fix it.

3 Make sure the vertical fence is snug against the edge of the workpiece by using long clamps tightened across the two pieces, parallel to the slot, as shown in photo C. Clamp the tee at the top end of the jig down to the bench.

4 Set the depth of cut to about ³⁄₁₆", guide the router into the slot, and rout across both side pieces, running the bearing against the left side of the slot. Once you've routed both pieces and the bit has traveled beyond the far edge of the workpiece, slide the router to the other side of the slot so the bearing runs on the right side of the slot and pull it toward you.

5 Stop the router, set the depth of the final cut to ³⁄₈", and make another run around the slot.

6 Repeat this procedure on the other dadoes.

Cutting dadoes for the top

Dadoes don't have to go the full width of the piece. You can use this jig to stop the dado at any point by slipping a ³⁄₄" x ³⁄₄" x 18" piece of scrap into the slot. Here's how it works: As you're routing along the left edge of the slot, the bearing encounters the stop and prevents any further forward motion.

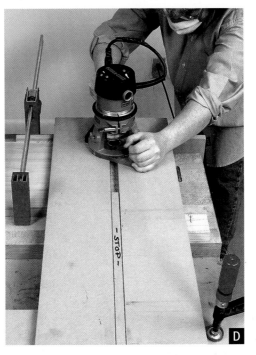

Slide the bearing against the right side of the slot and bring the router home. This leaves a stopped dado with rounded corners. Later you'll chisel them square.

Rather than measuring to find the proper length for the slot, follow this procedure.

1 Clamp the jig in place square against the edge of the workpiece and over the penciled dado. Because the jig is near the edge of the workpiece, you can't get clamps on both sides of the jig, so clamp across only one side and clamp the end to the bench, as shown in photo D.

SKILL BUILDER | Template Routing with a Straightedge

What You'll Need

- Router
- Template router bit with a ¼" shank, a ½" diameter and a ¾" cutting length
- Plywood or MDF fence, ¾" (or ½") x about 6" wide x 50" long
- ¾ x ¾ x 18" molding stock for stop
- Sliding square
- Four clamps
- Safety gear

Straight-sided router bits with a bearing mounted on the shank are called template bits (for more on this, see p. 35). They're most often used with a template (straight or curved) clamped atop the workpiece. The bearing runs against the template, and the bit cuts the material below it exactly flush with the template.

As always when using a router, be sure to wear a dust mask, hearing protectors, and safety glasses.

Setting Up

Use a piece of plywood or MDF with a perfectly straight and smooth edge that's a little wider than your router's base and at least a couple of inches longer than the edge to be routed. Make sure there are no dings or voids in the edge—the cut edge will exactly match the template's edge, including flaws.

1 Clamp the workpiece to the bench and use a sliding square to mark ¼" in from the edge on both ends of the workpiece.

2 Clamp your straightedge along this line, with the clamps well back from the edge so the router won't interfere with them.

Setting Template Router Bit Depth

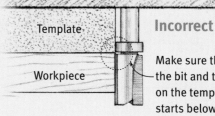

Incorrect

Make sure the gap between the bit and the bearing is fully on the template. If not, the cutter starts below the surface of the workpiece and leaves a ridge.

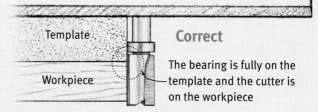

Correct

The bearing is fully on the template and the cutter is on the workpiece

3 With the bit secured in the collet, place the router on the left end of the fence where it overhangs the workpiece, and raise or lower the bit until the bearing and the space between it and the workpiece are wholly on the fence, as shown in the illustration above, or it leaves a ridge.

The lower end of the bit should extend below the workpiece—but it doesn't matter by how much.

Template Routing

1 Start the router well away from the edge, get your stance, and push the bearing against the template. Rout from left to right, as shown in the photo at right.

2 Using a sliding square, make a vertical mark on the inside of the slot and a horizontal one on the face of the jig at the end of the dado, as shown in photo E.

3 Put a piece of ¾" x ¾" molding stock that's clearly too long into the slot, and push it up against the top end (it'll be a little loose in the slot but that's okay). Draw a line on the molding that aligns with the mark you made in step 2.

2 Listen to the router to judge the feed rate; it will tell you what to do. If you're going too fast, you'll hear the motor slow down a little. If you feed too slowly, the surface of the wood will burn.

3 If your router seems to complain too loudly, don't try to cut the full depth in one pass. Slide the router back an inch or two so it's not cutting, and turn it off. Raise the bit a little and make a cut the full length of the workpiece. Then lower the bit to the final depth and make another full-length pass. Make sure that after you raise the bit, the bearing still rides on the fence.

Crosscut the molding to length, and check that its end aligns with the mark on the jig.

4 Cut the stopped dado in two passes, just as you did the dadoes in the side pieces. Start the router as you did for the sides, and run the bearing down the left edge of the slot. When it reaches the molding stop, push into the stop and over to the right side of the slot. Then pull the router toward you, keeping the bearing against the right side of the slot.

Rout the Edge Treatment on the Top

To give the top edge of the bookcase more visual interest, rout a profile in the front and sides using an edge-trimming bit with a tip-mounting bearing. The process is the same as that used to make the rabbets, including starting and stopping without turning the corners.

1 Set the depth of cut by testing it on offcuts that are the same thickness as the top of the bookcase. Clamp the offcut to the bench, and put a classical pattern bit into the router (for more on these bits, see p. 35). Flip the router over, and set the depth by eye so the corner of the bit is about $\frac{1}{16}$" above the base, as shown in photo F.

SKILL BUILDER | Making a Dado Cutting Jig

What You'll Need

- ¾" MDF or plywood 4" to 26" wide (two pieces 30" long, two pieces 20" long)
- Plywood or MDF, ¾" x 1" x 4" (scrap okay, size is approximate)
- Stop, ¾" x ¾" molding stock , about 18" long
- Two bar clamps
- Two panel clamps (must open at least 30")
- Pocket-hole jig
- 1¼" pocket-hole screws
- 1¼" flat-head screws
- Combination square
- Sticky notes
- Block plane and/or hand-sanding block
- Two offcuts from shelf material, each about 6" long
- Backsaw

There are several ways to cut dadoes, but the safest, easiest, and most precise way is to use a jig like this. Clamp the jig down tightly with the fence against the edge of the board, and it makes identical dadoes that are always square to the edge and exactly the right width. You'll make two passes with the router to make each dado—the first with the bit set to cut into the wood to a depth of about ³⁄₁₆", the second to cut to the full ⅜".

It's critical that the fence on this jig be square to the slot. The sequence of assembly is important to achieving this result.

1 Draw a line perpendicular to the edge of one of the 30" pieces. Using a 12" combination square with the base against a long edge, make the line about 2½" back from one end.

2 One of the 20" pieces is the fence that fastens on its edge with pocket-hole screws along the line you just drew. Using the pocket-hole jig, drill pocket holes in the piece as shown in the illustration at right. Place the fence on the line and drive a pocket-hole screw at just one end. Make sure the other end is also on the line, perfectly square to the edge. Fasten the other end in place. Double-check

using your sliding square to make sure the fence is perpendicular to the slot, and drive the remaining pocket-hole screws.

3 Fasten the base (the other 20" piece) face down to a line squared across the other end about 4" back from the edge.

4 Flip the piece over, with the fence against the edge of the bench. Peel two sets of two sticky notes from a pad and stick one set to each end of each shelf offcut. The sticky notes act as shims to make the slot a little wider than the shelf. Position the shelf offcuts along the inside long edge of the 30" piece, with one offcut at each end.

5 Place the other 30" piece along side the offcuts. Align the ends with the other 30" piece, and clamp the two long pieces together near both ends, as shown in the photo at right. This puts the second long piece perfectly parallel to the first, separated

■ Murphy's Law Dado Jig

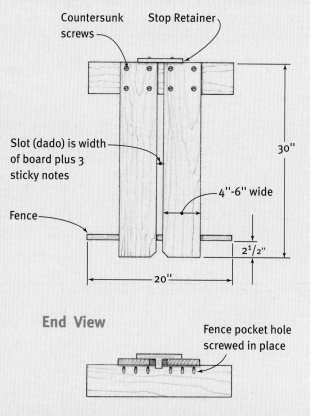

Countersunk screws

Stop Retainer

Slot (dado) is width of board plus 3 sticky notes

Fence

30"

4"-6" wide

2¹/₂"

20"

End View

Fence pocket hole screwed in place

WORK SMART

Position a clamp so the router base bumps into it before the bearing plows a groove in the side of your bench.

by the shelf offcuts. Fasten the fence and the base to the second long piece with the appropriate screws. Don't use glue because you might want to make an adjustment later. Remove the clamps and the offcuts.

6 The jig needs a retainer across the slot at the top end so you can slip a stop in place to limit the length of the dado (see "Cutting Dadoes for the Top" on p. 147 for details on fitting and using the stop). Use a small piece of scrap (a piece of leftover hardboard is perfect), and fasten it with a couple of pocket-hole screws. Their washer heads are perfect for this, since you won't have to countersink them into the thin hard-board.

7 Using a backsaw, cut away the inside corners of the long pieces, widening the mouth of the slot, which makes a good place to start the router.

8 Break all of the edges using a block plane or hand-sanding block so the jig is easy on the hands and has a neater, more finished appearance.

2 Run this bit set-up on the test piece for a few inches to see if you like the way the profile looks. Experiment with raising and lowering the bit slightly for different effects.

3 When you like the depth setting, clamp the top to the bench (dadoes down and rabbet toward the back of the bench) with the left end overhanging about 18". Start routing at what will be the left back corner of the top. Rout down the left end, around the corner (go slowly and keep the bearing in contact), and down the front until you get close to the bench, as shown in photo G on p. 152.

4 Reposition and reclamp the top (twice if necessary) to rout all the way around it—right up to the back right corner. When resuming your routing after repositioning, back up a few inches and start the router away from the edge. Push inward, and make the bearing contact the edge at a place you've already cut. Move the router to the

G

WORK SMART

Practice with the corner chisel before working on your bookcase.

WORK SMART

If the fit of the dado is tight, it's easier to alter the board that fits into the dado rather than the dado.

H

right and continue cutting the profile. You'll never see where you started and stopped.

Square the Stopped Dadoes

The rabbet has a rounded front edge, but your side pieces have square corners. Make the stopped dado fit the sides by squaring its ends using a chisel. You can make a square corner with a bench chisel, but it's far easier with a proper corner chisel (for more on this, see p. 21).

1 Put the arms of the chisel against the end of the dado made by the router, with the corner against your penciled layout marks.

2 Hold the chisel perfectly vertical, as shown in photo H, and whack it with a mallet. Clean out the excess down to the bottom of the dado, using a bench chisel if necessary, as shown in photo I.

3 Check the fit of the side pieces in the dadoes. If the fit is tight, it's probably because there's some cup in your side pieces. First try planing a chamfer

I

around the upper end of the side piece. If that doesn't work, use a block plane to take a few strokes off one or both faces of the upper end where they slip into the dado.

Fasten cleats to the sides

1 Now work on the lower ends of the sides. Use a sliding square to make a mark ¾" from the front edge of the bookcase and another mark ¾" in from the rabbet on the back edge. Measure the distance between these lines.

2 Crosscut two pieces about 10"-long from the ¾" x 2½" poplar, and clamp or

tape together and cut two identical pieces to fit between the marks. These are the cleats.

3 Clamp a cleat to one side piece so its top edge is flush with the bottom of the dado, as shown in photo J.

4 Turn the piece over and drive three screws to hold the cleat in place. Drill pilot holes from the inside out. Don't countersink too deeply. The heads need to be only about ⅛" below the surface.

5 Remove the screws and clamps, apply glue to both surfaces, reclamp, and fasten in place. Wipe up any glue drips with a wet paper towel.

Drill Pilot Holes All Around

To increase the strength and stiffness of the bookcase, the dadoes are reinforced with long screws into the end grain. Rather than guessing where the screws go or measuring to find their location, just drill the pilot holes before assem-

bly—from the outside in, just as you did when installing the cleat on the back of the Outdoor Easy Chair.

1 Drill three fairly evenly placed pilot holes in the dadoes in the sides and top as shown in photo K.

2 Flip the pieces and countersink a 2" screw in each pilot hole from the outside.

Cut the Aprons

The aprons fit between the the side pieces at the bottom. Their length is exactly the same as the distance between the inside edges of the stopped dadoes in the top.

1 Rather than using your tape measure that will require reading and remembering fractions, take a direct measurement using the apron itself. Start by slipping a piece of ¾" scrap into one of the stopped dadoes.

2 Use the scrap as a stop: Place the squared end of a length of ¾" x 2½" apron stock against the stop, and let it extend across the top and over the other stopped dado. Mark the location of the inside edge of the other dado on the wood, being sure to put an X on the waste side. Clamp or tape it to a companion piece for the other apron, and cut both pieces to length.

3 Double-check that the length is correct by laying the aprons between the stopped dadoes on the top.

4 Put two pocket holes in each end of both aprons.

Assemble the Case

As always, put the case together with clamps to check both your clamping strategies and to make sure the pieces are correctly made before gluing.

Dryfitting

1 Screw the aprons to the front and back of one of the side pieces, as shown in photo L. Use your thumb to keep the top edge of the aprons flush with the bottom edge of the dadoes.

2 Lay the assembly on its back edge and fasten the front apron to the other side piece. Use a piece of ¾" scrap in the dado for alignment, as shown in photo M.

3 Gently flip the assembly to rest on the front edges, and fasten the back apron in place.

4 Place the top on the bench with the dadoes up, and insert the assembly into the stopped dadoes. Use long panel clamps and clamp from the top to the bottom of the side pieces if necessary to hold them in place.

5 Check that the case is square. Use your largest square to make sure the inside angle between the top and the

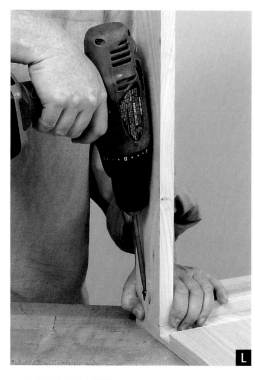

side is 90 degrees. Also make sure the rabbets are flush at the upper back corners. If they're not, make sure the side pieces are all the way into the stopped dadoes.

6 Stand back and take a look at the bookcase from a distance. Look for racking and out of squareness. When everything checks out, remove the clamps and aprons, and sand all the pieces to 220 grit using a random-orbit sander.

Gluing up

1 Apply glue to the ends of the aprons, the end grain of the cleats, the tops of the side pieces, and in the stopped dadoes, as shown in photo N. Replace the clamps.

2 Put the case face down on the bench and measure the diagonals to check squareness before driving the screws.

3 Hook the tape measure over an upper corner of the case and measure the diagonal to the lower corner, as shown in photo O. Exactly where you hook it isn't as important as being able to hook it in the same relative location when you measure the other diagonal.

4 Measure the other diagonal and compare. If the sides are all the way in the dadoes and the aprons are the correct length, the diagonals will not be very

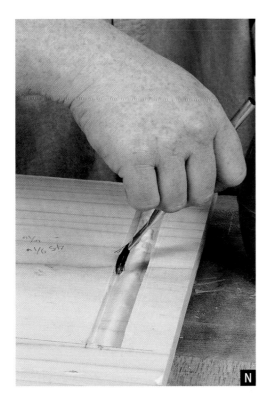

different. If they are, try shoving the bookcase into square and see if that works. If not, loosen the clamps and make larger adjustments.

5 When the diagonals match (or are within about ⅛6"), drive 2" screws into the pilot holes in the top, as shown in photo P.

Install the Shelves

Position the bookcase on the bench with the rabbet side up and the top overhanging the edge so the front is flat on the bench.

Cutting to length

Since the rabbets are the same depth as the dadoes, you can get the length of the shelves by measuring the distance between the rabbets on the back.

1 Push the hook of your tape measure against the rabbet at the upper dado, and open the tape until its case is against the rabbet on the other side, as shown in photo Q. Lock the tape open.

2 Move to the other rabbet and check that the distance is the same. Keep the tape measure locked.

3 Next, transfer the measurement to the workpiece. Hook the tape measure on the squared end of a ¾" x 9¼" shelf piece and put a mark on one edge at the far end of the tape case. Put an X on the waste side.

4 Clamp the two shelf pieces together or use double-sided tape, then crosscut to length.

Checking the fit

The shelves should slide easily into the dadoes. If they don't, deal with them in the same way you dealt with the sides—by chamfering the ends or by planing the faces. Once they're in place, you'll note that even with their fronts resting on the bench, the back edges stick up above the rabbet, making it impossible to fit the back. The shelves must be made narrower by an amount equal to the depth of the rabbet. You could remove this material with a circular saw and guide, but the point of this project is learning to use the router. So, you'll remove the excess using a router and a template-cutting bit.

1 Make a pencil mark at the bottom of the rabbet on both ends of each shelf, as shown in photo R. Remove the shelves from the case.

2 Clamp a shelf to the bench, then clamp a straightedge to the shelves. Align each end of the straightedge with

Q

your marks and rout away the excess with the template bit against the straightedge.

Testing your clamping strategy

Gluing the shelves in place requires long panel clamps on each shelf front and back.

1 Keeping the case on the bench with the front side down, insert the bottom shelf and put a clamp across the back. Place the bar right down on the edge, as shown in photo S. Repeat with the other shelf.

2 Set the case upright, then apply two more clamps across the front, as shown in photo T.

3 Stand back and take a look to see that the sides fit properly. If the sides bow outward at a shelf, it's too long. If they bow inward, the shelf is too short. Adjust as necessary.

4 When the shelves fit, sand both sides smooth using a random orbit sander and 220-grit disks. Break the edges using sandpaper and a hand-sanding block.

Gluing and screwing the shelves in place

1 Apply glue to the dadoes and to the ends of the shelves and clamp as before.

2 Drive 2" screws through the pilot holes, and let the glue dry.

Install the Base Molding

Decorative moldings meet at the corner in nonstructural miter joints, as shown in the illustration below. Measuring and cutting perfect miters around all four sides can be tricky—it requires perfect measuring, perfect cutting, and perfectly adjusted tools. In this project, you'll ace all that by simply applying molding to only three sides. That way, you can concentrate on getting the front corners right.

Before installing any molding, make sure the aprons are flush with the front and back edges of the side pieces. If they stand proud, plane them flush. If they're a little below flush, just leave them alone.

■ The Elements of a Mitered Corner

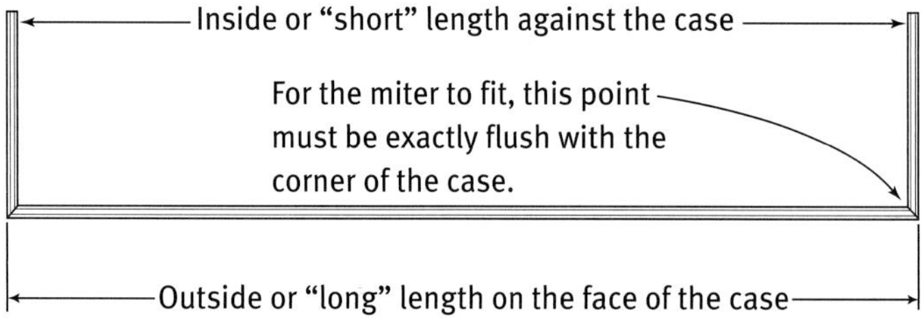

Inside or "short" length against the case

For the miter to fit, this point must be exactly flush with the corner of the case.

Outside or "long" length on the face of the case

Fitting the molding

1 Cut the longest piece first so if you make a mistake, you can use it to make shorter pieces.

2 Cut the miter in one end. Set your miter box or chopsaw to cut a 45-degree angle, and clamp the molding in place with the decorative edge up and the longer end on the face of the molding.

3 Clamp the molding to the front apron at each end. Keep it flush to the bottom of the apron—it looks fine if the shelf is a little higher than the molding. Make sure the inside of the miter (on the back side of the molding) is right at the corner of the case.

4 Draw a line on the back side of the molding along the outside edge of the case. Remove the molding and square the line around both edges.

5 Once more, set up the molding in the miter saw to cut right the other miter on the line, with the long side of the molding facing outward, away from the fence.

6 Clamp the molding in place again, and check the fit. Leave the clamps in place.

7 Rough-cut a piece of molding about 12" long, and miter one end with the long side on the face.

8 Hold this piece of molding against the front molding piece that's clamped in place, pushing firmly to get a tight fit at the miters, as shown in photo U. Clamp it in place.

9 Using your square, mark on the molding where to cut it flush with the back edge of the case, as shown in photo V. Set the saw to 90 degrees and make the cut.

10 Repeat with the other corner.

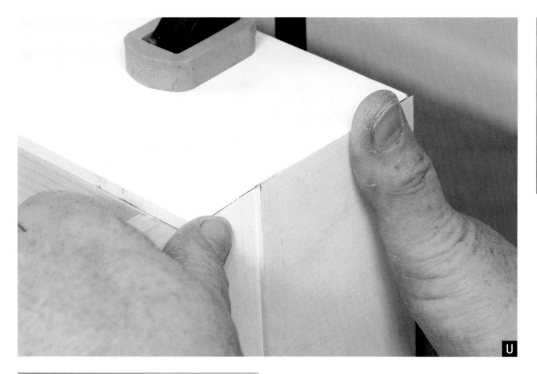

■ **WORK SMART**

If the joint at the miter doesn't fit, check that the apron is flush or perhaps you can angle the molding slightly to improve the fit. It could also be that the miter is rough or not sawn properly, or the front molding piece shifted.

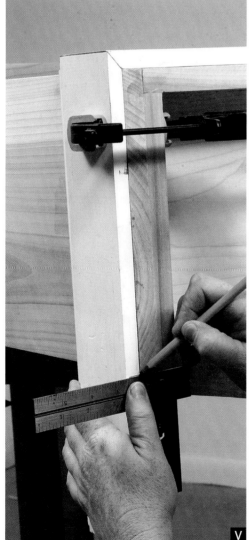

Gluing and nailing the molding

Traditionally, furniture makers fasten molding and trim with tiny brads, although very small finishing nails will also work (see p. 50 for more information). The small heads of brads don't make much more than a dimple in the wood, even when they're countersunk with a nail set. For painted work such as this, you can also use small-headed trim screws and fill the holes with putty.

1 Using 1" brads and a Warrington hammer, start the brad with the straight end of the hammer so you don't mash your fingers (see photo W on p. 160).

2 When the brad is set in the wood and no longer needs to be held, switch to the face of the hammer. Stop driving just before the head is flush so you don't dent the surface of the bookcase.

3 Set the brad head below the surface with a nail set by putting the tip of the nail set into the dimple on the brad

and driving it slightly below the surface, as shown in photo X. Drive a brad every 6" or so.

Leveling the bottom

When the molding is fastened, flip the case upside down (protect the top from scratches by using a piece of clean plywood, cardboard, or carpet), and plane the bottoms of the side pieces, cleats, and moldings flat so the case will sit level, as shown in photo Y.

Install the Back

If your case is square, cutting the back to fit is a simple job. If something went wrong and the case isn't square, you'll have to cut the back to match.

Cutting the back to fit

1 Once more, set your tape measure for the inside distance between the rabbets at the top of the case. Transfer the measurement to the beadboard by hooking the end of the tape over one

edge (perpendicular to the beads) and mark at the back side of the tape case. Repeat for the bottom of the case, resetting the length of the tape if required.

2 Using a circular saw and a 50"-long guide (see p. 128 for more information), cut the piece to width with the guide on your marks.

3 Measure the distance from the rabbet on the top of the case to the bottom edge of the apron and transfer this measurement to the edge of the beadboard, going parallel to the beads. Repeat on the other side of the case and transfer this measurement to the other edge of the beadboard. Cut with your circular saw and guide.

4 Slip the back into place to check the fit. If the fit is very tight, you may have to flex the back a little to get it in. If the back is still too big, use your block plane to shave down one edge. If the back is a little small and some gaps show on the sides, don't worry because you'll have a chance to fill them before painting.

5 Once the back fits, use a straightedge to draw light lines on the back to show you where the shelves lie underneath the beadboard. That way you'll know where to put the nails.

Fastening the back

To fasten the back to the narrow rabbet, use 1" brads or finishing nails rather than screws. Screws are relatively large and would make a mess if you ran through the edge of a shelf. The hole made by a misplaced brad is a much smaller problem, easily filled with a little putty and sanded smooth.

Finishing

Eighty percent of getting a great paint job is preparation. When you start with a flat, smooth, clean surface, it's hard to get bad results. But prep work requires a lot of patience. You just have to be disciplined, and settle down to doing your best on each rather dull step, even though what you really want is to get the paint on so you can see your finished project.

Filling and sanding

1 Fill all the countersinks, any small gaps in the dadoes that show in the front of the bookcase, knots, dings, and other imperfections with a readily sandable filler (for more information, see p. 58). Apply it with a putty knife or a plastic spreader. Push down hard to get the filler to go into the hole, then scrape off the excess, as shown in photo Z.

2 For any gaps in the back or in the mitered corners of the molding, use some soft, paintable caulk that comes

in a tube. It's much easier than standard fillers to mold it into a nice radius with your finger. That way you'll get a smooth surface that won't require sanding.

3 Once the filler is dry, hand-sand using a block and 150-grit paper. When you start, the area around the hole is smeared with a thin layer of filler. Sand the surface until the smear is gone from around the filled hole and the edges of the fill appear crisp, as shown in photo AA.

4 As you're sanding, look for holes you missed or areas that need a little more filler. Apply another round of filler, and sand it again.

5 Switch to 220-grit paper and sand a slightly wider area around the filler.

6 Since the rest of the piece was sanded before assembly, simply check it over for smoothness and break all the edges.

AA

Cleaning

Cleaning is the most overlooked step in getting a fine finish. If you neglect it, the painted surface will end up as rough as sandpaper, no matter how much you time you spent sanding.

1 Vacuum or brush the bookshelf inside and out. Clean up the surrounding area as well.

2 Wipe the surface with a paper towel wet with denatured alcohol to remove any hand oils or chemical contaminants. This step also picks up any remaining dust.

3 Wipe down the surface with a tack cloth to pick up any remaining dust. If you're using a water-based finish, make sure you have a compatible tack cloth.

Painting

You can use any type of paint you like for this project. Everything looks good on it, from faux-distressed milk paint to super-glossy enamel.

1 For the best finish, start with a primer coat. A primer paint is full bodied and designed to fill the grain, smooth the surface, and sand easily. Check with your paint dealer to find a product compatible with the paint you intend to use. Apply a thin coat or coats as specified by the manufacturer, as shown in photo BB.

2 Sand lightly with 220 grit using a random-orbit sander until smooth to the touch. Don't sand away the paint—remove as little as necessary to get a smooth surface. You won't be able to get right into the corners with the machine, so do that part by hand with the sandpaper on a hand-sanding block. Vacuum and wipe with a tack cloth.

WORK SMART

Most paint problems result from applying too much paint, often without allowing enough drying time between coats. Thin coats of paint self-level better, and they dry more quickly and completely.

3 Apply a thin coat of top-coat paint. When it's dry, sand lightly with 220-grit paper. You don't want to sand away all the paint, just smooth off the nibs. Vacuum up the dust.

4 To get the surface looking really good, apply at least two coats of paint. If you sand and clean carefully between each coat, the surface will be smooth and even.

Top-Drawer Lateral File

Whether a home office is used for paying bills or making a living, space is usually at a premium. Because a home office is often carved out of a living space, the standards for functionality and appearance are high. A home office needs furniture that looks great and can do double duty. Hence this lateral file.

The large horizontal surface is intended for a printer—most of which are now too wide to fit atop a regular file cabinet—and for a homey lamp or a no-nonsense inbox. The height matches that of most desks, so the printer is easy to operate while you remain seated, plus it can serve as a desk annex in a pinch. The height also puts the file drawer closer to your lap, making it easier to find what you need. It has one moderately sized lateral file drawer, because most of what used to go in a file drawer is now stored on hard drives, and one generous top drawer to keep close at hand the printer's varied diet of paper (letter quality, draft, three hole, photo, cards, labels, etc.).

It's a totally practical piece of furniture, and it's a satisfying woodworking project designed to give you a thorough grounding in the methodology of building plywood cabinetry. If you have any notion of building your own kitchen, bathroom, or shop cabinets, this is important information. You'll also learn the fundamentals of using a table saw safely and efficiently, plus some tips for using stains and water-based clear-coat finishes. ∎

What You'll Learn

- Ripping on the table saw
- Making and using featherboards
- Building and using a table-saw crosscut sled
- Cutting dadoes on the table saw
- Cutting rabbets on the table saw
- Making grooves using the table saw
- Installing face frames
- Installing full-extension drawer slides
- Two methods of edging plywood
- Installing drawer pulls with a shopmade jig
- Using water-based clear-coat finishes

With this lateral file, you step up to the next level in woodworking. In building this project, you'll be working with lumber and plywood dimensioned to your own specs, rather than using standard sizes. You'll turn that wood first into drawers, which must be alike, and then you'll build (to close tolerances) a case to fit the drawers. Finally, you'll be installing hardware—drawer slides and pulls. This is a whole new level of complexity, and if you want to be successful at it, you need to understand the whole building process before you begin.

▼ Using a table saw to build drawers takes you to a new level of woodworking. Building this project will give you a firm foundation for safe and accurate table-saw operation.

Top-Drawer Lateral File

Plan View

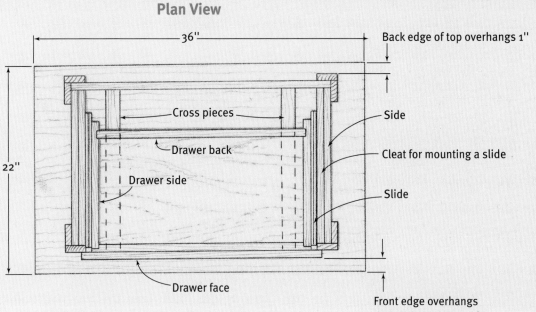

36"

Back edge of top overhangs 1"

22"

Cross pieces

Drawer back

Drawer side

Side

Cleat for mounting a slide

Slide

Drawer face

Front edge overhangs
drawer face about 1 1/2"

Front View

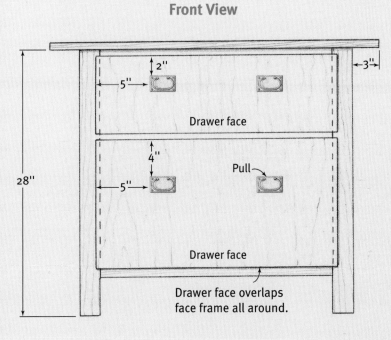

2"

5"

Drawer face

4"

Pull

5"

28"

Drawer face

3"

Drawer face overlaps
face frame all around.

Face Frame Detail

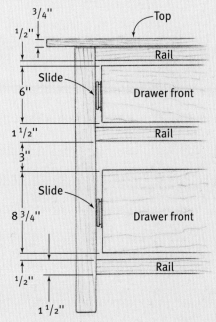

3/4"

1/2"

Top

Rail

Slide

6"

Drawer front

1 1/2"

Rail

3"

Slide

8 3/4"

Drawer front

Rail

1/2"

1 1/2"

■ Making Informal Sketches of Key Points

Detail of corner construction

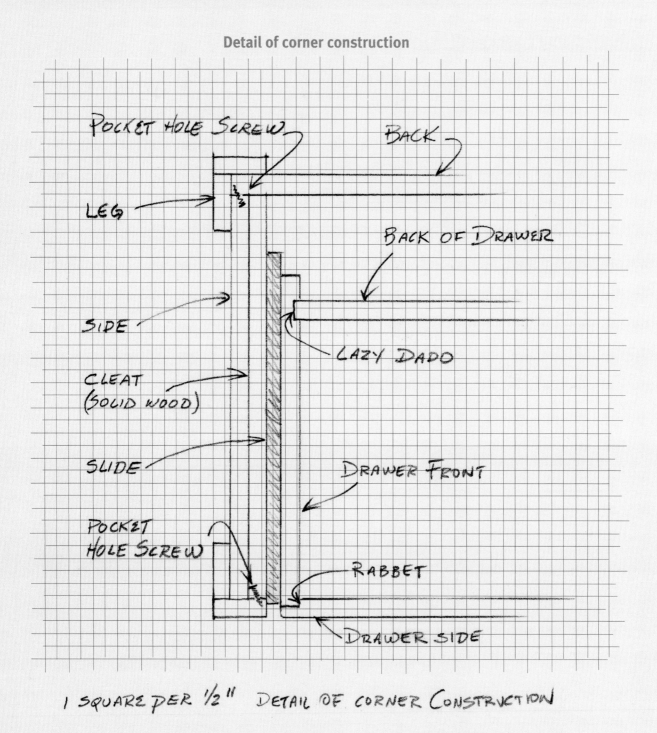

POCKET HOLE SCREW

BACK

LEG

BACK OF DRAWER

SIDE

LAZY DADO

CLEAT
(SOLID WOOD)

SLIDE

DRAWER FRONT

POCKET
HOLE SCREW

RABBET

DRAWER SIDE

1 SQUARE PER ½" DETAIL OF CORNER CONSTRUCTION

Drawer Details

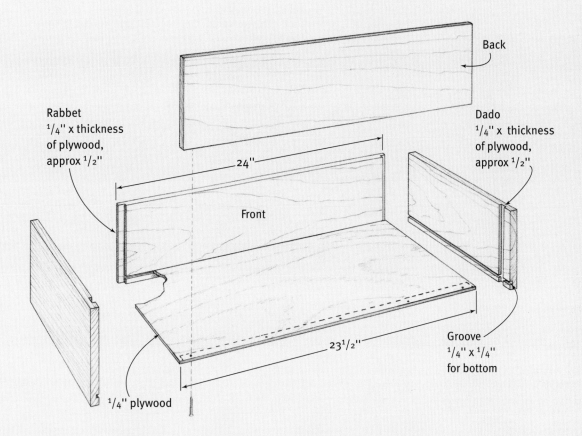

Back

Rabbet
$^{1}/_{4}$" x thickness
of plywood,
approx $^{1}/_{2}$"

Dado
$^{1}/_{4}$" x thickness
of plywood,
approx $^{1}/_{2}$"

24"

Front

23$^{1}/_{2}$"

Groove
$^{1}/_{4}$" x $^{1}/_{4}$"
for bottom

$^{1}/_{4}$" plywood

Tools

- Table saw with a good combi-nation blade
- Circular saw with a blade for plywood and a fence
- Chopsaw or mitre box
- Cordless drill/driver
- Small sliding square
- 12" combination square
- Pocket-hole jig
- Pocket-hole step drill

- Square-drive bits, 6" and 2"
- #8 countersink drill bit
- 1/8" brad-point drill
- 1/4" brad-point drill
- Tape measure
- Ruler
- Panel clamps
- Bar clamps
- Table-saw height gauge

- Block plane
- Random-orbit sander
- Scraper
- Hand-sanding block
- Safety glasses
- Hearing protection
- Dust mask
- Push stick
- Rubber-bottom push block

MATERIALS

Quantity	Actual Dimension*	Length	Description	Notes
1 sheet	¾"	4' x 8'	Cabinet	Birch, cherry, maple, luan, and oak plywood are all good choices. If possible, have the yard rip the sheet into 25" x 8' and 23" x 8'.
½ sheet	½"	4' x 4'	Drawers	Birch or Baltic birch (which has more plies) plywood are readily available and less expensive. Could be any nice-looking plywood.
½ sheet	¼"	4' x 4'	Drawer bottoms	Birch or Baltic birch plywood or hardboard.
2	¾" x 5½"	8'	Legs, face frames, rails	Buy 1x6. The longest leg is 28¼".
1 roll	¾"		Edging tape for drawers	
		1¼"	#7 or #8 pocket-hole screws	
		1"	#7 or #8 self-drilling screws	Square drive preferred.
		1¼"	#7 or #8 self-drilling screws	Square drive preferred.
2 pairs		12"	Accuride® 4034 lateral file slides	If you make substitutions, make sure the slides are full-extension slides rated for use in lateral files.
4			Drawer pulls	Shown are Craftsman-style, large-size pulls available from various woodworking catalogs.
1			File folder insert	Available from office-supply stores.
1		24"	Miter slide bar	For making a crosscut sled. Adjustable metal slide is preferred.
			Yellow glue	
			120-, 180-, and 220-grit sandpaper	Hand-sanding.
			180- and 220-grit sanding disks	Random-orbit sanding.
			Shellac or water-based grain filler	To reduce blotchiness when staining birch.
1			Squegee for applying stain conditioner/grain filler (if used)	
1 quart			Water- or alcohol-based dye stain	
1 quart			Water-based semi-gloss clear finish	
			Tint for water-based finish	Optional—to warm up the color of the clear coat.
	2"		Bristle or foam brushes	Good quality suitable for water-based finishes.
			Paper towels or rags	Lint-free for wiping stain.

*See p. 44–45 for a discussion of actual vs. nominal dimensions.

Take some time to plan, sketch, and rehearse your actions before you get into the shop. It's time well spent. Mentally break down the project into its component pieces and think about how they are joined. Work through each step in your mind, making informal full-sized sketches on four- or eight-square-per-inch graph paper as shown in the illustration on p. 168. The work will flow more smoothly, you'll make fewer mistakes, and you'll have a lot more fun.

You can fit this planning into odd moments of daily life. You can sketch details while watching TV, or doodle them while on hold on the phone. Jot down notes while waiting in line at the bank, talk yourself through it while driving, or build the project in your mind as you're falling off to sleep.

As part of this process, you should keep Murphy's Law in mind and think about what could go wrong and what you need to do to prevent it, or how you could repair the damage. This line of thinking will often lead you to new ways to solve a problem or use a tool. You'll soon realize that there is usually more than one means to an end.

For instance, you already know how to cut rabbets and dadoes with a router—this project teaches you how to make them on a table saw. You'll make jigs to hold the workpieces securely for safety and accuracy, and by the time you've completed the project you'll understand both methods well enough to choose the right one for your future projects. You'll have done the basic table-saw operations and with a little more practice will be ready to tackle more advanced joinery, such as raised panel doors and slip mortises.

Building the Top-Drawer Lateral File

Start by milling the solid wood to learn the basics of table-saw operation, then move on to cutting the plywood and then the more complex table-saw operations involved in making the drawers.

Mill the Solid Wood

A 9' piece of solid wood is heavy and difficult to run through the table saw unassisted. Crosscutting to rough length before ripping makes more manageable pieces. See the illustration above for a cutting guide.

1 Using a chopsaw, miter saw, or a circular saw and guide, crosscut one ¾" x 5½" piece to yield three 30" pieces, plus waste.

2 Set up your table saw as described in "Skill Builder: Ripping on the Table Saw" on p. 176, and rip to yield four 2¼" x 30" boards.

3 Rip the remaining material to yield seven 1½" x 30" boards for legs and rails.

Assemble the Legs

The two sides of the leg are glued into a simple right angle, but be careful how you assemble it. Each side must end up 2¼" wide. One face is the wide piece; the other face shows the side grain of the wide piece and the face grain of the narrow piece.

1 Plane each piece smooth to remove saw marks and irregularities. Use a sharp plane and a sliding square to check to make sure you're planing square.

2 Put a 1½"-wide piece in a vise and place the 2¼" piece on top, using a piece of scrap to support the back edge of the wider piece, as shown in photo A. Apply glue to the upper surface of the piece in the vise and to the overlapping portion of the back of the 2¼" piece. Don't apply glue to the whole surface, just ¾" along one side, and don't use too much glue or the wood will skate around, making clamping difficult.

3 Put the pieces back together, making sure the ends and the edges are flush. You can fix minor discrepancies later using a plane or saw, but if the edges or the ends are off by more than about 1/16" it won't look right in the end.

4 Align one end and clamp in place, then align the other end and clamp. Most pieces spring a bit in the middle, so you may have to use a clamp horizontally in the middle to force the edges into alignment, as shown in photo B. Pad the clamps as necessary to protect the legs from dents.

5 After the glue is thoroughly cured (roughly two hours), scrape off any excess glue, and plane away any irregularities in the joint.

Which Plywood?

The grainy fir sheathing used in homebuilding is just the tip of the plywood iceberg. You can get plywood made from hundreds of other woods, from apple and oak to exotic Carpathian elm burl and crotch mahogany. Most lumberyards and home centers stock just a few species—typically birch, fir, luan, oak, and pine—but many are willing to special-order cherry, maple, and a few other local favorites. For anything more exotic, you'll have to go to a specialty house (see Resources on p. 198).

I've seen this cabinet built with a variety of wood combinations: cherry panels with maple legs, birch panels with maple legs, maple panels with mahogany legs, mahogany or luan panels with mahogany legs, and oak on oak. They all look great. Just keep in mind that hardwoods like maple and oak are more difficult to saw and plane.

- Birch has a light creamy color and can range from interestingly figured to bland in appearance, depending on what grade you buy. Shop-grade birch has a smooth surface, but the grain can have wild figure or mismatched colors. It's fine for painting. If you want to stain your birch plywood, go for premium grade (sometimes called stain grade), but keep in mind that birch tends to be blotchy like pine.

- Baltic birch is a kind of super-quality birch made in the northern reaches of Scandinavia and Siberia. It has a stain-grade surface, and its more numerous plies are good looking enough to leave bare. Standard sheet size is 5' x 5', and it's often sold in half and quarter sheets.

- Luan is a type of mahogany and has a medium-brown tone when finished. It's inexpensive, and its close grain stains well.

- Oak plywood is made from red oak, which has a golden-pink tone. Be sure to get red oak solid wood if you want the tone to match. Oak has a wide-open grain, which is accentuated when stained.

- Pine plywood tends to be of the knotty variety and made with narrow veneers. The look is great for paneled walls but isn't quite right for this project.

- Maple is similar in color to birch but is less likely to blotch. You may be able to get maple that's prefinished on one side, a favorite with pro cabinetmakers, who put the prefinished side in so they don't have to do anything to it once the cabinet is built.

- Cherry plywood has a rich color and close, even grain. It takes stain well, but you may want to simply put a clear coat over it without staining, since its red-brown color darkens over time.

WORK SMART

Since each leg has to stay in clamps for at least an hour, start making legs now and move on to the next steps while the glue is drying.

6 Using a chopsaw or miter saw and a stop block, crosscut each leg to 28¼".

7 Break the corners lightly using a block plane, as shown in photo C, then use a random-orbit sander and 220-grit paper to smooth the outside surfaces of the legs.

8 If you intend to stain the legs a different color from the case, do so now (see p. 196). Be sure to stain the inside of the legs at the bottom where it will show, but not where they will be glued to the case.

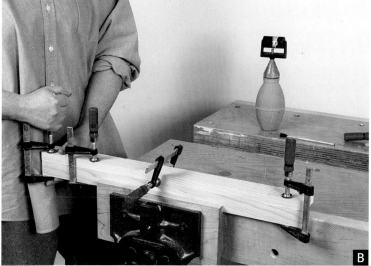

Mill the Drawer Components

The drawers must fit the case perfectly or else the slides won't work, which is why you should build the drawers first. If you build the case first, you're faced with making two complex drawers to very precise dimensions, a difficult process for an inexperienced drawer-maker. If you build the drawers first their actual measurements are not

Avoiding Kickback

Most of the danger in using a table saw has the same root cause: binding on the back edge of the blade. When that happens, the power of the rotating blade can lift the wood off the table and propell it back at the operator with enough force to cause serious injury. Known as **kickback,** this process draws the wood forward as it rises, sometimes bringing the operator's hands into the blade.

The most common cause of kickback is when the kerf gets out of parallel with the fence. This can occur when the piece isn't held tightly against the fence or when the fence is not adjusted correctly. Before ripping on the table saw, make sure the fence is parallel to the blade. Check your owner's manual or a book on tuning up your table saw (see Resources on p. 198).

This dangerous out-of-parallel situation is likely to occur when trying to crosscut on a table saw. The geometry is against you—the leverage makes it likely the workpiece will twist a little and bind against the blade. Never crosscut on a table saw without using a miter gauge (see p. 17 for more information on choosing and using a miter gauge) or a crosscut sled (see the sidebar on p. 182 for details on how to build and use one).

When ripping on a table saw, always keep your eye on the fence just in front of the blade and make sure the wood is tight up against it. To help keep it against the fence, you can use a featherboard (see "Skill Builder: Ripping on a Table Saw" on p. 176).

Ripping can release tensions in the board that are the result of how the tree grew. A piece may spring as soon as it has been cut, binding against the back of the blade. You can prevent kickback in such situations by using a splitter, a piece of shaped wood or metal that sits behind the blade to keep the kerf open (see the photo below). If the tension is so great that the workpiece binds against the splitter and makes pushing it through the saw difficult, turn off the saw, back the workpiece out of the cut, and try again. The second cut usually widens the kerf enough to remove the difficulty. If this doesn't get rid of the problem, rough-cut the piece by using another method (with a circular saw and fence, for example), and use the table saw to cut it to final width. A narrow falling board usually gives no problem.

What is Kickback?

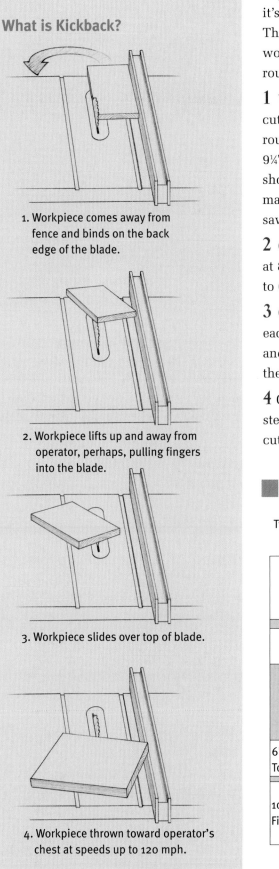

1. Workpiece comes away from fence and binds on the back edge of the blade.

2. Workpiece lifts up and away from operator, perhaps, pulling fingers into the blade.

3. Workpiece slides over top of blade.

4. Workpiece thrown toward operator's chest at speeds up to 120 mph.

important as long as they're alike, and it's easy to build the case around them. The drawers are made from ½" plywood. See the illustration below for a rough cutting guide.

1 Use a circular saw with a plywood-cutting blade to rip the plywood to rough width, yielding two pieces 9¼" x 48" and two pieces 6½" x 48", as shown in photo D (see p. 129 for information on building and using a circular saw fence).

2 On a table saw, rip two wider pieces at 8¾", and then the narrower ones to 6".

3 Crosscut one of the 48" pieces in each width to yield one piece 24" long and another piece 23½" long. These are the drawer fronts and backs.

4 Crosscut the drawer sides in two steps to get identical pairs. First, crosscut to 13¾" and clamp or tape that

■ Cutting Guide for ½" Plywood

Two drawers fit easily into a 4' x 4' half sheet of plywood.

Grain

$10^1/_2$" x 24" File drawer front	$10^1/_2$" x 23 $^1/_2$" File drawer back	
6" x 24" Top drawer front	6" x 23$^1/_2$" Top drawer back	
Waste		
6" x 13$^1/_2$" Top drawer side	6" x 13$^1/_2$" Top drawer side	Extra
$10^1/_2$" x 13$^1/_2$" File drawer side	$10^1/_2$" x 13$^1/_2$" File drawer side	Extra

SKILL BUILDER   Ripping on a Table Saw

What You'll Need

- Table saw
- Fence
- Scrap wood, 1" or ¾" x about 6" x at least 20"
- Push stick
- Safety gear

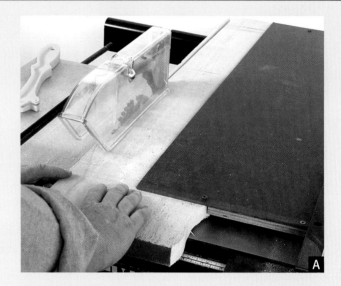

A

Preparing to Rip

1 Check your board by sighting down it to make sure one edge is straight. Always run a straight, smooth edge against the fence. Even a little curve can cause a kickback, and even if you're lucky, it won't yield a parallel-sided piece. Most dimensional lumber is straight enough to run through the table saw as is, but check it to be sure. If needed, rip one edge straight by screwing your circular saw jig to one edge, as shown in photo A, and running its straight edge along the fence. Then you can safely run the edge so produced against the fence to rip the board to the desired width. You can also straighten an edge using a router and a template routing bit and a straightedge.

2 Adjust the blade height so the gullets are above the surface of the workpiece at the top of the blade so they can clear the sawdust from the kerf.

3 Set the fence to the desired width, check that the splitter and guard are in place, and put your push stick in a handy place (typically to the right of the fence) so you can grab it quickly to guide the wood at the end of the cut. Also be sure to don safety gear.

Ripping

1 Stand with your right hip just to the left of the blade so that a board, if kicked back, will pass you by.

2 Place the heel of your left hand on the table near the edge. Push the board against the fence with your left middle finger and thumb, while your right hand holds the board parallel to the

floor. Hook your left forefinger over the top of the board to press it down onto the table, as shown in photo B.

3 Adjust the pressure of your left thumb and forefinger to allow the board to slide through while maintaining side pressure against the fence. The heel of your hand should remain on the table, never moving as the board slides through. Keep your eyes on the fence just in front of the blade, and make sure the board remains in contact with it.

4 When the end of the board reaches your left hand, reach for the push stick. Place it against the back edge of the board, toward the blade side to maintain the pressure against the fences as well as forward, as shown in photo C.

5 Now that the end of the board is past your left hand, move it so it's palm down in a comfortable position well to the left of the blade. Put some weight on it. You're now a stable tripod, and you'll feel secure as you push the push stick past the blade, which pushes the work beyond the back edge of the blade, as shown in photo B.

6 Turn the saw off and walk around to collect your workpiece. Never reach across the blade. A thin or small offcut sometimes dances around on the left side of the blade, and the rotation of the blade will

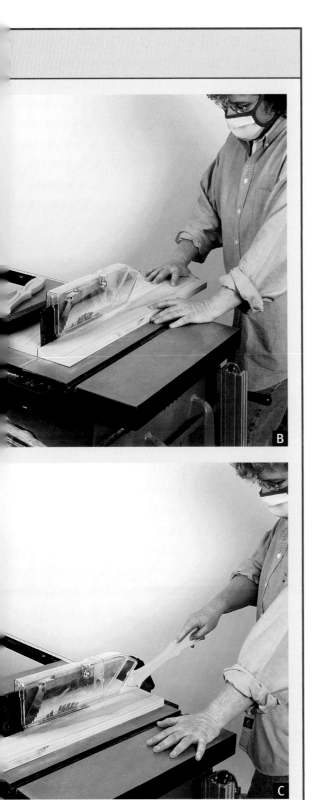

often shoot it back like an arrow. Don't even think about touching a small off-cut, no matter what. Just step out of the way and let it go.

piece on top of the remaining piece with the ends and sides flush. Then crosscut the two pieces at once to 13½". Cut two sides at 6" wide and two at 8¾".

Rabbet the Drawer Fronts

Rabbeting on a table saw is a two-step process: You run the piece through on edge, then put the face that was against the fence down on the table and saw at 90 degrees to the first cut, as shown in the illustration on p. 178. Rotate it 90 degrees and take another cut. Rabbeting along the grain on a table saw is similar to ripping, but cutting a cross-grain rabbet requires some simple but specialized jigs to ensure the workpiece is under your control at all times.

It always takes some trial and error to get the saw and jigs set up properly. You can run through a fair number of scraps in the process, but don't worry if it seems to take forever. It almost always takes longer to set up a machine than it does to make the final cuts.

WORK SMART

Sawblades tend to tear out the grain in plywood on the last surface the blade cuts as it rotates. On corded circular saws, this will be the bottom edge, but some cordless saws rotate in the opposite direction and tear out the top of the plywood. When cutting, orient your plywood so the inside is the side that gets torn out.

■ Cutting Rabbets on a Table Saw

Step 1—Vertical Cut

Inside
face

Place the inside face
against the fence

Raise the blade
to $1/2$".

Position
of blade

The result is
a groove $1/2$" deep

Step 2—Horizontal Cut

Place the inside face
on the saw table.

The result is
a rabbet.

Inside
face

Position
of blade

Falling
board

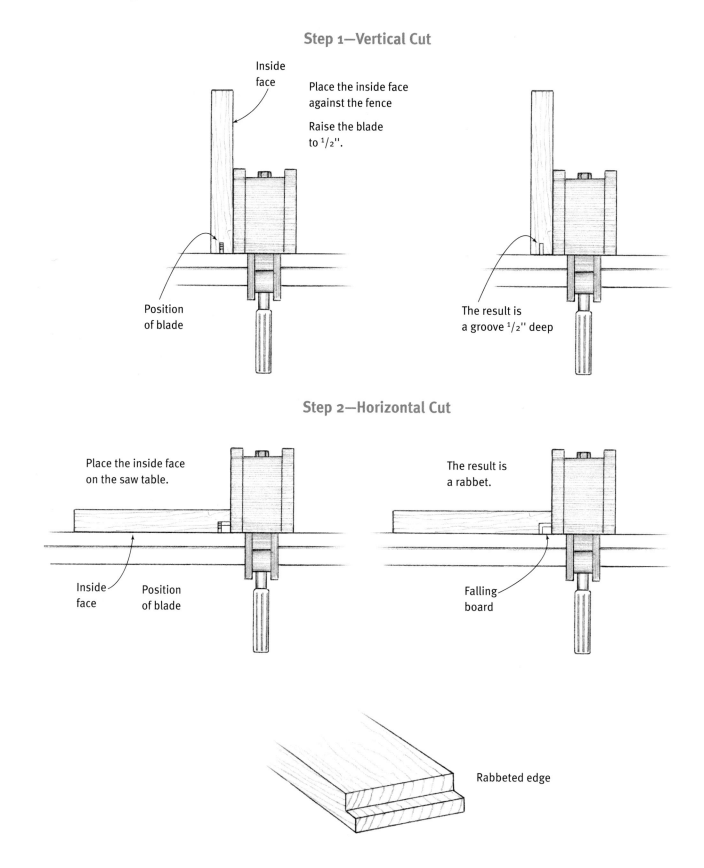

Rabbeted edge

Making vertical cuts

1 Make the rabbeting saddle shown in the illustration below, and put it in position over the fence.

2 Raise the blade to a height equal to the thickness of the plywood, as shown in photo E on p. 180, and clamp the drawer front to the saddle with the inside face against the fence (mark it "inside" so you won't get confused). Adjust the fence so the distance from the blade to the face of the rabbeting saddle is ¼", as shown in photo F on p. 180. Draw the saddle to the front of the saw so it's not touching the blade when the saw goes on.

3 Turn on the saw and push the workpiece over the blade saddle until its back edge of the workpiece is beyond the blade, as shown in photo G. Leave it in position and turn off the saw. When the blade has stopped turning, unclamp the drawer front and remove it.

4 Rotate the piece end for end and cut the other side. Make sure the inside is still toward the fence.

5 Make the vertical cuts in the other drawer front following steps 1 through 4.

Making horizontal cuts

Build a crosscut sled following the instructions in the sidebar on p. 182.

WORK SAFE

Get in the habit of unplugging the table saw before working close to the blade—removing splitters, setting blade height, and positioning fences.

■ Rabbeting Saddle for Drawer Fronts

This tablesaw fence saddle holds a long drawer front vertically for the first cut of the rabbet. It's safe, secure, and nearly foolproof as long as you use two clamps.

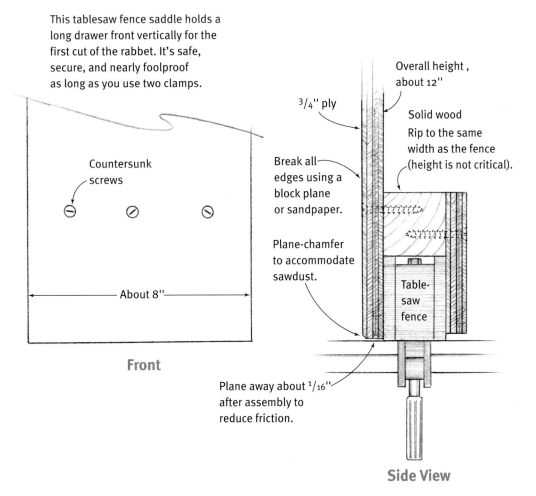

Countersunk screws

About 8"

Front

³/₄" ply

Break all edges using a block plane or sandpaper.

Plane-chamfer to accommodate sawdust.

Overall height , about 12"

Solid wood
Rip to the same width as the fence (height is not critical).

Table-saw fence

Plane away about ¹/₁₆" after assembly to reduce friction.

Side View

E

F

G

WORK SMART

Run tests on all machine setups before you cut actual workpieces. Do the tests using the same wood as the project. Once you've got it set up right, run an extra couple of pieces through to use for setting up subsequent steps.

Test the set up on the extra pieces of scrap.

1 Slip the miter bar on the bottom of the sled into the left-hand slot of the table saw and raise the blade ¼" above the surface of the sled. Use a saw height gauge, as shown in photo H.

2 Place the blade of your sliding square on the end of the kerf made with the

saddle and on the base along the inside face of the drawer front. Draw a line across the edge, as shown in photo I.

3 Position the drawer front on the sled with the inside face down. Align the mark with the edge of the sled, then push the sled past the blade to make the cut. Turn off the saw and wait for the blade to stop before removing the piece or pulling the sled back to its starting position.

4 Check that the two cuts that make the rabbet meet cleanly and that the inside corner of the rabbet has no deep grooves or high ridges, as shown on the right in photo J. Adjust the blade height up and down until the two cuts meet cleanly, as shown on the left in photo J. It may take a few tries to get it right.

5 When you can make a perfect rabbet on scrap, cut the rabbets on the inside of both sides of the two 24" drawer fronts.

Dado the Drawer Sides

If you're cutting a lot of dadoes, you can buy a set of dado blades for your table saw. A set allows you to make any width dado (up to about ⅞") in one pass by stacking various combinations of blades and shims. That complication isn't necessary for the four drawer dadoes needed here. For so few dadoes, you can use the lazy dado method. Just make multiple passes over your regular combination blade holding the workpiece in a crosscut sled. The bottom of the dado won't be as smooth as you'd get with a set of dado blades, but it does the job.

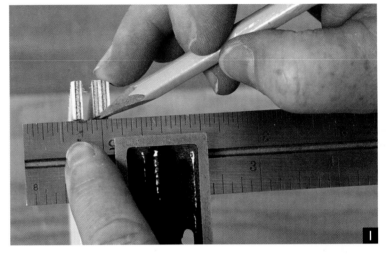

1 Using a sliding square, draw the dado on the inside face of each drawer side. First draw a line 1" from the back, then another line 1½" from the back. Square both lines across the top and bottom face as shown in photo K.

2 Place the crosscut sled on the table saw and raise the blade ¼" above it.

3 Put one of the drawer sides on the sled with the dado down. Align the right edge of the dado with the right side of the blade from the back side of the piece, as shown in photo M. Make

sure the drawer side is firmly against the cleat. Pull it away from the blade, turn on the saw, and run it through. Let the blade stop before you bring it back.

SKILL BUILDER   Building a Crosscut Sled

What You'll Need

- Table saw
- Three pennies
- Double-sided tape
- 24" adjustable miter bar kit to fit the miter slot on your table saw (metal is better than wood or plastic)
- ½" plywood about 13" wide x about 26" long, sized to suit your table-saw table
- Cleat
- Square
- Scrap wood, ¾" x 2" x 14"
- 1¼" self-drilling screws

A cardinal rule of table saws is never to crosscut without holding the workpiece in a guide or jig that slides in the miter slot. For purposes of this rule, a crosscut is any cut on a square workpiece, or cutting the short side of a rectangle. A miter gauge is fine for guiding medium-sized pieces, but when you're working with small or large ones, it's safer to use a crosscut sled, as shown in photo A. This is because the workpiece sits on the sled and not on the table where the friction of sliding might cause the piece to twist or bind.

This simple jig produces accurate repeatable results and is easy to build and master. Start by lowering the sawblade and unplugging the saw.

1 Place three pennies in the table saw's miter slot, and place the miter bar (from the miter bar kit) in the slot bottoms up, that is, with the countersinks down.

2 Put double-sided tape on the bar, and then place the plywood squarely (by eye) on the tape. Make sure the right side of the plywood extends beyond the blade by at least ½", as shown in photo B. Turn off the saw. Press down on the plywood to ensure contact, then gently lift the assembly out of the slot and turn it over.

3 Drive the short screws that came with the kit into the countersunk holes and use a knife to cut away any tape that shows on either side of the bar.

4 Remove the pennies and slide the sled back and forth to make sure it runs free. Adjust to fit without slop as per directions in the kit.

5 Raise the blade, turn on the saw, and run the sled along its slot. The saw will remove all of the material to the right of the blade. Turn off the saw, and slide the sled back toward you.

C

6 Lower the blade, and fasten a cleat to the back edge of the sled. Let it hang off the right edge at least ¼" and put a single screw near the right corner. Use your longest square to orient the cleat so it's perfectly square to the edge you just cut, as shown in photo C. Drive another fastener at the left edge.

7 Raise the blade high enough to cut off the overhanging edge on the cleat, and run a test piece through, holding it as shown in photo A.

8 Test the resulting end for squareness and adjust the cleat as necessary. If the cleat is square but the jig still doesn't cut square, make sure the miter bar is not sloppy in the miter slot.

9 Once the jig cuts a square end, drive four screws, evenly spaced along the cleat.

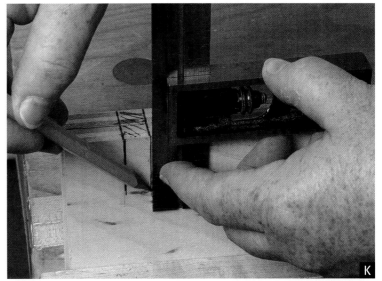

K

L

4 Next, align the left side of the dado with the edge of the sled. Run the sled through the saw, turn off the saw, and bring the sled back, as shown in photo L.

5 Slide the piece to the left and remove the material between the two cuts in two or three passes as necessary.

6 Test the fit by trying to insert the drawer back into the dado. Widen the dado as necessary (make very light cuts), following the steps above.

7 Repeat steps 3 through 6 for all four drawer sides.

WORK SMART

If your dado ends up a little too wide, you can glue it with gap-filling epoxy rather than yellow glue.

M

N

O

Cut the Groove for the Drawer Bottom

The ¼" plywood bottom fits in a groove cut in the front and the two sides of the drawer. The back of the drawer is not grooved—it's narrower so the bottom can be held in place by being screwed to the underside of the back.

1 Set the table-saw blade height to ¼", and set the fence to ½" from the blade.

2 Since the drawer sides are mirror images of one another, mark their correct orientation by putting the dadoes facing inward, and open them as a book with the bottom edge as the spine. Label the bottom edge, as shown in photo N.

3 Standing to the side of the blade, use a rubber-bottomed push block to run a drawer front over the blade with the inside down, as shown in photo O. Keep pushing the workpiece against the fence. Stop the saw when the blade comes out the back of the workpiece.

4 Run the other drawer front and all four sides (with the inside down) over the blade with the bottom edge against the fence. Also run a piece of scrap at least 2' long through, which you'll use for testing the setup for the second cut.

5 Unplug the saw and hold the piece against the fence. Position the fence and the piece so the next cut is slightly less than one kerf width to the left of the first.

6 Reconnect the saw to the power, and run about 4" of the test piece through the blade. Stop the saw, and remove the piece when the blade stops turning. Test to see if the ¼" plywood for the bottom fits in the groove. If the plywood doesn't fit, adjust the fence, cut the 4" off the end of the scrap with the chopsaw, and run another test.

7 When the plywood slides into the groove, run the two front and four side pieces through at that setting to widen the groove.

Cut Out the Drawer Bottoms

The width of the drawer bottom is equal to the distance between the two rabbets on the front plus ½". The length of the drawer bottom is equal to the distance from the front end of a side piece to the back of the dado plus ¼". Lay out these dimensions on the ¼" plywood and cut two drawer bottoms.

Assemble the Drawers

The actual size of the drawers is not critical, since you'll build the case to fit. However, it is critical that the drawers be exactly the same in size and that they be square. Make both drawers smaller if necessary, but be sure they're identical.

Dry-fitting

1 Drill three ⅛" pilot holes from the inside of each dado, then countersink from the outside. Be careful not to countersink too deeply (see photo 31 on p. 187).

2 Clamp the drawer front to the drawer sides at the top and bottom with panel clamps. Make sure the bottom of each piece is flat on the bench. Drive 1¼" screws through the dadoes into the sides.

3 Remove the clamps, upend the drawer, and slide the bottom into the groove, as shown in photo P.

4 Drop the back into the dadoes on the two sides. Because the back is the same height as the sides and it's now sitting on the bottom, the back sticks up above the sides. That's how much you're going to cut off. Mark the height of the side on one end of the back as shown in photo Q.

5 Remove the back and rip off the excess at the line. Slide the back into the dado to check that the top edge is flush with the top edges of the sides.

P

Q

R

6 Once the back is set, add clamps across the back of the drawer at both the top and the bottom as shown in photo R.

7 Check the drawers to make sure the corners are square and that the joints fit well, then remove the clamps and screws for glue-up.

Gluing and screwing the drawers

1 Apply glue to the grooves, rabbets, and dadoes, then assemble and clamp the drawer.

2 Drive 1¼" screws from the sides into the back through the dadoes.

3 Once the glue has cured, drill and countersink for three 1¼" screws from the plywood bottom through the bottom edge of the back, as shown in photo T.

Applying edgebanding

Depending on the plywood you used and your taste, you may want to cover the plywood edges that show when you open a drawer. The easiest way to cover the edges in the drawers is with ⅞"-wide birch or maple iron-on edgebanding.

1 Heat an ordinary iron to high, with no steam. Cut a length of edgebanding an inch or so longer than the edge you want to cover, then place the band over the plywood (don't bother to align the edge; it just slows you down) and simply iron the band. The heat of the iron melts the glue and the pressure makes it stick. Keep the iron moving, as shown in photo U on p. 188.

2 Allow the glue to cool for 10 to 15 minutes, then use a sharp knife to cut the overhanging edgebanding close to the plywood, as shown in photo V on p. 188.

3 Lightly sand the edges to make them flush with the sides and break the sharp corners, but be careful because the edgebanding veneer is very thin.

Sanding and smoothing the drawers

When the drawers are complete, break all of the sharp edges and sand the surface inside and out using coarse grits as required but finishing with 220 grit. You can use a random-orbit sander for the open spaces, but because of the corners, you'll have to do much of it by hand (use a hand-sanding block).

Build the Case

This case has a somewhat unusual method of construction, with solid-wood legs concealing the unsightly plywood end grain. Fastened with pocket-hole screws and glue, the case is easy to build, strong, and good looking.

Cutting the plywood panels

The dimensions of the panels depend on the final size of the drawers. Measure the drawers first, and then lay out your panels to suit. The back panel is 4" longer than the width of the drawers, the side panels are ¼" longer than the drawer sides, and all panels are 24" high. The drawer faces are 2" longer than the drawer front.

1 Referring to the illustration on the facing page as a guide, cut the plywood panels with the grain oriented as shown using your own measurements.

2 Cut the back to final dimensions using a circular saw and guide. Position the guide carefully so the corners are square.

3 Using a circular saw, cut the side panels at about 13¾" x 24", then tape them together with one side flush and rip them to 13½" so they'll be identical.

4 Sand the panels on both sides using a random-orbit sander. Start with 180-grit paper and finish with 220-grit paper.

Drilling pocket holes

Set up your pocket-hole jig according to the directions on p. 117, and drill pocket holes in the inside back and front edges of the two side panels. Before drilling, double-check that the pocket holes are on the inside face (the face with the least attractive surface). Put a pair of holes at the top and bottom and another pair in the middle.

Crosscutting the rails

1 Using a chopsaw or miter saw, crosscut three face frame rails to a length that is the same as the width of the drawer front plus 1".

2 Put two pocket holes in each end of each face frame rail.

Assemble the Case

1 Clamp a piece of scrap plywood to one side of the bench (or in your vise), and clamp the back panel down to the bench with one side against this scrap plywood. Lay the edge of the side panel on the back, with its outside face against the scrap plywood, as shown in photo W on p. 190. Draw a light line on the back panel along the inside edge of the side panel to show where to put the glue. Remove both panels and apply glue to the mating surfaces.

2 Put the panels back in position against the scrap plywood, and fasten the side panel to the back with pocket-hole screws, as shown in photo X.

3 Repeat for the other side.

4 Apply glue to the inside of a leg, but don't put any on the lower 4¼". Next, apply glue to the back corner of the case, and clamp the leg in place. The part without glue is at the bottom, with the top of the leg flush with the top of

Cutting Guide for ¾" Plywood

Have the lumberyard rip plywood to about 25" and 23" x 8'. When cutting plywood, lay out the first panel, cut it, then lay out the second panel and cut it. Otherwise, your measurements will be off by the cumulative thickness of the kerfs.

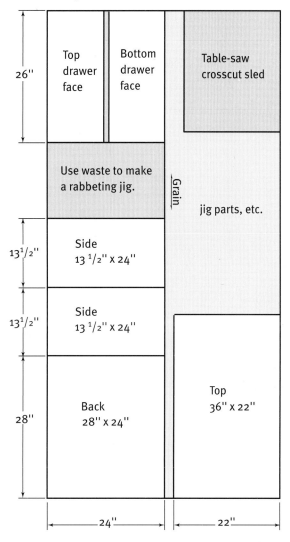

the case. The easy way to do this is to put the case upside down on the bench. Drive four 1¼" screws through the plywood into the leg.

5 Repeat for the other side.

6 Apply glue to the front edges of the side panels, and clamp the front legs in place with the tops flush with the top of the case. Fasten in place with pocket-hole screws.

> **WORK SMART**
>
> Before drilling pocket holes in the panels, test the drill cutting depth in an offcut.

W

X

Install the Face Frames and Crosspieces

The face frames cover the plywood edge on the front of the case and divide the opening for the drawers. Two crosspieces run fore and aft at the top of the case between the face frame and the back of the case. They keep the face frame from bending and give you a solid surface to which the top is fastened.

1 Use pocket-hole screws and clamps to fasten the bottom rail across the bottom of the panels (flush with the bottom edge) and the top rail across the top (also flush). Fasten the top edge of the middle rail 9¼" down from the top, as shown in photo Y.

2 Using leftover ¾" plywood, make two crosspieces about 2" wide and the same length as a side panel. Put two pocket-hole screws in each end, and fasten them flush with the top of the case about 6" inward from the side panels, as shown in photo Z.

Install the Drawer Slides

Before you install the slides, play with them a bit to understand how they work. The drawings in the installation guide are quite helpful, but the directions are complex and nearly incom-

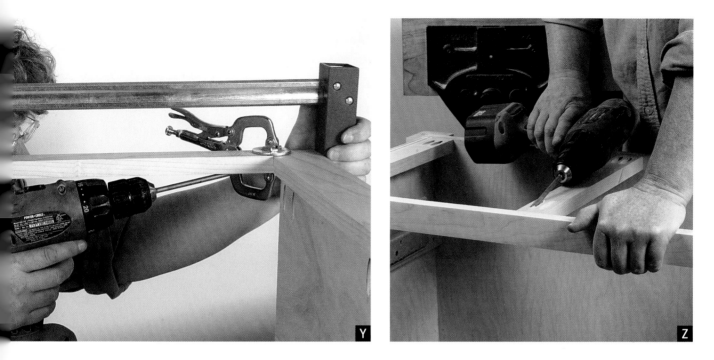

prehensible. By comparing them with the following steps, you should come to understand exactly how they work.

Screwing the slides to the case

The slides fasten to ¾" cleats screwed to the inside of the case so their inside face is flush with the edge of the face frame. The following steps will help you interpret the installation guide that came with your slides.

1 Rip leftover solid wood to 2" wide. To make four cleats, you'll need enough wood to rip a total of 56" in length.

2 Crosscut to yield four pieces each 13½" long. Using a sliding square, draw a centerline the full length of each piece.

3 Set your combination square to 6½". Placing the base of the square on the bottom edge of the side panel, draw a line at the end of the blade from front to back on each side (parallel to the floor). Fasten the bottom edge of the cleats along this line on each side using 1¼" screws. Be careful not to countersink too deeply.

4 Set the square to 2⅜", and place the base against the front of the face frame and draw a line vertically across the centerline drawn on the cleat. At the intersection of these lines, drill a ⅛" pilot hole for the screws that came with the slides, as shown in photo AA (crosspiece removed for clarity).

5 Close the slide and fasten it to the cleat through the oversize hole in its front.

6 Open the slide fully and position it so the line drawn on the cleat shows through the center of the holes. Drill another pilot hole on the line in the center of the slotted hole about two-thirds the way along the slide. Install only two screws at this point. Later you'll adjust the position of the slide and install the rest of the screws.

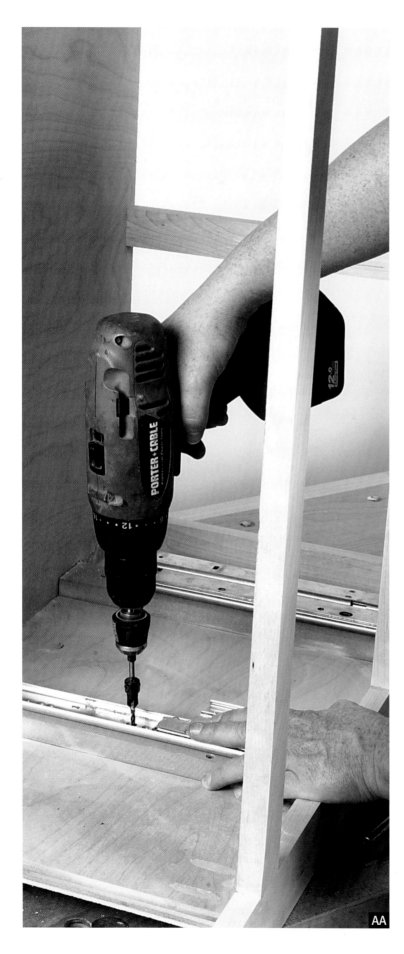

AA

7 Repeat steps 1 through 6 to install the other lower drawer slide.

8 Fasten the top drawer slides in the same way, except run the square 4½" down from the top edge of the panel. Locate the upper edge of the top drawer cleats along the line.

Installing the rails on the drawers

The rails fasten to the drawer sides on a line running fore and aft a set distance above the centerline of the drawers. The difficult fractions are specified by the slide manufacturers.

1 Measure the height of the file drawer side and mark the midpoint. Using a ruler, measure and make a mark 2⅞" up from the midpoint. Place the base of the sliding square on either edge of the drawer and set the blade to this mark, then draw a line down the length of the drawer side. Repeat on the other side of the drawer.

2 Measure the height of the top drawer side and mark the midpoint. Using a ruler, measure and make a mark 2¹¹⁄₁₆" from the midpoint. Place the base of the sliding square on the edge of the drawer side and set the blade to this mark. Draw a line down the length of the drawer side. Repeat on the other side of the drawer.

3 Set your sliding square to 1¹⁹⁄₃₂", put the base on the front of the drawer, and draw a vertical line that crosses the lines you made in steps 1 and 2. This marks the location of the first screw. Drill a ⅛" pilot hole and fasten with one of the screws that came with the slide.

4 Align the rail so the line shows through the center of the holes, and drill a pilot hole in the middle of the other vertical slot, as shown in photo CC. Drive the second screw.

5 Repeat on the remaining rails.

Checking the fit

1 Pull the slides about two-thirds of the way out, and position the drawer with its rails resting on the slides. Holding the drawer steady, pull the slide all the way out until the plastic key snaps into the slot in the slider, as shown in photo CC.

2 Open and close the drawers to make sure they glide smoothly. If they don't, check for loose or misaligned rails or slides.

3 Remove the drawers by opening them all the way, then raising the plastic levers while lifting the drawer from the slides.

Install the Drawers

The directions that follow assume plywood faces, but you could also make the drawer faces from solid wood, eliminating the need for edgebanding. Rip the boards to width on the table saw, and glue them up into wide panels. You can even make the top of solid wood as well.

Cutting the drawer faces

1 Using a sliding square, make marks ½" outward from the drawer openings on the rail and the face frame at each corner. This is where the finished drawer face will end. Measure the length and width between these marks to get the final dimension, as shown in photo DD.

2 Cut out the plywood faces using a circular saw and/or a table saw using methods described earlier.

BB

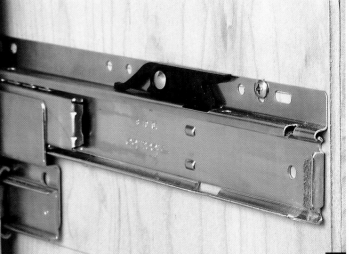

CC

3 Iron on edgebanding around the exposed edges of the plywood, using the same techniques used previously.

Fastening the faces to the drawer

1 Place the file drawer in the case and push it all the way in. Clamp the drawer face to the face frames within the lines drawn ½" from the edges, as shown in photo EE.

2 Position the cabinet face down on the bench, and screw the face in place from the back with four 1¼" pocket-hole screws.

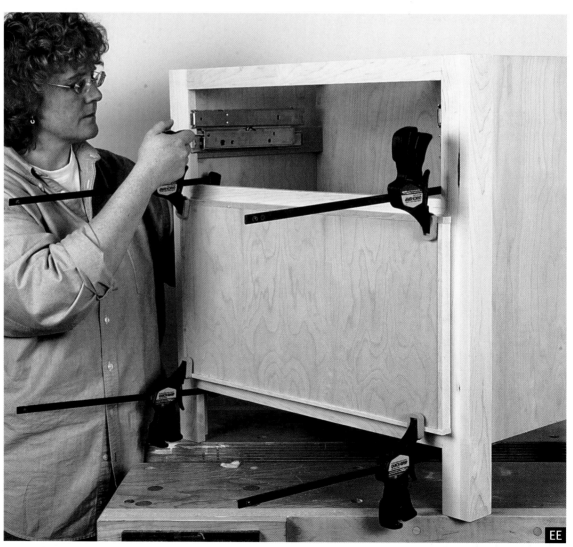

3 Remove the file drawer and put the top drawer in place. Clamp its face to the face frames and fasten in place in the same manner.

Fitting the drawers

The two screws holding each of the rails and sliders in place are in slots to allow for fine-tuning the fit of the drawers. The most common problem when fitting drawers is for the drawer face to be out of parallel with the floor. Fix this by loosening the screws in the rail and raising or lowering the drawer as necessary. If the face is not flush at the bottom, lower the back of the slides. If one side isn't flush, slide the runner back. It's a trial-and-error process that may involve removing the drawer several times. When you're done, remove the drawers and set them aside.

Installing the hanging file holder

Assemble the hanging file holder according to its directions so that it fits into the lower drawer.

Install the Drawer Pulls

1 Make the jig shown in the illustration above.

2 Align the left edge of the jig with the left edge of the face of the top drawer. Drill one set of holes using the upper holes as guides as shown in photo FF on p. 196.

3 Align the right edge of the jig with the right edge of the drawer face. Drill the upper two holes.

4 Repeat for the lower drawer, using the lower set of guides.

▉ Drawer-Pull Boring Jig

Make this jig out of plywood offcuts, it'll be easy to install the drawer pulls level and square. If you're using different hardware, the principle is the same, though the location of the holes will be different.

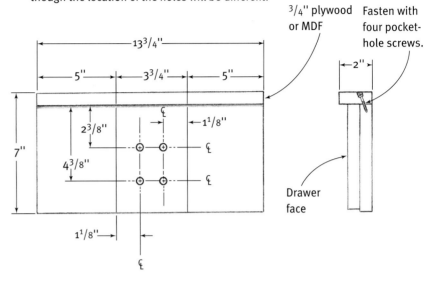

5 Install the pulls to check the fit and position.

6 Remove the pulls for now, so you won't get finish on them. You will reinstall them after finishing.

▉ WORK SMART

If you are finishing the inside of your cabinet, do so before you screw the top in place.

Install the Top

1 From the remaining plywood, lay out and cut the top 36" x 18½".

2 Following the procedure used on the drawers, apply edge banding to the sides and then the front and back.

3 Plane the banding flush and break the edges as described previously.

4 Set the top upside down on the bench, and center it just as you did for the top on the coffee table (see p. 134).

5 Once you've marked the corners to reposition the case correctly, remove the case and apply glue to the surface of the crosspieces. Reposition the case and drive three 1¼" screws through each crosspiece and into the top to hold it in place.

WORK SMART

If you're staining the drawer faces, apply the stain to the whole project and a protective coat or two of clear coat before fastening them to the drawer.

Finishing

Furniture is used hard in an office, even a home office, so the surface of the file cabinet needs to be tough. A water-based semigloss clear-coat finish fits the spec and is fast and easy to apply. You may want to tint it to add some warmth to the finish (for more on this, see p. 157).

Because birch tends to be blotchy, I chose to start with a water-based grain filler to reduce the amount of stain the wood absorbed. You could use a thin coat of shellac instead, as described on p. 133.

Every staining job is different: You never know what you're going to get until you see it. Run tests on offcuts of the same material that have been sanded and prepared using the same sanding procedure as used on the project. Make notes of what you've used in each sample, and let the samples dry before you decide which you want to use. In fact, live with the samples for a while and look at them in various kinds of light, from lamplight to the afternoon sun, to make sure you pick a color you'll like for years to come.

It's not necessary to stain the parts of the drawer made from ½" material. In fact, it's customary for drawer sides and bottoms to be made of a material with a contrasting color.

1 Using water-based grain filler, trowel it on with a plastic squeegee, pushing it down into the grain. Be careful not to get too much in the corner between the legs and the panels (see photo GG). Wipe it down with a tough paper towel

GG

or cotton rag before it dries, rubbing across the grain.

2 After the filler is dry, sand with 220-grit sandpaper (use a random-orbit sander for most of it, but hand-sand near the legs), vacuum thoroughly, and apply a water- or alcohol-based stain with a rag or foam brush, as shown in photo HH.

3 Once the stain is dry, sand very lightly with the grain using a hand-sanding block and 220-grit paper, being especially careful not to cut through the stain at the edges.

4 Apply a thin coat of semigloss water-based clear finish using a foam or natural bristle brush, as shown in photo II.

5 Apply at least four coats, lightly sanding (or wetsanding if you choose) between each with a maroon synthethic steel wool pad. The more coats you apply, the richer the finish will look.

6 If you like, finish with a couple of coats of wax for a rich, smooth glow.

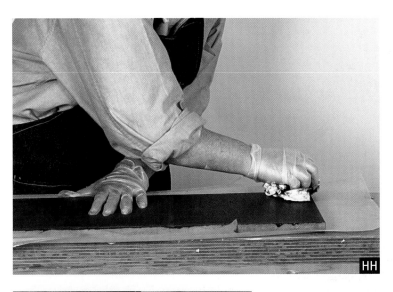

HH

II

WORK SMART

Several thin coats of finish dry smoother and more quickly than a few thick coats.

Resources

Suppliers

Accuride International Inc.
Corporate Headquarters
12311 Shoemaker Ave.
Santa Fe Springs, CA 90670
(562) 903-0200
www.accuride.com
Maker of the 4034 12" drawer slides used in the lateral file project.

American Clamping Corporation
50 Franklin St.
P.O. Box 399
Batavia, NY 14621
www.jamesmorton.com
Distributors of German-made Bessey clamps.

Garrett Wade
161 Avenue of the Americas
New York, NY 10013
(800) 221-2942
www.garrettwade.com
Retailer of fine woodworking tools.

Jamestown Distributors
500 Wood St. Building #15
Bristol, RI 02809
(800) 423-0030
www.jamestowndistributors.com
Specializes in fasteners of all kinds but also offers tools, sandpaper, adhesives, etc. Offers tool kits for projects in this book.

Kreg Jig
201 Campus Dr.
Huxley, IA 50124
(800) 447-8638
www.kregtool.com
The pros' choice for pocket holes.

Lee Valley
P.O. Box 1780
Ogdensburg, NY 13669-6780
(800) 513-7885
www.leevalley.com
This company's excellent catalog is an education in woodworking.

Lie-Nielsen Toolworks
P.O. Box 9
Warren, ME 04864-0009
(800) 327-2520
www.lie-nielsen.com
Maker of superb planes, chisels, and saws.

McFeely's Square Drive Screws
1620 Wythe Rd.
P.O. Box 11169
Lynchburg, VA 24506-1169
(800) 443-7937
www.mcfeelys.com
A wide selection of specialized and general purpose square drive screws for a variety of uses.

Osborne Wood Products Inc.
8116 Hwy. 123 N.
Toccoa, GA 30577
(800) 849-8876
www.osbornewood.com
Maker of turned wooden table legs, including the Jumbo English Country Legs used for the coffee table project.

Porter-Cable Corporation
4825 Hwy. 45 N.
P.O. Box 2468
Jackson, TN 38302-2468
(800) 487-8665
www.porter-cable.com
Quality hand power tools.

Roberts Plywood
45 N. Industry Ct.
Deer Park, NY 11729
(631) 586-7700
Outside NY State:
(800) 422-4944
www.getwood.com
An astonishing variety of specialty plywoods, available in slightly less than half-sheets via UPS.

Rockler
4365 Willow Dr.
Medina, MN 55340
(800) 279-4441
www.rockler.com
Tools, hardware, and more. The website has product info sheets on many items; a good resource.

System Three Resins, Inc.
3500 W. Valley N.
Ste. 105
Auburn, WA 98001
(800) 333-5514
www.systemthree.com
Maker of high-performance epoxies, paints, and varnishes, including the self-mixing gun used in the Outdoor Easy Chair.

Tried and True Finishes
14 Prospect St.
Trumansburg, NY 14886
(607) 387-9280
www.triedandtruefinish.com
Maker of the oil/wax finish used on the box project.

Waterlox Coatings Corporation
9808 Meech Ave.
Cleveland, OH 44105
(800) 321-0377
www.waterlox.com
Maker of the tung oil varnish used on the outdoor easy chair project.

Woodcraft
P.O. Box 1686
Parkersburg, WV 26102-1686
(800) 225-1153
www.woodcraft.com
Catalog retailer of tools, materials, wood, and hardware.

The Woodworkers' Club
215 Westport Ave.
Norwalk, CT 06851
(203) 847-9663
www.woodworkersclubnorwalk.com
Offers kits of tools and materials for projects in this book.

www.aofraser.com
Companion website to this book. Features photo gallery, drawings of variations, articles, links, message board, and more.

Reading List

The Basics of Craftsmanship: Key Advice on Every Aspect of Woodworking Joinery: Shaping & Milling. The Taunton Press, 1999. *Reprints from* Fine Woodworking *magazine.*

Care and Repair of Shop Machines. John White. The Taunton Press, 2002. *A complete reference for assembling, tuning, maintaining, and repairing major shop tools.*

The Complete Guide to Sharpening. Leonard Lee. The Taunton Press, 1990. *An in-depth guide to sharpening all kinds of edge tools.*

Encyclopedia of Furniture Making. Ernest Joyce. Sterling Publications, 1987. *This is the old standby reference for furniture makers in the United States and United Kingdom.*

***Fine Woodworking* Magazine.** 63 S. Main St., P. O. Box 5506, Newtown, CT 06470-5506, (800) 477-8727. www.taunton.com/finewoodworking/index.asp. *How to do all kinds of woodworking, from the humble to the sublime.*

Great Wood Finishes: A Step-By-Step Guide to Consistent and Beautiful Results. Jeff Jewitt. The Taunton Press, 2000. *Details on finishing. This book is a necessity if you want to do anything other than oil your projects.*

Mastering Woodworking Machinery. Mark Duginske. The Taunton Press, 1992. *The best guide on how tune up and use the table saw and other woodworking machines.*

Methods of Work: The Best Tips from 25 Years of *Fine Woodworking* (Methods of Work Series). The Taunton Press, 2000. *A collection of neat tips and tricks from 25 years of* Fine Woodworking *magazine.*

The Router Book: A Complete Guide to the Machine and Its Accessories. Pat Warner. The Taunton Press, 2001. *A great guide to learning to use this essential tool.*

Router Joinery. Gary Rogowski. The Taunton Press, 1997. *Jigs and setups for routing joints.*

Router Magic: Jigs, Fixtures and Tricks to Unleash Your Router's Full Potential. William H. Hylton. Reader's Digest Adult, 1999. *How to do almost anything with a router.*

Setting Up Shop: The Practical Guide to Designing and Building Your Dream Shop. Sandor Nagyszalanczy. The Taunton Press, 2000. *What you need to know to set up a shop right. Interesting peeks into a variety of shops.*

***ShopNotes* Magazine.** www.shopnotes.com. *Projects and info to get your shop in shape.*

The Table Saw Book. Kelly Mehler. The Taunton Press, revised edition 2002. *A no-frills, easy to understand book on all aspects of the table saw.*

Table Saw Magic. Jim Tolpin. Popular Woodworking Books, 1999. *Choosing, using, and mastering the table saw.*

Tage Frid Teaches Woodworking 1 & 2: A Step-By-Step Guidebook to Essential Woodworking Technique. Tage Frid. The Taunton Press, 1994. *Classical European woodworking with an emphasis on hand tools.*

Traditional Woodworking Handtools: A Manual for the Woodworker. Graham Blackburn. The Lyons Press, 1999. *A lot of history but solid practical information for those who want to learn more about hand tools.*

Understanding Wood: A Craftsman's Guide to Wood Technology. R. Bruce Hoadley. The Taunton Press, revised edition, 2000. *The standard reference on why wood does what it does.*

Woodworking with the Router: Professional Router Techniques and Jigs Any Woodworker Can Use. Bill Hylton and Fred Matlack. Reader's Digest Adult, 1999. *Everything you want to know about the router. A great reference.*

The Workbench Book. Scott Landis. The Taunton Press, 1998. *A cultural history of the workbench that's actually useful. Photos and plans for a variety of proven designs. Pick the one that suits your style.*

Glossary

Acme Thread—A powerful coarse thread that's designed to work without sloppiness even after years of use. Used on clamps, vises, and jacks.

Adjustable Clamps—Another name for the modern type of bar clamp where the handscrew end slides up and down the bar.

Aluminum Oxide—An aggressive sandpaper abrasive often distinguishable by its light gray color. Best suited for sanding bare wood.

Apron—A horizontal member connecting the upper parts of the legs of a table. The aprons also support the tabletop.

Assembly Bench—A low workbench without a vise used for assembling and finishing.

Baltic Birch Plywood—Formerly a trade name now used generically for a high-grade birch plywood manufactured in the Baltic region of many very thin veneers. For a given dimension, Baltic birch is stronger and more stable than other birch plywood.

Baluster—The upright portion of a railing.

Bar Clamp—Properly any clamp with a bar, including throat clamps and panel clamps. Many people use the term to refer to panel clamps.

Beadboard—Sold in 4' x 8' sheets like plywood, beadboard is essentially plywood or MDF with grooves cut in it to look as though it was made up of individual boards.

Bearing Surfaces—The portion of the joint or surface that bears a load.

Bench Chisel—A moderately sized chisel on which the back edges are lightly chamfered. A good all-around chisel.

Bit—A replaceable tool chucked into a rotating holder that does the intended job. Types of bits include router bits, drilling bits, and driver bits.

Board Foot—A cubic measure that equals the amount of wood in a piece that's 1" thick, 12" wide, and 12" long. For example, a board ¾" x 6" x 2" equals ¾ of a board foot, and so does a piece 2" x 6" x 9". The formula for calculating board feet is: [length (inches) x width (inches) x thickness (inches)] ÷ 144. Wood sold in bulk can vary in length, width, and thickness and is therefore sold by volume.

Bore—To make a hole using a drill or similar tool and a suitable bit.

Bow—A condition in which a board is not flat along its length but rather bent like a bow.

Brad—A short, thin nail used for light-duty work.

Brad-Point Drill Bit—A drill bit designed for boring holes in wood, featuring a sharp point to prevent skidding over the surface and spurs to start the cut.

Burr—The thin wire edge you can feel on the back edge of a blade after honing the bevel. When the very end of the blade gets quite thin, the metal bends back under the pressure of honing. You can use this burr to tell you when you've honed enough: When you can feel the burr across the whole back of the blade, the entire edge has been abraded to the same level.

Cabinet-Grade Birch—A general-purpose grade of plywood with a knot-free surface, but where the veneers may not match for appearance.

Cam-Out—A condition whereby the torque on a driver bit forces it out of the head of a screw. It usually occurs as the head of the screw nears the surface of the wood, when the friction increases considerably.

Cathedral Figure—The familiar slightly V-shaped pattern of grain that shows on the face of a flatsawn board.

C-Clamp—A clamp with a fixed head and a handscrew shaped like the letter of its namesake.

Chamfer—A beveled edge.

Checks—Longitudinal cracks in the ends of boards that occur as the result of drying.

Chopsaw—A powered circular saw mounted on guides with a fence to ensure accurate cuts at any angle.

Chuck—The part of a tool that holds a bit.

Circular Saw—A hand power tool with a circular blade used for ripping and crosscutting with guides. Not suitable for cutting curved lines.

Clear Coat—A term for a clear film finish, generally applied to colorless water-based finishes.

Cleat—A piece fastened to or across something to give it strength or hold it in position.

Clutch—A mechanism between two drive shafts that enables them to be disconnected or connected at will. Most cordless drill/drivers have clutches that allow you to set the level of torque at which the bit stops turning, even when the trigger is still depressed. Using the clutch prevents driving screws too deeply or turning them beyond their breaking point.

Collet—A device that holds a bit in a chuck by compression.

Combination Square—A measuring and layout tool that combines a sliding rule with a base capable of measuring both 45 degrees and 90 degrees.

Common Pine—A grade of pine that is structurally sound but that allows for knots. #1 pine has the fewest knots, whereas #5 has the most.

Compound Miter Saw—A miter saw capable of tilting the blade off the vertical, a critical attribute for cutting crown moldings.

Conditioner, Stain or Prestain—A sealer coat used on hard-to-stain woods. It soaks into the thirsty parts and seals them, making subsequent coats of stain absorb more evenly.

Corner Chisel—A chisel with two adjoining faces used for squaring corners.

Counterbore—(verb) The act of making a larger-diameter enlargement in the outer end of a hole for accepting a plug or a nut and washer. (noun) The bit used for counterboring a hole.

Countersink—(verb) The act of making a funnel-shaped enlargement in the outer end of a hole for accepting the head of a fastener. (noun) The bit used for countersinking a hole.

Crook—A condition of a board that's not straight end to end along the edge.

Crosscut—A cut made across the width of a board.

Cup—A condition of a piece of wood in which it is warped across its width.

Cyanoacrylate Adhesive—Super Glue for woodworkers. Bonds quickly and is great for cosmetic repairs.

Dado—A square-bottomed groove running the width of a piece. Properly, a groove runs lengthwise, a dado across the width.

Dead-Blow Hammer—A hammer filled with a heavy substance such as sand or lead shot that reduces the tendency to bounce after striking.

Dimensional Lumber—Lumber that has been dried to about 10% moisture content and surfaced on four sides to standard dimensions.

Double Square—A measuring and layout tool with a sliding ruler and a 90°-degree base.

Drill—(noun) A device used for turning drill bits. (verb) Technically, any means of making a hole by cutting or piercing. Generally used to mean making a hole using a drill, although the proper word is to bore.

Dye Stain—A water- or alcohol-based stain that penetrates the surface of the wood and often enhances the appearance of the grain.

End Grain—The open grain showing at the end of a board.

Engineer's Square—An all-metal fixed square.

Epoxy—A waterproof glue that can be formulated to meet a variety of needs. Open times are typically short, with the cure time ranging from five minutes to overnight depending on the formulations and conditions. The only glue that forms a strong bridge across gaps.

Face Edge—The edge used as a reference edge for all measuring. It should be the edge that goes inside or down.

Face Side—The face used as a reference for all measuring. It should be the back or inside face.

Face Grain—The familiar cathedral grain pattern seen on the face of most flatsawn boards.

Falling Board—The part of the board that is waste after the workpiece has been cut from it. The falling board may or may not be scrap.

F-Clamp—Another name for a bar clamp.

Fixed-Base Router—A router in which the motor and bit are fixed while the bit is turning.

Fixture—A device for supporting work during machining.

Flatsawn—A method of sawing logs by cutting along the length of the boards. This is the most cost-effective way to produce lumber. Also said to be sawn through and through.

Forstner Bit—A type of drill bit used mostly for larger-diameter holes. Two or three spurs are surrounded by a toothed rim. Forstner bits work well for angled cuts or when part of the bit must be off the workpiece.

Full-Extension Drawer Slide—A drawer slide that allows you to open the drawer so that the back edge is flush with the face of the cabinet.

Garnet—A soft abrasive best suited for sanding bare wood. It leaves a slightly burnished surface that often results in a lighter, more even color when used before staining.

Gel Stains—Stains that are thickened for ease of use on vertical surfaces.

Grain—Generally refers to the direction of cells in a piece of wood, oriented in the living tree with their longitudinal axis on the vertical. The term also refers to the appearance of this grain, which is distinctive for each species of wood as well as for how the piece was cut from the log.

Groove—A wide kerf running the length of a piece. Properly, a groove runs lengthwise, a dado across the width.

Gullet—The valley between the teeth on a sawblade.

Hand-Sanding Block—A block of felt, cork, rubber, or wood around which sandpaper is wrapped. A sanding block ensures flatness when sanding.

Handscrew—The threaded handle on a clamp or similar mechanism.

Hand Tight—As tight as you can get by hand without straining.

Hardboard—A very dense homogeneous product made by combining finely milled sawdust with binders and adhesives. One side is often slick and shiny, the other textured. Strong, stable, and smooth. Dark brown in color, this is the material used to make pegboard. Often used for jigs and drawer bottoms. Masonite is a well-known brand of hardboard.

Hardwood—The wood of deciduous trees, which are those that lose their leaves in autumn.

Hatch Marks—Straight or squiggly lines drawn on a workpiece to show where the parts of a joint overlap. It's an informal marking, intended to delineate the area where glue is applied.

Heartwood—The mature wood in a tree between the pith in the center and the sapwood near the edges.

Honing—The part of the sharpening process where a blade's bevel is abraded with ever finer abrasives at a set angle (most often 30 degrees) to make it level, flat, and smooth.

Iron—A plane's blade.

Jacking—A condition that occurs in a screw-fastened joint when the threads grip the upper piece and force the two pieces apart as the screw is driven. Can be prevented by boring a properly sized pilot hole in the upper piece.

Jig—A device used to maintain parts in the correct position.

Jigsaw—A hand power tool with a reciprocating blade used for cutting curves.

Jobber's Drill Bit—The standard type of drill with a conical point. Works well in wood in most but not all cases.

Joinery—The process of joining pieces of wood together; the word embraces many methods.

Jointer—A stationary power tool with a rotating cutterhead set between two tables. Jointers are used to flatten and straighten the face of a board. When used in connection with a fence, a jointer is used to make an edge square to the face.

Kerf—The groove left by a saw. Sometimes refers to the material removed in making the groove.

Kickback—When a piece of wood binds on a table-saw blade, the speed and power of the blade can launch the wood back at the operator with lethal force.

Kiln—A chamber for drying wood using a complex interplay of heat, steam, and sometimes vacuum. Most lumber for woodworking is dried down to about 10% moisture content.

Lag Screw—A long, large-diameter coarse screw with a hex head.

Lazy Dado—A method of making dadoes on a table saw where multiple passes are made with a single blade until achieving the desired width.

Mallet—A tool used to strike wooden objects. Typically made of wood, plastic, leather, or rubber.

MDF—Stands for medium-density fiberboard. A homogeneous product made by combining finely milled sawdust with binders and adhesives. Sold in 4' x 8' sheets like plywood, MDF is strong, heavy, stable, and easy to machine and paint. Often used for paint-grade cabinets, as a substrate for fine veneers, and for jigs and fixtures. Normally light to medium brown in color.

MDO—Stands for medium-density overlay, a type of plywood with a tough, smooth coating. Also called signboard.

Miter—An angled cut. Usually refers to a 45-degree angle, but the usage is not limited to that.

Miter Box—A device for guiding a handsaw for making square crosscuts or angled miter cuts.

Miter Saw—An electric saw that swivels on a base used for making square crosscuts and angle cuts at virtually any angle from 0 degrees to about 50 degrees (depending on the brand).

Nibs—A slight roughness left on the surface of paint, varnish, shellac, and similar coatings that can be removed by a light sanding. In the first few coats of finish, nibs form until the coating fills in all the roughness of the grain. In later coats, nibs might be caused by pollen, dust, or other contaminants.

Oil Finish—In woodworking this usually refers to boiled linseed or tung oil. Takes a long time to dry but enhances the grain.

Oil/Wax Finish—A very old recipe that combines oils, beeswax, and some dryers. Imparts a soft patina.

Panel Clamp—A clamp used for joining wide panels. The work rests on the bars to keep the bottom side flat, while the narrow-throated jaws grip the edges of the panel. Sometimes called a sash clamp.

Phillips Head—A screw-head design with a slot shaped like a plus sign.

Pigment Stain—An oil- or water-based stain that colors the wood by applying a light film of pigment on the surface. These are the easiest to apply but can leave a muddy appearance if used too heavily.

Pilot Hole—A small-diameter hole used to guide a screw or larger drill. When used in reference to screws, it refers to a hole as long as the screw with a diameter slightly smaller than the root diameter of the screw.

Pipe Clamp—A type of clamp made up of removable head and screw mechanisms mounted on standard black iron pipe.

Pith—The center of a tree. Generally this wood is not desirable for woodworking.

Planer—A stationary power tool with a flattened table and a rotating cutterhead to remove wood from the top of a board until it reaches the desired thickness.

Plug—Also called bung. A round, tapered cylinder of wood set into a counterbored hole and cut flush. When installed properly, it is virtually invisible. Proper plugs are made with face grain showing at the top.

Plunge-Base Router—A router that is designed to be raised and lowered into position while the bit is turning.

Ply—A layer of veneer in a plywood panel.

Pocket Hole—A long, angled hole bored in the face of a board near the edge that nearly pierces the side of the board.

Pocket-Hole Jig—A tool used to drill the angled holes needed for pocket-hole joinery.

Polyurethane Adhesive—A waterproof adhesive that cures in the presence of moisture. It has an open time of about 20 minutes, needs about three hours in clamps, and the squeeze-out foams up, making it easy to remove. Requires tight joints and moderate clamping pressure.

Quartersawn—A method of sawing logs that involves rotating the log to yield the maximum amount of clear, straight, dimensionally stable lumber.

Rabbet—A groove cut in the edge of a board, which leaves a shoulder.

Rack—(verb) To be forced out of square and into a parallelogram shape.

Radiused—Heavily rounded. Usually used in reference to corners and edges.

Rails—The vertical part of the frame.

Ray Fleck—The peculiar grain structure shown in quartersawn lumber caused by the sectioning of storage pockets in the grain. The degree of flecking varies from species to species.

Riftsawn—A board that shows the growth rings on the end grain as lines running about 45 degrees off the vertical.

Rip—A cut made the length of a board, parallel to the run of the grain.

Root Diameter—The diameter of the core of a threaded object, such as a screw or drill bit.

S2S—Boards that are surfaced on two sides but where the edges are not necessarily machined.

S4S—Boards that are surfaced on four sides, usually as dimensioned lumber, but can refer to lumber machined to any specified dimension.

Sapwood—The younger wood near the bark of the tree. In many species this wood is a different color than the heartwood and less stable.

Select Pine—A grade of pine that is nearly clear, allowing for only a few pin knots.

Self-Drilling Screw—A term that refers to modern engineered wood screws that don't need a pilot hole or countersinking in most circumstances.

Shank—The unthreaded portion of a wood screw just below the head.

Shellac—A film finish that uses alcohol as a solvent. Very good as a sealer coat since it sticks to most finishes.

Shop Birch—An economy-grade birch plywood with no voids in the core but which may have knots or other defects in the face. Used around the shop for jigs, fixtures, and enclosures.

Side Grain—Straight, even grain running along the edge of a flatsawn board.

Silicon Carbide—A very aggressive sandpaper abrasive intended for use on finished surfaces.

Sliding Miter Saw—A miter saw on which the blade slides back and forth on rails to increase the width of board the saw can cut through.

Softwood—The wood of conifers.

Sole—The bottom of a plane; its plane of reference.

Splitter—A piece of shaped wood or metal that sits behind the blade to prevent kickback by keeping the wood from binding on the sawblade.

Square-Drive Screw—A screw-head design with a square recess for the screw driver.

Square—(adjective or verb) Measuring 90 degrees or making it measure so. (noun) A tool for marking and checking right angles.

Stain Conditioner—A thin coat of sealer or a specially formulated product that inhibits stain penetration to reduce blotchiness in hard-to-stain woods.

Step Drill Bit—A drill bit with two different diameters, where the diameter changes in a distinct step. Used most often for drilling pocket holes.

Stickering—A method of stacking wood that keeps air circulating around all sides. Rather than piling one board atop another, several pieces of wood about 1" high rest between each layer to allow air to circulate so the wood reaches the same moisture level as the air around it.

Stickers—Small pieces of wood placed between layers in a stack of wood to provide space for air to circulate.

Stile—The vertical member of a frame.

Stop Block—A square piece of wood clamped in place to set the length of a piece to be sawn.

Stop Collar—A ring that fastens in place around a drill bit or countersink to control the depth of cut.

Stretcher—A structural member between the legs of a chair or table.

Structural Lumber—Lumber used in the building trades, such as softwood 2x4s. Such lumber is often dried to a moisture content of 19%.

Template—A pattern made of thin board.

Throat Clamp—A type of clamp where the head and screw are at least 4" or so from the bar.

Throat Plate—The insert around the sawblade with a slot for the sawblade. In most modern saws, they're red, white, or yellow for safety.

Torque—A force that produces rotation; also the measure of that force.

Tung Oil—Natural oil made from the seeds of the tung tree. Slow drying but flexible.

Twist—A defect in a board in which the ends of the board are in the same plane.

Varnish—A durable, thick film finish made of oils and resins; mineral spirits or turps are the solvents.

Veneer—A very thin slice of wood. The term refers to a thin slice of decorative wood glued to the surface of a stable but less attractive substrate, and also refers to the thin layers of wood laid up into plywood.

Veneer Core—A type of decorative plywood with a core laid up of thin veneers. The contrast to this is solid-wood cored panels, where decorative veneers are used to face thin (about ¾") panels of solid wood.

Warrington Hammer—A light cabinetmaker's hammer with a rounded face and a cross peen for starting brads.

Wetsanding—Sanding with special sandpaper (or synthetic steel wool) soaked in water. Rather than making dust, wetsanding makes slurry. If you wipe down or hose off the slurry before it dries in place, you get a smooth finish with less mess.

Yellow Glue—The woodworker's most commonly used glue. With an open time of about 15 minutes, you can remove the clamps in an hour, and full cure occurs overnight. Requires close-fitting joints and tight clamping pressure.

Index